A CONCISE HISTORY OF CLASSICAL SANSKRIT LITERATURE

A CONCISE HISTORY OF
CLASSICAL SANSKRIT LITERATURE

GAURINATH SASTRI

MOTILAL BANARSIDASS PUBLISHERS
PRIVATE LIMITED • DELHI

*4th Reprint: Delhi, **2013***
First MLBD Reprint: Delhi, 1974
First Edition: Calcutta, 1943 (1960)
By arrangement with Oxford University Press

ISBN: 978-81-208-0027-4 (Cloth)
ISBN: 978-81-208-0175-2 (Paper)

MOTILAL BANARSIDASS
41 U.A. Bungalow Road, Jawahar Nagar, Delhi 110 007
8 Mahalaxmi Chamber, 22 Bhulabhai Desai Road, Mumbai 400 026
203 Royapettah High Road, Mylapore, Chennai 600 004
236, 9th Main III Block, Jayanagar, Bengaluru 560 011
Sanas Plaza, 1302 Baji Rao Road, Pune 411 002
8 Camac Street, Kolkata 700 017
Ashok Rajpath, Patna 800 004
Chowk, Varanasi 221 001

Printed in India

by RP Jain at NAB Printing Unit,
A-44, Naraina Industrial Area, Phase I, New Delhi–110028
and published by JP Jain for Motilal Banarsidass Publishers (P) Ltd,
41 U.A. Bungalow Road, Jawahar Nagar, Delhi-110007

PREFACE TO THE SECOND EDITION

The history of Sanskrit Literature is by itself a fascinating subject in which not only students of language but also the intelligentsia in general finds an abiding interest. This prompted me to undertake the first edition of the book under the title, An Introduction to Classical Sanskrit, in a short compass in 1943. It is indeed a matter of gratification to me that the edition was exhausted in a rather short time, and there has been a persistent demand for a new edition of it. But I have to admit that due to forces beyond my control it could not be brought out earlier. The present edition, however, is not just a reprint of the former; much new matter has been put into it and the whole book has been thoroughly revised and brought up-to-date. The scope of the book has also been suitably widened which will be evident from its rechristening A Concise History of Sanskrit Literature. I believe it will satisfy its users much more than its predecessor.

In preparing this edition Dr. Radha Govinda Basak, M.A., Dr. Benoy Chandra Sen, M.A.,P.R.S., and a former pupil of mine, Shri Kali Kumar Dutta Sastri, M.A., Kavya-Sankhyatirtha have rendered me much help, especially by drawing my attention to some of the omissions that crept in the first edition of the book. I am also much indebted to my colleagues Dr. Govindagopal Mukherjee, M.A., Sankhyatirtha, Dr. Sisir Kumar Mitra, M.A., LL.B., and also to my former pupils Shri Kalidasa Bhattacharyya, M.A., Shri Gopikamohan Bhattacharyya, M.A., and Shri Bimal Krishna Motilal, M.A. for rendering me invaluable assistance in preparing the present edition.

G.S.

PREFACE TO THE FIRST EDITION

The impetus to the writing of the present work came from my students at Presidency College, Calcutta. The paucity of suitable text-books on the subject intended for degree and post-graduate students of Indian universities was felt by myself in my college life, and in writing this book I have always borne in mind the difficulties which our students experience in tackling the subject.

In the preparation of the book I have freely consulted the two monumental works of M. Winternitz and A.B. Keith. To them, therefore, I am under a deep debt of gratitude. I must also acknowledge my indebtedness to all those authorities whose works have been mentioned in the 'References'.

In preparing the press copy, my former pupil, Prof. Sarojendranath Bhanja, Sahityasastri, Kavya-Puranatirtha, M.A., has rendered invaluable assistance. Another pupil of mine, Shri Taraknath Ghosal, M.A., prepared the major part of the Index. My ex-colleagues, Prof. Upendranath Ghosal, M.A., Ph.D., and Professor Subodh Chandra Sengupta, M.A. P.R.S., Ph.D., had the kindness, the former, to find out for me a few, references, and the latter, to read a considerable portion of the work while in the press. My teachers, Mahamahopadhyaya Haranchandra Shastri, Professor Sadananda Bhaduri, M.A., Ph.D., and Professor Somnath Maitra, M.A., have helped me much by offering valuable suggestions from time to time. I must also acknowledge the advice given so freely by my friend and colleague, Professor Taraknath Sen, M.A., Lastly, I must mention the deep interest which was taken by my cousin, Pandit Ashokanath Shastri, Vedantatirtha, M.A., P.R.S., in seeing the work through.

The occasion makes me remember, with deep and reverent gratitude, those of my teachers at whose feet I had the privilege of studying the subject-the late Professor Rakhaldas Banerjee, M.A., of Benares Hindu University, and Professor Nilmony Chakravarty, M.A., late Senior Professor of Sanskrit, Presidency College, Calcutta.

January, 1943 G.S.
Calcutta.

CONTENTS

	PAGES
Introductory	1—23
History of the Study of Sanskrit in the West—Origin of Indian writing—Vedic and Classical Sanskrit: their relationship—Prākrit—Was Sanskrit a spoken language?	
Chapter I : The Great Epics	24—39
Rāmāyaṇa: Story—Origin and Source—Character—Spurious element—The influence of the Rāmāyaṇa on Indian life and literature—Antiquity—Relation to Buddhism—Greek influence—Allegorical interpretation—Mythological interpretation	
Mahābhārata: General character and story—Gītā—Age of Gītā—Christian influence in Gītā—The Harivaṁśa—Authorship—Three stages of the Epic—Age—Literary and inscriptional evidence—Which of the two Epics is earlier?	
Chapter II : The Purāṇas	40—46
Introduction—Age and antiquity—Was there an original Purāṇa—Character and value—Name and number of Purāṇas—Classification of Purāṇas—The Bhāgavata Purāṇa—Devīmāhātmya—Name and number of Upapurāṇas	
Chapter III : The Tantras	47—50
Meaning, contents and classification—Relation to Vedic literature—Character—Antiquity—Home—Works	
Chapter IV : Post-Epic Kāvya	51—53
Chapter V : Kāvya in inscriptions	54—57
Renaissance Theory of Max Müller—Girnār, Nāsik, Allahabad and Mandasor inscriptions—Conclusions	

PAGES

Chapter VI : Early Buddhist works in Sanskrit ... 58—74

Introduction—Works belonging to Mahāyāna and Hīnayāna schools: (i) Poetical ; (ii) Philosophical ; (iii) Avadāna

Chapter VII : Court-epics ... ... 75—84

Introduction—Growth and development of court-epics—Lesser epic poems

Chapter VIII : Drama ... ... 85—118

Origin of Sanskrit drama—Characteristics—Classification—Growth and development—Less important dramas

Chapter IX : Lyric Poetry ... ... 119—125

Introduction—Growth and development—Lesser lyric poems and anthologies

Chapter X : Historical writings ... ... 126—129

Introduction—Growth and development—Minor historical works

Chapter XI : Prose Literature ... ... 130—138

Introduction—Romance—Fable—Lesser prose tales

Chapter XII : Campū literature ... ... 139—140

Introduction—Important Campūs

Chapter XIII : Grammar ... ... 141—148

Introduction—Pāṇini school—Other important schools—Sectarian schools—Some important grammatical works

Chapter XIV : Poetics and Dramaturgy ... ... 149—155

Introduction—Alaṅkāra school—Rīti school—Rasa school—Dhvani school—Works on Poetics and Dramaturgy

PAGES

Chapter XV : Metrics 156

Introduction—Works on Metrics

Chapter XVI : Lexicography ... ... 157—158

Introduction—Major lexicons—Minor lexicons

Chapter XVII : Civil and Religious Law ... ... 159—161

Growth and development—Important legal works

Chapter XVIII : Politics ... ... 162—164

Introduction—Works on Politics

Chapter XIX : Erotics 165

Introduction—Works on Erotics

Chapter XX : Medicine ... ... 166—167

History of medical literature—Earlier and later medical works

Chapter XXI : Astronomy, Mathematics and Astrology 168—171

History of Astronomy—Works on Astronomy—Works on Mathematics—Works on Astrology

Chapter XXII : Miscellaneous Sciences ... ... 172—173

Archery—Sciences of elephants and horses—Architecture—Sciences of jewels, stealing, cooking, music, dancing and painting

Chapter XXIII : Philosophy ... ... 174—202

Orthodox systems: Nyāya, Vaiśeṣika, Sāṅkhya, Yoga, Mīmāṁsā and Vedānta—Heterodox systems: Buddhism, Jainism and Materialism—Miscellaneous works on philosophy

Index ... ... 203—220

ABBREVIATIONS

ABORI	Annals of the Bhandarkar Oriental Research Institute
Aṣṭ	*Aṣṭādhyāyī*
Har	*Harṣacarita*
HOS	Harvard Oriental Series
IA	Indian Antiquary
JRAS	Journal of the Royal Asiatic Society
Kād	*Kādambarī* (M. R. Kale, 2nd edition)
KL	*Kāvyālaṅkāra*
KS	*Kāmasūtra*
MB	*Mahābhāṣya*
Mbh	*Mahābhārata*
Nir	*Nirukta*
Rag	*Raghuvaṁśa*
Rām	*Rāmāyaṇa*
RV	*Ṛgveda*
SBE	Sacred Books of the East, Oxford
SD	*Sāhityadarpaṇa*
SV	*Śiśupālavadha*
Vās	*Vāsavadattā*

INTRODUCTORY

A. HISTORY OF THE STUDY OF SANSKRIT IN THE WEST

It was in the seventeenth century that the European people, particularly missionaries and travellers, came to know of the Indian languages. In A.D. 1651 Abraham Roger published a Portuguese translation of Bhartṛhari's poems. In A.D. 1699 the Jesuit Father Johann Ernst Hanxleden came to India and after getting himself acquainted with the Sanskrit language wrote the first Sanskrit grammar in a European language. The book, however, was not printed but was consulted by Fra Paolino de St Bartholomes who wrote two Sanskrit grammars besides a number of important works. It was during the administration of Warren Hastings that the work called *Vivādārṇavasetu* was compiled. Under the title *A Code of Gentoo Law* it was published in English in A.D. 1776. Nine years later, the *Bhagavadgītā* was translated into English by Charles Wilkins who also rendered into English the *Hitopadeśa* and the Śakuntalā episode of the *Mahābhārata*. It was, however, Sir William Jones who did most to arouse the interest of Europeans in Indian literature. In A.D. 1789 he published his English translation of Kālidāsa's *Śakuntalā*. The English translation of Kālidāsa's immortal drama was followed by a German translation by Georg Forster in A.D. 1791 which attracted the attention of men like Herder and Goethe. It was again through the enthusiasm of Jones that the *Ṛtusaṁhāra* of Kālidāsa was published in the original text in A.D. 1792. A third work of Jones was the translation of the *Manusmṛti*, the most important legal literature of ancient India. The work of Jones was followed up by Henry Thomas Colebrooke who published

A Digest of Hindu Law on Contracts and Successions based on a composition in Sanskrit by orthodox Indian scholars. He also edited a number of Sanskrit works including the *Amarakośa*, the *Aṣṭādhyāyī*, the *Hitopadeśa* and the *Kirātārjunīya*. Another Englishman who studied Sanskrit in India was Alexander Hamilton who, while returning to England in A.D. 1802, was imprisoned with other Englishmen at Paris under orders of Napoleon Bonaparte. During the period of his imprisonment Hamilton trained up a band of European scholars who took to the study of Sanskrit with earnest zeal. This is commonly referred to as the 'Discovery of Sanskrit' in the West. One of Hamilton's most distinguished students was the great German scholar and poet Friedrich Schlegel, who wrote that epoch-making work *On the Language and Wisdom of the Indians*. This work introduced for the first time the comparative and the historical method. It also contained translations in German of many passages from the *Rāmāyaṇa*, the *Bhagavadgītā*, the *Manusmṛti* and other early works. Friedrich Schlegel's brother August Wilhelm von Schlegel, a student of Professor A. L. Chézy, the first French scholar in Sanskrit, not only contributed much to the study of Comparative Philology but also helped the study of Sanskrit by editing texts and writing translations. One of Schlegel's students was Christian Lassen who was deeply interested in Indian culture. The science of Comparative Philology was founded by Franz Bopp, a student of Professor Chézy and contemporary of August Wilhelm. Bopp also rendered great service to the investigation of Sanskrit literature by incorporating in his work *Conjugations-system*, translations from the *Rāmāyaṇa* and the *Mahābhārata*. His Sanskrit Grammars considerably furthered the study of Sanskrit in Germany. The work of Bopp in the domain of Comparative Philology was developed in a most comprehensive manner by Wilhelm von Humboldt whose interest in the philosophical works of the Indians was of an abiding character. Another noted German, Friedrich Rückert, was also highly interested in Indian poetry. The Latin translations of the Upaniṣads in the beginning of the nineteenth century inspired German philosophers. Schelling, Kant, Schiller, and Schopenhauer were highly charmed to discover 'the production of the highest human wisdom' The actual investigation of Vedic literature was first undertaken by Friedrich Rosen in A.D. 1838 and was subsequently continued by a band of illustrious students of the great French orientalist Eugéne Burnouf, including Rudolph Roth and F. Max Müller, who brought out his famous *editio princeps* of the *Ṛgveda* with the commentary of Sāyaṇa in the years 1849-75. One of Roth's distinguished students was H. Grassmann who published a complete translation of the *Ṛgveda*. It was during this period that Horace Hayman Wilson who came to Calcutta represented the orthodox interpretation of the *Ṛgveda* by translating it on the lines of Sāyaṇa's commentary. Similar work was done by Alfred Ludwig, who is looked upon as a forerunner of R. Pischel, and K. F. Geldner, the joint authors of *Vedic Studies*. The name of Theodor Aufrecht is also associated with Vedic investigations.

The publication of the great *St Petersburg Dictionary* (*Sanskrit-Wörterbuch*) in 1852 is an important event in the history of progressive studies in Sanskrit in the West. The dictionary was compiled by Otto Böhtlingk and Rudolph Roth and published by the Academy of Fine Arts and Sciences, St Petersburg. *The History of Indian Literature* which was published by Albrecht Weber in A.D. 1852 and was edited for the second time in A.D. 1876, is another important work. The edition of the *Śatapathabrāhmaṇa* by the same author is another outstanding contribution. The *Catalogus Catalogorum* published by Theodor Aufrecht in the years 1891, 1896, and 1903, forms a most comprehensive list of Sanskrit authors and works and is a monumental work of its kind. Arthur Anthony Macdonell's *Vedic Grammar* and *Vedic Mythology* and the *Vedic Index* by Macdonell and Arthur Berriedale Keith, have all proved helpful works for the study of Sanskrit in Europe. Maurice Bloomfield's *Vedic Concordance* is another great work which has been of immense help to Vedic studies in the West. William Dwight Whitney's *Sanskrit Grammar* is yet another important treatise. Edward Byle Cowell, who was Principal, Government Sanskrit College, Calcutta, gave a distinct fillip to Sanskritic studies by his translations of the *Sarva-darśanasaṁgraha* and many other important Sanskrit works. Arthur Venis, Principal, Government Sanskrit College, Varanasi, also did a lot to help Sanskritic studies. Amongst European scholars who lived in India and took interest in Sanskrit learning and literature, mention may be made of J. F. Fleet, Vincent A. Smith, Sir Alexander Cunningham, Sir John H. Marshall, Sir M. A. Stein, Sir George Grierson and J. Ferguson.

Among western Indologists who have done invaluable service to the cause of Sanskrit studies, the names of George Bühler, J. Muir, Frank Kielhorn, E. Röer, H. Lüders, Hermann Jacobi, E. Senart, Sylvain Lévi, Edward Washburn Hopkins, Eugen Hultzsch, Arthur Coke Burnell, Monier M. Williams, Theodor Goldstücker, Richard Garbe, Paul Deussen, Julius Eggeling, George Thibaut, Julius Jolly, Maurice Winternitz, F. W. Thomas, L. D. Barnett, T. Tscherbatsky, Sten Konow, Vallée Poussin, Otto Strauss, C. R. Lanman and Giuseppe Tucci are known to all lovers of Sanskrit.

B. ORIGIN OF INDIAN WRITING

Introduction

THE immemorial practice with students of Sanskrit literature has been to commit to memory the various subjects of their study, and this practice of oral tradition has preserved the ancient Vedic texts. This fact has led scholars to surmise that writing was perchance unknown in the earliest period of Indian civilization and that the later forms of the alphabet were not of pure Indian growth.

Evidence of Vedic and Sūtra works

The earliest references to writing in Sanskrit literature are to be found in the *Dharmasūtra* of Vaśiṣṭha, which, as Dr Bühler thinks, was composed about the eighth century B.C. There are, however, some scholars who would like to assign a much later date to the work, namely, the fourth century B.C. There we obtain clear evidence of the widely spread use of writing during the Vedic period, and in Ch. XVI. 10, 14-15, mention is made of written documents as legal evidence. Further, the *Aṣṭādhyāyī* of Pāṇini contains such compounds as *lipikara* and *libikara* which evidently mean 'writer' [III. ii. 21]. The date of Pāṇini, however, is not fixed. Professor Goldstücker wants to place him in the eighth century B.C., while the general body of scholars hold that his age is the fourth century B.C. In addition to the few references set forth above, it may be said that the later Vedic works contain some technical terms such as 'akṣara', 'kāṇḍa', 'paṭala', 'grantha' and the like, which some scholars quote as evidence of the use of writing. But there are others who differ in their interpretations of these terms.

The aforesaid references do not help us much

Evidence of Brāhmaṇical works

in determining the genuine Indian growth of writing, inasmuch as none of the works in which they are found can be safely dated earlier than the period of inscriptions. In the same way, evidences in the Brāhmaṇical works such as the Epics, the Purāṇas, the Kāvyas and the like, are of little or no help. Among them, the Epics are by far the oldest, but it is difficult to prove that every word of their text goes back to a high antiquity. One fact is, however, undeniable, namely that the Epics contain some archaic expressions, such as, 'likh', 'lekha', 'lekhaka', 'lekhana', but not 'lipi', which, as many scholars think, is after all a foreign word. This may suggest that writing was known in India in the Epic age.

Evidence of Indian civilization

There are two other facts which also suggest the same thing. It is believed that the Aryans were in an advanced state of civilization—there was a high development of trade and monetary transactions, and that they carried on minute researches in grammar, phonetics and lexicography. Do not the above facts presuppose the knowledge of the art of writing among ancient Indians? Nevertheless, one will have to adduce evidence, without which nothing can be taken for granted. So we turn to the Buddhist works.

Evidence of Buddhist writings

There are quite a large number of passages in the Ceylonese *Tipiṭaka,* which bear witness to an acquaintance with writing and to its extensive use at the time when the Buddhist canon was composed. 'Lekha' and 'lekhaka' are mentioned in the *Bhikkhu Pācittiya* 2, ii and in the *Bhikkhunī Pācittiya* 49, ii. In the former, writing has been highly praised. In the Jātakas, constant mention is made of letters. The

Jātakas know of proclamations. We are also told of a game named akṣarikā in which the Buddhist monk is forbidden to participate. This game was in all probability one of guessing at letters. In the rules of *Vinaya*, it has been laid down that a criminal, whose name has been written up in the King's porch, must not be received into the monastic order. In the same work, writing has been mentioned as a lucrative profession. Jātaka No. 125 and the *Mahāvagga*, I. 49 bear witness to the existence of elementary schools where the manner of teaching was the same as in the indigenous schools of modern India. All these references prove the existence of the art of writing in pre-Buddhistic days.

Piprāwā vase inscription

The earliest written record is the Piprāwā vase inscription which was discovered by Colonel Claxton Peppe. This inscription is written in Brāhmī character and is in a language which does not conform to any of the standard Prākrits. Some of the case-endings tend towards Māgadhī. No compound consonant has been written. They have been either simplified or divided by epenthesis. No long vowel, excepting two '*e*'s, have been used. The inscription has been differently interpreted. According to some scholars the relics that were enshrined were the relics of Buddha, while others maintain that the relics were those of the Śākyas, who were massacred by Virulaka, son of Prasenajit, King of Kośala. In any case the inscription belongs to the early part of the fifth century B.C.

Next in order of antiquity comes the Sohgaura copper-plate which, as Dr Smith thinks, may be

Sohgaura Copper plate

dated about half a century prior to Aśoka.[1] The characters of the document according to Dr Smith are those of the Brāhmī of the Maurya period and his statements, according to Dr Bühler, are incontestable as everyone of them is traceable in the Edicts. About the proper import of the inscription none is sure. Dr Smith says that he cannot find out any meaning from it. The value of the inscription rests on the fact that it is an evidence for the assumption that in the third century B.C., the use of writing was common in royal offices and that the knowledge of written characters was widely spread among the people.

Inscriptions of Aśoka, Nahapāna and Rudradāman

The inscriptions of Aśoka, are found almost all over India and are written in two different scripts, viz., Brāhmī and Kharoṣṭhī. Two of these inscriptions—that of Shāhbāzgarhī and Mānsehrā, are written in the latter. The rest are written in Brāhmī. The language of early Indian inscriptions is not Sanskrit, but vernacular, which is known as Prākrit. In the inscriptions of Aśoka, local varieties are to be found. Those in the north-western part of India incline more towards Paiśācī, than those found in the eastern part. It is interesting to note that all the Indian inscriptions from the earliest times down to the second century A.D., are in Prākrit. The earliest inscription in Sanskrit is the Nāsik Cave No X inscription of Nahapāna, which was written, in all

[1] The English translation of Dr Bühler's version is given below: 'The order of the great officials of Śrāvastī (issued) from (their camp at) Mānavasitikaṭa—"These two store-houses with three partitions (which are situated) even in famous Vaṁśagrāma require the storage of loads (bhāraka) of Black Panicum, parched grain, cummin-seed and Āmba for (times of) urgent (need). One should not take (anything from the grain stored)." '—IA. Vol. XXV, p. 265.

probability, in the year 41 of the Śaka era, corresponding to A.D. 119. But there are scholars who do not like to call this inscription the earliest in Sanskrit, and in their opinion the well-known Junāgaḍh inscription of Rudradāmaṅ, dated A.D. 150, heads the list of Sanskrit inscriptions. Sanskrit gradually encroached upon Prākrit in the field of epigraphy and it was from the fifth century A.D., that Prākrit disappeared from the field of inscriptions.

Kharoṣṭhī

As for the history of the two scripts, Brāhmī and Kharoṣṭhī, mentioned above, Dr Bühler thinks that the latter was derived from the Aramaic or Phœnician character used by the clerks of the Persian Empire. The north-western parts of India came under the Achæmenian or Persian rule about the sixth century B.C. And it is in those parts of India that inscriptions and coins in Kharoṣṭhī character have been discovered. Dr Bühler has taken sufficient pains to show how from some borrowed letters the full alphabet of the Sanskrit language came into being. There are some scholars who have gone so far as to suggest a meaning of the word Kharoṣṭhī. Thus it is held that the name Kharoṣṭhī has been derived from the shape of letters which generally resemble the lip of an ass. Professor Lévi thinks that the word is derived from the name of the inventor, Kharoṣṭha, an inhabitant of Central Asia.

Brāhmī: South and North Semitic origin

There are several theories regarding the origin of the Brāhmī character. According to Dr Taylor and others, the Brāhmī character was borrowed from a Southern Arab tribe. This theory has not gained any popularity. The theory started by Dr Weber and illustrated by Dr Bühler is generally accepted.

Dr Weber was the first man to discover that some of the old Indian letters are practically identical with certain Assyrian letters and several letters in some inscriptions of the ninth and the seventh centuries B.C., found in Assyria. About one-third of the twenty-three letters of the North Semitic alphabet of that period is identical with the oldest forms of the corresponding Indian letters. Another one-third is somewhat similar, while the rest can with great difficulty be said to correspond to letters of the Indian alphabet. Dr Bühler took advantage of this theory of Dr Weber, and he next proceeded to show that as a result of the prolonged contact between Indian merchants, mostly, Dravidians, and Babylonians in the eighth and the seventh centuries B.C., the former availed themselves of the opportunity to bring the Assyrian art of writing over to India, which later on was enlarged to suit the requirements of the Indian people. Nearly a thousand years later, this form of writing came to be styled as Brāhmī. It has been said that originally the letters were written from right to left, as a single coin has been discovered in a place named Eran, on which the legend runs from right to left. But as the Brāhmiṇs believed the right hand direction to be sacred, they changed the direction and began to write from left to right.

Pre-Semitic origin

According to Professor Rhys Davids, the Indian letters were developed neither from the Northern nor from the Southern Semitic alphabet, but from the pre-Semitic form current in the Euphrates valley. But this theory is not accepted on the ground that this supposed pre-Semitic form of writing has yet to be explored.

Sir Alexander Cunningham had wanted to derive each letter from the indigenous hieroglyphic, but his theory was discarded on the ground that no such hieroglyphic could be found in India. But the recent excavations at Mohenjo-Daro and Harappa have brought to light an original Indian hieroglyphic and a further examination of the theory once started by Sir A. Cunningham may be undertaken.

Hieroglyphic origin

Until the discovery of the Indus Valley civilization, extant archaeological evidence relating to the use of writing in India could not be carried far beyond the Maurya period. But the seals which have been recovered from Mohenjo-Daro and Harappa, although not yet deciphered, clearly show that some form of writing must have been in existence at least two millenniums before the birth of Christ. Some attempts have been made to decipher the seals and trace their origin from or affinities with forms of writing current in the ancient world. According to one view, the Indus valley inscriptions are composed of symbols, each of which is an ideogram. Hrozny tries to discover similarities between the Hittite script and the Indus Valley script. Diringer on the other hand is convinced that no script existed from which the derivation of the Indus script could be reasonably proved. He expresses the view that the latter may have originated from a yet unknown script which was the common ancestor of the cuneiform and the early Elamite writing. Hunter and Langdon regard the Mohenjo-Daro script as the prototype of Brāhmī but it is impossible to expect any final or conclusive results from speculations based on a series of unknown factors or mere probabilities, especially when

Conclusions

the sound-values of the signs in the Indus Valley still remain unascertained. Ancient Indian traditions recorded in a number of works, Brāhmaṇical, Jaina and Buddhist, ascribe the invention of writing to Brahmā. A Chinese reference seems to indicate that the particular writing meant by this tradition was the Brāhmī. Thus the Indians in ancient times believed that their system of writing was national in character, indigenous in origin and of remote antiquity. But if the name Brāhmī is to be given to the script used in the inscriptions of Aśoka as well as the Piprāwā Vase inscription and the Eran coin legend, that name cannot consistently be applied to the script used by the Indus Valley people, as no similarity between the two has yet been established.

Both on grounds of developed form of the Brāhmī script as indicated in the Aśokan edicts and its supposed origin from the North Semitic writing used in certain inscriptions of the ninth and eighth centuries B.C., Bühler proposes to place the beginning of the Brāhmī at some date in the neighbourhood of 800 B.C. This date according to his line of argument may be the starting-point of the form of Brāhmī which passed through certain fundamental changes, modifications and enlargements to reach the stage as exhibited in the Aśokan edicts and the one or two supposedly earlier inscriptions. But it can no longer be regarded as the date marking the beginning of writing in India in view of the discoveries made in the Indus Valley. Nor, as Bühler himself admitted, can his theory explain how without some kind of writing being current among the Vedic people the technicalities and complexities of their literature, their phonetics, grammar, economic transactions, numerical calculations and the like assumed such a pronounced form with the help of memory alone unsupported by written symbols. But as no specimen of writing or any hint about its form which may have been connected with the culture and civilization of the Vedic people has been found, it is still impossible to frame an acceptable hypothesis about the course of evolution of writing in India preceding the advent of Brāhmī in the form known to us and the nature of its affiliation to the earlier script the existence of which is not considered unlikely.

The foreign origin of Brāhmī, though advocated by many, has not been definitely proved. In fact many eminent scholars maintain that writing in India was of indigenous origin. No final conclusion can be arrived at in the matter until the Indus Valley script has been correctly deciphered and fresh material discovered filling in the long gap that separates the Indus Valley period from the Maurya period in the history of writing in India and also new light thrown on the system of writing that may have been quite possibly used by the Vedic people. The genius of the Indian people was responsible for an extraordinary development of regional scripts out of the original Brāhmī. Local varieties which are not wanting in the Aśokan Brāhmī used throughout his empire in the North and the South, gathered a momentum in the succeeding centuries, and the numerous regional or provincial scripts which came into being and advanced towards maturity can be traced to Brāhmī with scientific precision. Two early Jain Sūtras, the *Samavāyāṅga Sūtra* and the *Paṇṇavāṇa Sūtra* furnish a list of eighteen varieties of writing including Brāhmī and Kharoṣṭhī, Dāmili (Dravidian) and Javanāliya. The last named script is to be identified with Yavanānī (i.e. the Greek script) mentioned by Pāṇini. The *Lalitavistara* gives a list of sixty four scripts which include Brāhmī, Kharoṣṭhī and foreign scripts like Cīnalipi, Huṇalipi and regional scripts like Aṅgalipi, Vaṅgalipi, etc. Indian scripts were introduced into different countries of Asia ; inscriptions and other valuable documents have been discovered in widely separated areas in Asia written in Indian characters which also became the basis of developments of national scripts in some countries with which India had been in active communication for many centuries in the past.

REFERENCES

Banerjee, R. D.: *The Origin of the Bengali Script*
Bühler, G.: *Indian Paleography*
The Origin of Brāhmī Alphabet
The Origin of the Kharoṣṭhī Alphabet (IA. Vol. XXIV)
Indian Studies III.
Cunningham, A.: *The Coins of Ancient India*
Cust, R. N.: *On the Origin of the Indian Alphabet,* JRAS. Vol. XVI (New series)
Diringer, D.: *The Alphabet*
Hunter, G. R.: *The Script of Mohenjo-Daro,* etc.
Lévi, S.: *Indian Writing* (IA. Vol. XXXIII)
Kharoṣṭrī Writing (IA. Vol. XXXV)
Kharoṣṭra and the Kharoṣṭrī Writing
Mitra, P.: *New Light from Pre-historic India* (IA. Vol. XLVIII)
Ojha, G. H.: *Bhāratīya Prācīna Lipimālā*
Pandey, R. B.: *Indian Paleography,* Part I
Shamasastry, R.: *A Theory of the Origin of the Devanagri Alphabet* (IA. Vol. XXXV)
Śivamūrti, C.: *Indian Epigraphy and South Indian Scripts*
Taylor, I.: *The Alphabet*
Thomas, E.: *Princep's Essays,* Vol. II

C. VEDIC AND CLASSICAL SANSKRIT: THEIR RELATIONSHIP

Introduction

INDIAN tradition knows Sanskrit as the language of the gods, which has been the dominant language of India for a period covering over four thousand years. Viewed from its rich heritage of literature, its fascinating charm of words, its flexibility of expression in relation to thought, Sanskrit occupies a singular place in the literature of the world.

Vedic and Classical: difference in matter and spirit

The Sanskrit language is generally divided into Vedic and Classical. In the Vedic language was written the entire sacred literature of the Aryan Indians. Within this Vedic language several stages may be carefully distinguished, and in course of its transition from the one to the other it gradually grew modern till it ultimately merged in Classical Sanskrit. But when we pass on from the Vedic lyrics to the lyrics of Classical Sanskrit, we seem to enter a 'new world'. Not only are the grammar, vocabulary, metre and style different, but there is also a marked distinction in respect of matter and spirit. Thus the Classical Sanskrit period is marked by a change of religious outlook and social conditions. Vedic literature is almost entirely religious; but Classical Sanskrit has a 'profane' aspect as well which is not in any way inferior to the religious aspect. The religion in the Epic period has become different from what it was in the Vedic age. The Vedic Nature-worship has been superseded by the cult of Brahmā, Viṣṇu and Śiva, and it is in the Epic period that we find for the first time the incarnations of Viṣṇu who has come to be looked upon as the Supreme Deity. New gods and goddesses unknown to the Vedas have arisen, and Vedic gods have either been forgotten or reduced to a subordinate position. Indra is, indeed, the only god who still maintains high status as the lord of heaven. Vedic literature in its earlier phase was marked by a spirit of robust optimism ; but Classical Sanskrit literature has a note of pessimism owing probably to the influence of the doctrine of *karman* and transmigration of souls. The naive simplicity of Vedic literature is strikingly absent in Classical Sanskrit where the introduction of the supernatural and the wonderful is full of exaggeration. So kings are described as visiting Indra in heaven and a sage creating a new world by means of his great spiritual powers. The tribal organization of the state has lessened much in importance in the Epic period where we find the rise of many territorial kingdoms.

Difference in form : (i) accent

In respect of form also Classical Sanskrit differs considerably from Vedic. Thus the four Vedas and the Brāhmaṇas are marked with accents (*udātta*, *anudātta* and *svarita*) which only can help us in finding out the meaning of different words. Thus, for instance, the word 'Indraśatru' with one kind of accent will mean 'Indra as enemy', and the same word with a different kind of accent will imply 'enemy of Indra'. But in Classical Sanskrit literature, accent has no part to play.

(ii) grammar

Phonetically Vedic and Classical languages are identical, but grammatically they differ. The change in grammar is not generally due to the introduction of new formations or inflexions, but to the loss of forms.[1] In respect of mood, the difference between

[1] Certain grammatical forms which occur in the Vedic language disappear in the Classical. Thus in declension a number of forms has

Classical and Vedic Sanskrit is specially very great. In the Vedas the present tense has besides its indicative inflexion, a subjunctive (requisition), an optative (wish) and an imperative (command). The same three moods are found, though with much less frequency, as belonging to the perfect and they are also made from the aorist (*luṅ*) and the future has no moods. In Classical Sanskrit, the present tense adds to its indicative an optative and an imperative. But the subjunctive (*leṭ*) is lost in Classical Sanskrit.[1] In the Vedic period no less than fifteen forms of infinitive were used[2] of which only one (*tum*) survives in the Classical period. Vedic Sanskrit differs from Classical Sanskrit in respect of the use of prefixes (*upasargas*). Thus in Classical Sanskrit the *upasarga* must invariably precede the root and should form a part of it. But the use of *upasargas* was unrestricted in Vedic Sanskrit. It was used before the root and after it and was also sometimes separated from the root itself.[3] Compounds of more than two words, which are rare in the Vedas and the Brāhmaṇas, are frequent in Classical Sanskrit.

(iii) Vocabulary

The aforesaid changes in respect of forms were mainly due to the efforts of grammarians who exercised considerable influence on the development of the language. The vocabulary also underwent many changes. It was largely extended by derivation, composition and compilation. Many old words that

been dropped: (i) the nominative and accusative dual forms of '-*a*' stems ending in *ā*, e.g., *narā*, (ii) the nominative plural form of '-*a*' stems ending in -*āsaḥ*, e.g., *devāsaḥ*, (iii) the instrumental plural form of '-*a*' stems ending in -*ebhiḥ* e.g., *devebhiḥ*.

[1] *adya jīvānā, śataṁ jīvāti śaradaḥ.*

[2] *Aṣṭ.* III. iv. 9

[3] *ā kṛṣṇena rajasā vartamāno.*

could not be found in Vedic literature came to be added in Classical Sanskrit and many new words were borrowed.

(iv) Metre Vedic language again differs from Classical with regard to the use of metres. Beside the principal seven metres of the Vedas (*gāyatrī, uṣṇik, anuṣṭubh, bṛhatī, paṅkti, triṣṭubh* and *jagatī*), Classical Sanskrit presents a limitless variety of metres.

REFERENCES

Ghate, V. S.: *Lectures on the Ṛgveda*
Kielhorn, F.: *A Grammar of Sanskrit Language*
Macdonell, A. A.: *A History of Sanskrit Literature*
A Vedic Grammar
Vedic Mythology
Weber, A.: *The History of Indian Literature*
Whitney, W. D.: *A Sanskrit Grammar*
Williams, M.. *A Practical Grammar of the Sanskrit Language*
Winternitz, M.: *A History of Indian Literature*, Vol. I

D. PRĀKRIT

Antiquity THE beginnings of the Prākrits go back to a period of great antiquity. Even at the time when Vedic hymns were composed, there existed a popular language which differed from the literary dialect. In the Vedic hymns, there are several words which cannot be phonetically other than Prākrit. Buddha and Mahāvīra preached their doctrines in the sixth century B.C., in the language of the people in order that all might understand them. The language of the Buddhist texts which were collected during the period between 500 B.C. and 400 B.C., was Māgadhī. The extant Buddhist texts of Ceylon, Burma and Siam are in a form of popular language to which the name Pāli has been given. There is difference of opinion amongst scholars regarding the place and origin of Pāli. The only inscription, the language of which is akin to Pāli, is the Hāti-Gumphā inscription of Khāravela, dated the 160th year of the Maurya era.

Relation of Sanskrit to Prākrit

Patañjali says that Sanskrit was a spoken language but it was confined to the cultured section of the people. The popular dialect of India was known by the general name of Prākrit. From the distribution of languages in Sanskrit dramas it appears that the masses while speaking Prākrit, could understand Sanskrit. It has been said in Bharata's *Nāṭyaśāstra* that Prākrit and Sanskrit are different branches of one and the same language. In the earliest known forms of Prākrit, there are passages which can be easily translated into Sanskrit by the application of simple phonetic rules.

European view

According to European scholars, Prākrit, which represents the Middle Indian period of the Indo-Aryan languages, may again be sub-divided into three stages: (1) Old Prākrit or Pāli, (2) Middle Prākrit, and (3) late Prākrit or Apabhraṁśa. They would like to say that if Prākrit had been a language derived from Sanskrit, Prākrit would have taken the name Sāṁskṛta. Moreover, there are many words and forms in Prākrit which cannot be traced in Classical Sanskrit. If however, by the word Sanskrit is included the language of the Vedas and all dialects of the old Indian period, it will be correct to assume that Prākrit is derived from Sanskrit. But the word Sanskrit is generally used to refer to the Pāṇini-Patañjali language.

Orthodox view

Indian grammarians, however, would say that the name Prākrit is derived from the word *prakṛti*, which means 'the basic form', viz., Sanskrit. Further, in Prākrit there are three classes of words, e.g., (i) *tatsama*—words which are identical in form and meaning in both Sanskrit and Prākrit, e.g., *deva, kamala,* (ii) *tadbhava*—words that are derived from Sanskrit by the application of phonetic rules, e.g., *ajjautta* < *āryaputra, paricumbia* < *paricumbya,* and (iii) *deśin*—words that are of indigenous origin and the history of which cannot be accurately traced, e.g., *chollanti, caṅga.* A careful examination of Prākrit vocabulary reveals the fact that the majority of Prākrit words belong to the second class ; words belonging to the other classes are comparatively small in number. The derivatives are in most cases the result of phonetic decay.

Varieties of Prākrit

The following are the more important literary Prākrits: Mahārāṣṭrī, Śaurasenī and Māgadhī are the dramatic Prākrits, while Ardha-Māgadhī, Jaina-Mahārāṣṭrī and Jaina-Śaurasenī are the Prākrits of the Jaina canon. The last is the Apabhraṁśa.

REFERENCES

Bhandarkar, R. G.: *Wilson Philological Lectures* (Lecture III)
Cowell, E. B.: *A Short Introduction to Prakrit*
Vararuci.: *Prākṛtaprakāśa*
Woolner, A. C.: *An Introduction to Prākrit.*

E. WAS SANSKRIT A SPOKEN LANGUAGE?

European view

A SECTION of European scholars believes that in spite of the vast extent of Sanskrit literature, Sanskrit was never used in actual speech. It was a purely literary and artificial language and the language that was spoken even in ancient times was Prākrit.

But there are evidences to show that to all intents and purposes, Sanskrit was a living language and that it was spoken by at least a large section of the people. Etymologists and grammarians like Yāska and Pāṇini describe Classical Sanskrit as *Bhāṣā*, the speech, as distinguished from Vedic Sanskrit,[1] and it will not probably be incorrect to suggest that this description serves to draw out the special character of Classical Sanskrit as a living speech. Moreover, there are many sūtras in the *Aṣṭādhyāyī* of Pāṇini which are meaningless unless they have any reference to a living speech.[2] Yāska, Pāṇini and even Kātyāyana have discussed the peculiarities in the usages of Easterners and Northerners.[3] Local variations are also noticed by Kātyāyana, while Patañjali has collected words occurring in particular districts.[4] Patañjali again tells us that the words of Sanskrit are of ordinary life and describes an anecdote in which a grammarian converses with a charioteer and the discussion is carried on in Sanskrit.[5]

Orthodox view

From all that has been said above, it is clear that Sanskrit was a living speech in ancient India. But the question which still remains to be discussed is whether Sanskrit was the vernacular of all classes of people in the society or of any particular section or sections. Patañjali says that the language spoken in the days of Pāṇini could be mastered if it was heard

Extent of Sanskrit as a spoken language

[1] *Nir.* I. iv. 5 & 7, II. ii. 6 & 7, *Aṣṭ.* III. ii. 108, etc.
[2] *Aṣṭ.* VIII. iv. 48, etc. Also *Gaṇasūtras,* Nos. 18, 20, 29.
[3] *Nir.* II. ii. 8. *Aṣṭ.* IV. i. 157 & 160.
[4] Cf. *Vārttika, sarve deśāntare,* referred to in the *Paspaśāhnika, MB.*
[5] *MB.* under *Aṣṭ.* II. iv. 56.

from the learned Brāhmaṇas of the day (*śiṣṭa*) who could speak correct Sanskrit without any special tuition.[1] It is gathered from the *Sundarakāṇḍa* of the *Rāmāyaṇa* that the language spoken by the twice-born castes was Sanskrit.[2] It is stated in the *Kāmasūtra* of Vātsyāyana that men of taste should speak both in Sanskrit and the vernacular of the province, and this means that Sanskrit was not the spoken language of each and every section of the people in the society.[3] Hiuen Tsang, the Chinese traveller (seventh century A.D.), tells us that the language in which official debates were arranged, was Sanskrit and not any provincial dialect. The *Pañcatantra* informs us that the medium of instruction for the young boys of the ruling class was Sanskrit and not any vernacular.

Conclusions

We may draw from this the conclusion that Sanskrit was the vernacular of the educated people but it was understood in still wider sections. Our conclusions may find support from the evidence of the dramatic literature where we observe that Brāhmaṇas, kings and ministers speak Sanskrit while women and all the common people use Prākrit, except that nuns and courtesans occasionally converse in Sanskrit. Uneducated Brāhmaṇas are introduced speaking popular dialects. But it is highly significant that dialogues between Sanskrit-speaking and Prākrit-speaking persons are very frequent and this suggests that in real life Sanskrit was understood by those who would not speak it themselves. This statement may be further corroborated by the fact that

[1] *MB.* under *Aṣṭ.* VI. iii. 109.
[2] *Rām.* V. xxx. 18.
[3] *KS.* iv. 20.

common people would gather to hear the recital of the popular Epics in the palaces of kings and in temples; they would not attend such functions unless they could understand the content of the recital.

REFERENCES

Bhandarkar, R. G.: *Wilson Philological Lectures* (Lecture VII)
Keith, A. B.: *A History of Sanskrit Literature*
Macdonell, A. A.: *A History of Sanskrit Literature*
Pathak, K. B.: *The Age of Pāṇini and Sanskrit as a Spoken Language* (ABORI. Vol. XI)
Rapson, E. J.: JRAS. 1904

CHAPTER I

THE GREAT EPICS

A. RĀMĀYAṆA

Story

THE Indian tradition makes Vālmīki, the author of the *Rāmāyaṇa,* the first poet (*ādikavi*) who is reported to have been deeply moved by the piteous wailings of the female curlew when her husband was killed by the dart of a forester. Vālmīki's feelings found an expression through the medium of metre,[1] and at the bidding of the divine sage Nārada who brought messages from Brahmā he composed the immortal Rāma-Epic which tells the story of Prince Rāma, the dutiful and devoted son of King Daśaratha of Ayodhyā, banished from his kingdom for fourteen years through the jealousy of his step-mother Kaikeyī who secured possession of the throne for her own son Bharata. So Rāma and Sītā, his beloved wife, accompanied by the third prince Lakṣmaṇa went to the forest. There the adventures of the banished prince, Sītā's abduction by Rāvaṇa, King of Laṅkā, the help given to Rāma by Hanumat, a chief of the monkeys, the destruction of Rāvana and his party, the fire-odeal of Sītā to prove her chastity—these and many other incidents have been described in all the glowing colours of poetry.

Origin and source

From a perusal of the *Rāmāyaṇa* itself we come to know that the story of the Epic was recited by pro-

[1] *Rām.* I. ii. 15.

fessional minstrels. The story was handed down by oral transmission from Vālmīki to the twin brothers, Kuśa and Lava, who sang it in the royal court of Rāma. The above facts have led scholars to surmise that the exploits of the great heroes of the Ikṣvāku race inspired the bards of Ayodhyā to compose narrative ballads. Such were utilized by Vālmīki who turned them into a full-fledged Epic. In this connexion, it may be remembered that Epics and Purāṇas are derived from a common ancient source which may be traced in the Vedas. The famous dialogue hymns of the Ṛgveda are but ancient ballads consisting of some narrative and some dramatic elements. These are believed to be the sources of epic poetry as well as dramas. It is opined again that the Epics owe their origin to the 'Songs in praise of men' known as Gāthā Nārāśaṁsī.

Character

The *Rāmāyaṇa* which is essentially a poetic creation has influenced the thought and poetry of later centuries in course of which new matters were added to the original composition. The work, in its present form and extent, comprises seven books and contains 24,000 verses approximately. But it must be remembered that the text of the Epic has been preserved in three recensions, the West Indian, the Bengal and the Bombay, and curiously enough each recension has almost one third of the verses occurring in neither of the other two. Of the three, the Bombay recension is believed to have preserved the oldest form of the Epic, for here we find a large number of archaic expressions which are rare in the Bengal and the West Indian recensions. According to Professor Jacobi, the Rāma-Epic was first composed in the Kośala country on the basis of the ballad poetry recited by the rhapsodists. In course of time there naturally arose difference in the tradition of the recitations made by professional story-tellers, and this difference adequately explains the variations in the three recensions when they had been assuming their definite forms in the different parts of the land. But it must be borne in mind that inspite of the variations in the three recensions it is not difficult to detect the spurious and recognize the nucleus. As Jacobi rightly puts it: As on many of our old venerable cathedrals every coming generation has added something new and repaired something old, without the original construction being effaced, in spite of all the added little chapels and turrets, so also many generations of singers have been at work at the *Rāmāyaṇa* ; but the old nucleus, around which so much has grown, is to the searching eye of the student, not difficult to recognize, if not in every detail, yet in its principal features.[1]

Spurious element

Internal evidence proves almost conclusively that the whole of the *Rāmāyaṇa* as it is found today was not written at one time. It is said that of the seven books in the *Rāmāyaṇa*, the last one and portions of the first are interpolations. In the first place, there are numerous passages in the genuine books which either make no reference to the incidents in the first book or contain statements which contradict those to be found in the first book. Secondly, in the first and third cantos of the first book we find two tables of contents, the first of which does not mention the first and the seventh books. Thirdly, the style and

[1] *Das Rāmāyaṇa*, p. 60.

language of the first book do not bear comparison with that of the five genuine books (II-VI). Fourthly, the frequent interruption of the narrative in the first and the seventh books and the complete absence of any such interruption in the other five books cannot but suggest that the two books were composed by subsequent poets of less eminence and talent than the author of the genuine books. Lastly, the character of the hero as drawn in the first and the seventh books differs from what we find in the remaining books. Thus in those two books Rāma is not a mortal hero which he is in the other five books, but a divine being worthy of reverence to the nation.

The influence of the Rāmāyaṇa on Indian life and literature

The *Rāmāyaṇa* is a highly popular epic which has become the property of the entire Indian people and it is not an exaggeration if it is said that it has influenced more than any other poem the thought and poetry of a nation for thousands of years. People in different walks of life are all quite familiar with the characters and stories of the great Epic. In the eyes of Indians Rāma is the ideal prince, the embodiment of all conceivable virtue and Sīta the ideal of conjugal love and fidelity, the highest virtue of woman. Popular sayings and proverbs bear unmistakable testimony to the acquaintance of the Indian people with the stories of the Epic. Preachers belonging to different sects draw upon the story of the Epic at the time of religious discourses meant for the mass. Beginning with Aśvaghoṣa who composed the *Buddhacarita* on the model of the *Rāmāyaṇa* and coming down to such later writers as Bhaṭṭi and Bhavabhūti we are amazed to observe the extent of influence of the Epic on them and their poetical creation. Even the folklores and vernacular literature of the various provinces have been deeply influenced by the story of the *Rāmāyaṇa*. And it would not be wrong to say that even upto present times the life and literature in India are considerably moved by the great Epic. The conception of Rāmarājya (Kingdom of Rāma) owes its origin to the *Rāmāyaṇa*.

Antiquity

It has been already observed that the original work of Vālmīki assumed different forms as with years rhapsodists introduced into it newer elements. It is, therefore, very difficult, if not absolutely impossible, to fix any specified age for the whole poem. Dr Winternitz says that the transformation of Rāma from a man to the Universal God through a semi-divine national hero, cannot but take a sufficient length of time. It should be noted, however, that not only the Rāma-legend but the *Rāmāyaṇa* of Vālmīki also was known to the *Mahābhārata* which contains the *Rāmopākhyāna* in the *Vanaparvan*, of course, in a condensed form. On the other hand, the poet or the poets of the *Rāmāyaṇa* nowhere refer to the Bhārata story. These facts have led scholars like Professor Jacobi to presume a very early existence of the Rāma-Epic[1] though it still remains a disputed point whether it was earlier than the original story of the *Mahābhārata*, the passage in the *Vanaparvan* containing the reference to the *Rāmāyaṇa*, being absent in that very early form of the Bhārata Epic. Dr Winternitz believes that 'if the *Mahābhārata* had on

[1] Scholars like Jacobi, Schlegel, M. Williams, Jolly and others point out that the *Rāmāyaṇa* is earlier than the *Mahābhārata*, because the burning of widows does not occur in it, but it is mentioned in the *Mahābhārata*.

the whole its present form in the fourth century A.D., the *Rāmāyaṇa* must have received its final form at least a century or two earlier".

Relation to Buddhism

From a study of Jātaka literature it would appear that the stories of some of the Jātakas naturally remind us of the story of the *Rāmāyaṇa* though it must be admitted that we seldom observe any 'literal agreement' between the two. To cite an instance, the *Daśaratha-jātaka* relates the story of the *Rāmāyaṇa* in a different way, where Rāma and Sītā are described as brother and sister. But it is highly significant that while the Jātakas give us innumerable stories of the demon-world and the animals, they never mention the names of Rāvaṇa and Hanumat and the monkeys. It is not, therefore, improbable that prior to the fourth or the third centuries B.C. when the Buddhist *Tipiṭaka* is believed to have come into existence, the *Rāmāyaṇa* in its Epic form was not available though ballads dealing with Rāma were known to exist. Traces of Buddhism cannot be found in the *Rāmāyaṇa* and the solitary instance where the Buddha is mentioned is believed to be an interpolation.[1] Dr Weber, however, suggests that the *Rāmāyaṇa* is based on an ancient Buddhist legend of Prince Rāma. He thinks that the hero of the *Rāmāyaṇa* is essentially a sage in spirit and not merely a hero of war and that in Rāma we observe the glorification of the ideal of Buddhist equanimity. Dr Winternitz also approves of the idea of explaining the extreme mildness and gentleness of Rāma by 'Buddhistic undercurrents'. But we must say that by thinking in this way

[1] Lassen on Weber's *Rāmāyaṇa* (IA. Vol. III)

Dr Weber has ignored the fact that a poet like Vālmīki could easily draw his inspiration from his own heritage. Our conclusion, therefore, is that there was no direct influence of Buddhism on the *Rāmāyaṇa*.

Greek influence

It is certain that there is no Greek influence on the *Rāmāyaṇa* as the genuine *Rāmāyaṇa* betrays no acquaintance with the Greeks. Dr Weber, however, thinks that the *Rāmāyaṇa* is based on the Greek legend of Helen and the Trojan war. But an examination of the contents of the poem shows that the expression *yavana* occurs twice in the passages of the *Rāmāyaṇa* which are evidently interpolations.

Allegorical interpretation of the Epic

Professor Lassen was the first scholar to give an allegorical interpretation of the *Rāmāyaṇa*. In his opinion the Epic represented the first attempt of the Aryans to conquer Southern India. According to Dr Weber it was meant to account for the spread of Aryan civilization to South India and Ceylon.

Mythological interpretation

Professor Jacobi gives us a mythological interpretation and says that there is no allegory in the Epic. Thus he points out that in the *Ṛgveda,* Sītā appears as the field-furrow and invoked as the goddess of agriculture. In some of the Gṛhyasūtras Sītā is the genuine daughter of the plough-field and is a wife of Parjanya or Indra. In the *Rāmāyaṇa* also Sītā is represented as emerging from the plough-field of Janaka. Rāma can be identified with Indra and Hanumat with the Maruts, the associates of Indra, in his battle with demons. But we would only add that to read allegory or mythology in a first rate work of art is without any justification.

REFERENCES

Davids, R.: *Buddhist India*
Hopkins, E. W.: *The Great Epics of India*
Jacobi, H.: *Das Rāmāyaṇa*
Macdonell, A. A.: *A History of Sanskrit Literature*
Smith, V. A.: *Oxford History of India*
Weber, A.: *On the Rāmāyaṇa* (IA. Vol. III)
The History of Indian Literature
Williams, W.: *Indian Wisdom*
Winternitz, M.: *A History of Indian Literature*, Vol. I

B. MAHĀBHĀRATA

General character and story

Dr Winternitz describes the *Mahābhārata* as a whole literature and does not look upon it as one poetic production which the *Rāmāyaṇa* essentially is. The nucleus of the *Mahābhārata* is the great war of eighteen days fought between the Kauravas, the hundred sons of Dhṛtarāṣṭra and the Pāṇḍavas, the five sons of Pāṇḍu. The poet narrates all the circumstances leading up to the war. In this great Kurukṣetra battle were involved almost all the kings of India joining either of the two parties. The result of this war was the total annihilation of the Kauravas and their party, and Yudhiṣṭhira, the head of the Pāṇḍavas, became the sovereign monarch of Hastināpura. But with the progress of years new matters and episodes, relating to the various aspects of human life, social, economic, political, moral and religious as also fragments of other heroic legends and legends containing reference to famous kings, came to be added to the aforesaid nucleus and this phenomenon probably continued for centuries till in the early part of the Christian era the Epic gathered its present shape which is said to contain a hundred thousand verses. It is, therefore, that the *Mahābhārata* has been described not only as a heroic poem, but also as a 'repertory of the whole of the old bard poetry'. The Epic in its present form is divided into eighteen books[1] with a supplement called the *Harivaṁśa*.

[1] The eighteen books which are known as *parvan* are the following: *Ādi, Sabhā, Vana, Virāṭa, Udyoga, Bhīṣma, Droṇa, Karṇa, Śalya,*

Gītā

The famous *Bhagavadgītā* is a chapter of the *Bhīṣmaparvan* and contains eighteen sections. The *Gītā* is a simplification in verse of the general doctrines in Hindu philosophy and is a book specially meant for the dwellers of the society rather than for one who has renounced it. The book is no doubt one of the finest fruits of Indian philosophy and has gained world-wide recognition in the hands of philosophers. The theme of this book is the advice, given by Kṛṣṇa for consoling depressed Arjuna, mainly dwelling on the doctrines of *karman*, *jñāna* and *bhakti*.

Age of Gītā

The *Gītā* has been widely read and admired for many centuries past, ever since Alberūnī spoke highly of it. According to Winternitz it is the sacred book of the Bhāgavatas, a Vaiṣṇava sect which as early as the beginning of the second century B.C. had found adherence even among the Greeks in Gāndhāra. Indian scholars like Telang and Bhandarkar hold that the *Gītā* was composed not later than the fourth century B.C. Its language, style and metre prove that the poem is one of the earliest parts of the *Mahābhārata*.

Christian influence on Gītā

There is a fantastic theory of Christian influence on the *Gītā* attempted by F. Lorinser. It is held that the author of the *Gītā* not only knew and frequently utilized the Scripture of the New Testament, but also wove into his system the Christian ideas and views in general. This view has been discarded on the ground

Sauptika, Strī, Śānti, Anuśāsana, Āśvamedhika, Āśramavāsika, Mausalya, Mahāprasthānika and *Svargārohaṇika.*

It is not definitely known whether this division into eighteen books is purely traditional, there being a somewhat different form of division as surmised from the writings of Alberūnī.

that the doctrine of *bhakti* in Indian literature is found earlier than the Christian era and that the *Gītā* was composed at least two hundred years before the birth of Christ.

Hari-vaṁśa

The *Harivaṁśa* is regarded as a supplement or appendix (*khila*) to the *Mahābhārata* but the connexion between the two is purely external and is limited essentially to the fact that the same Vaiśampāyana is the speaker in both. The *Harivaṁśa* which is a work of 16,374 verses does not appear to have been composed by a single author. It is, in fact, a jumbled mass of texts. It consists of three sections, namely, *Harivaṁśa-parvan* containing geneology of Hari, *Viṣṇuparvan* dealing almost exclusively with Kṛṣṇa and *Bhaviṣya-parvan,* a loose collection of Purāṇa texts.

Authorship

In spite of all the diverse elements of which the *Mahābhārata* consists, the poem is regarded by the Indians as a unified work complete in itself. The author is the sage Kṛṣṇa Dvaipāyana, also called Vyāsa. The story runs that the sage imparted the work to his pupil Vaiśampāyana who recited the whole poem in the intervals of the great snake-sacrifice of King Janamejaya. On the occasion it was heard by Sūta Ugraśravas, son of sage Lomaharṣaṇa. The present text of the *Mahābhārata* is what Sūta Ugraśravas narrated in the assembly of sages at the twelve-yearly sacrifice of Śaunaka in the forest of Nimiṣa. Thus Ugraśravas is the reciter of the outline story while in the poem itself Vaiśampāyana is the speaker. Within the narrative of Vaiśampāyana numerous inserted stories are put in the mouth of different persons and it must be remembered that such insertion of stories within stories is a very common device in Indian literature. A careful study of the above facts will suggest the gradual growth of the Epic from a smaller poem to its present extent and thus convince us of the truth of the contention that the work is not from the pen of a single author or even a careful compiler. It is maintained by Winternitz that 'unpoetical theologicians and commentators and clumsy copyists have succeeded in conglomerating into a heterogenous mass parts which are really incompatible and which date from different centuries'. But the very fact that the *Mahābhārata* represents a whole literature and should not be looked upon as a single unified poetic production has made it a valuable record enabling us to gain 'an insight into the deepest depths of the soul of the Indian people'.

Three stages of the Epic

It is extremely difficult for us to separate at this distant date the chaff from the real. However, in the first book of the *Mahābhārata* there is a statement that at one time the Epic contained 24,000 verses while in another context we find that it consisted of 8,800 verses. These statements may definitely lead one to conclude that the Epic had undergone three principal stages of development before it assumed its present form.

Age

It is impossible to give in one line the exact date of the *Mahābhārata*. To determine the date of the *Mahābhārata* we should determine the date of every part of this Epic. In the Vedas there is no mention of the incident of the great Kurukṣetra battle. In the Brāhmaṇas, however, the holy Kuru-field is described as a place of pilgrimage where gods and mortals celebrated big sacrificial feasts. We also find the names of Janamejaya and Bharata in the

Brāhmaṇas. So also the name of Parīkṣit as a ruler of Kuru-land is found in the *Atharvaveda*. We find frequent mention of the Kurus and the Pāñcālas in the *Yajurveda*. The *Kāṭhakasaṁhitā* mentions the name of Dhṛtarāṣṭra, son of Vicitravīrya. In the *Sāṅkhyāyana-śrautasūtra* we find the mention of a war in Kuru-land which was fatal for the Kauravas. But the names of the Pāṇḍavas do not occur therein. The *Gṛhyasūtra* of Āśvalāyana gives the names of Bhārata and *Mahābhārata* in a list of teachers and books. Pāṇini gives us the derivation of the words Yudhiṣṭhira, Bhīma and Vidura and the accent of the compound *Mahābhārata*. Patañjali is the first to make definite allusions to the story of the battle between the Kauravas and the Pāṇḍavas. Although the Buddhist *Tipiṭaka* does not mention the name of the *Mahābhārata*, the Jātakas betray a slight acquaintance with it.

Literary and inscriptional evidence

Moreover, it is proved by literary and inscriptional evidence that already about A.D. 500, the *Mahābhārata* was no longer an actual Epic but a sacred book and a religious discourse. It was on the whole essentially different from the Epic as it is found today. Kumārilabhaṭṭa quotes passages from the *Mahābhārata* and regards it as a Smṛti work. Both Subandhu and Bāṇa knew it as a great work of art[1] and Bāṇa alludes to a recital of the *Mahābhārata*.[2] It must be admitted on all hands that though an Epic *Mahābhārata* did not exist in the time of the Vedas, single myths, legends and poems included in the *Mahābhārata* reach back to the Vedic period. The

[1] *Vās.* p. 37 & *Har.* p. 2.
[2] *Kād.* p. 104.

Mahābhārata has also drawn many moral narratives and stories of saints from its contemporary 'ascetic-poetry'. An Epic *Mahābhārata,* however, did not exist in the fourth century B.C., and the transformation of the Epic *Mahābhārata* into our present compilation probably took place between the fourth century B.C. and the fourth century A.D. In the fourth century A.D., the work was available in its present extent, contents and character, though small alterations and additions might have continued even in later centuries.

Two Epics: which is earlier?

To the strictly orthodox Indian mind, the *Rāmāyaṇa* appears to have been composed earlier than the *Mahābhārata*. Indians believe that of the two incarnations of the Lord, Rāma and Kṛṣṇa, the former was born earlier. Western critics do not attach any importance to this belief, for it is argued by them that the hero of the genuine portion of the *Rāmāyaṇa* which is older, does not appear as an incarnation but as an ordinary mortal hero.[1] Professor Jacobi also thinks that of the two poems, the *Rāmāyaṇa* is the earlier production, and he bases his theory on the supposition that it is the influence of the *Rāmāyaṇa* which has moulded the *Mahābhārata* into a poetic form.[2]

That the *Rāmāyaṇa* is earlier than the *Mahābhārata* may be proved on the strength of the following points. The *Vanaparvan* of the *Mahābhārata* contains references to the Rāma story while no such

[1] There are a few passages in the genuine books, *e.g.*, the one in Bk. VI. where Sītā enters into the pyre, wherein Rāma is described as a divine being. Critics feel no hesitation in calling such passages interpolations.

[2] According to Mr Hopkins, the *Rāmāyaṇa* as an art-product is later than the *Mahābhārata*. (*Cambridge History*, I. p. 251)

reference to the Mahābhāratan story is to be found in the *Rāmāyaṇa:* Again, the *Mahābhārata* contains reference to the burning of widows as evinced in the story of Mādrī's *satīdāha*. But nothing akin to it is found in the *Rāmāyaṇa*. From the references of Megasthenes we come to know that the practice of burning of widows was in vogue in the third century B.C. In the Vedic period such a system was unknown in this country. Further, Pāṭaliputra is mentioned as a city in the *Mahābhārata* which according to Megasthenes was founded by Kālāśoka in the fourth century B.C. But it is interesting to note that this important city is not mentioned in the *Rāmāyaṇa* though many cities of lesser importance and some of them again very close to Pāṭaliputra have been alluded to. Furthermore, the territories occupied by the Aryans in the age of the *Rāmāyaṇa* appear to be much more limited than the Aryan-occupied territories in the *Mahābhārata*. But Winternitz does not attach any real importance to this theory and criticizes it by saying that the *Mahābhārata,* even in its present form, retains several characteristics of older poetry while the poem of Vālmīki reveals such peculiarities as would place him nearer to the age of Court-epics. Thus it is asserted by Winternitz that the *Rāmāyaṇa* appears to be an ornate poem having served as the pattern to which later Indian poets admiringly aspired. What Winternitz means by ornate poetry is that kind of poetic composition in which greater importance is attached to the form than to the matter and contents of the poem and in which literary embellishments are profusely used even to excess. The *Rāmāyaṇa* is the first literary work in which the aforesaid peculiarities of ornate poetry are found. These peculiarities, however, are not present in the *Mahābhārata* which is, therefore, presumed to be the earlier composition. Again, it has been pointed out that such expressions like 'Bhīṣma spake,' 'Sañjaya spake' which the poet of the *Mahābhārata*, uses to introduce a character, are reminiscent of ancient ballad poetry.[1] But in the *Rāmāyaṇa* the speeches are introduced in verses and therefore in a more polished form. The theory of Professor Jacobi may be further contested on the ground that from a perusal of the two Epics, the reader will unmistakably carry the impression that while the *Mahābhārata* describes a more war-like age, the *Rāmāyaṇa* depicts a comparatively refined civilization.

REFERENCES

Bhandarkar, R. G.: *On the Mahābhārata* (IA. Vol. I)
Goldstücker, T.: *The Mahābhārata*
Hopkins, E. W.: *The Great Epics of India*
Macdonell, A. A.: *A History of Sanskrit Literature*
Telang, K. T.: SBE. Vol. VIII
Vaidya, C. V.: *Mahābhārata, a critical study*
Weber, A.: *The History of Indian Literature*
Williams, M.: *Indian Wisdom*
Winternitz, M.: *A History of Indian Literature*, Vol. I

[1] The mixture of prose with poetry which we notice in the *Mahābhārata* is a fact that proves its antiquity. This view of Professor Oldenberg is not accepted by Dr Winternitz.

CHAPTER II

THE PURĀṆAS

Introduction

THE origin of the Purāṇas must be traced to that time of religious revolution when Buddhism was gaining ground as a formidable foe of Brāhmaṇic culture. Great devotees of Brāhmaṇic religion were anxious for the preservation of the old relics of Hindu culture, and Vyāsa, the great compiler, the greatest man of his time, was born to meet the demand of the age. The most important point to be remembered in this connexion, is that the entire Vedic culture lies at the background of the age of Buddhism and the Purāṇas.

Age

It was at one time believed by European scholars that not one of the eighteen Purāṇas is earlier than the eleventh century A.D. But this belief has been discarded on the discovery of a manuscript of the *Skandapurāṇa* in Nepal written in the sixth century A.D. Further, Bāṇabhaṭṭa in his *Harṣacarita* mentions that he once attended a recitation of the *Vāyupurāṇa*. Kumārila (A.D. 750) regards the Purāṇas as the sources of law. Śaṇkara (ninth century A.D.) and Rāmānuja (eleventh century A.D.) refer to the Purāṇas as sacred texts for their dependence on the Vedas. The famous traveller Albērūnī (A.D. 1030) also gives us a list of the eighteen Purāṇas.

Antiquity

The word Purāṇa means 'old narrative'. In the *Atharvaveda* (xi. 7.24), the Brāhmaṇas (*Śatapatha* and *Gopatha*), the Upaniṣads (e.g., *Bṛhadāraṇyaka,* ii. 4. 10) and the Buddhist texts, the word is found to be used in connexion with Itihāsa. Some scholars hold that the Purāṇas mentioned in these places do not refer to the works we have before us. But the references found in the *Dharmasūtras* of Gautama and Āpastamba (works belonging in all probability to the fifth or the fourth century B.C.) suggest that there were at that early period works resembling our Purāṇas. The close relationship between the *Mahābhārata* and the Purāṇas is another point in support of the antiquity of the latter. The *Mahābhārata* which calls itself a Purāṇa, has the general character of the latter, and it is not highly improbable that some integral parts of the Purāṇas are older than the present redaction of the *Mahābhārata.* The *Lalitavistara* not only calls itself a Purāṇa but has also much in common with the Purāṇas. The *Vāyupurāṇa* is quoted literally by the *Harivaṁśa.* The genealogical survey of all the Purāṇas reveals the fact that they generally stop with the accounts of the Andhra Bhṛtya and Gupta kings and that later kings like Harṣa are not mentioned. So it may be suggested that the Purāṇas were written during the rule of the Gupta kings. On the other hand, the striking resemblance between the Buddhist Mahāyāna texts of the first century A.D. and the Purāṇas, suggests the fact that the latter were written early in the beginnings of the Christian era. The characteristics of the Purāṇas are also found in books like the *Saddharmapuṇḍarīka* and the *Mahāvastu.* Dr Winternitz has, however, concluded that the earlier Purāṇas must have come into being before the seventh century A.D. But it may be pointed out that the worship of Śiva and Viṣṇu referred to in quite a good number of Purāṇas reach back to the pre-Christian era, if not the pre-Buddhist age. The Purāṇas are by no means 'quite modern'.

Was there one original Purāṇa?

It is quite interesting to note that some of the important Purāṇas, *e.g.*, the *Vāyu*, the *Brahmāṇḍa*, the *Viṣṇu* and others, speak of one original Purāṇa-saṁhitā which was compiled by Vyāsa and imparted by him to his disciple, Lomaharṣaṇa, the Sūta. The theory of the existence of one original Purāṇa which was supported by such scholars as A. M. T. Jackson, A. Blan and F. E. Pargiter, appears to point to the earliest Vedic age when the Vedic Indians were still undivided and consequently the Paurāṇic heritage was the same. As time went on and the population increased, the Vedic Indians could no longer remain undivided and with their division into groups and their movement into different territories scriptural, cultural, traditional and ritualistic unity could not be preserved. Hence in course of years the same Paurāṇic heritage was remodelled which ultimately resulted in the emergence of different Purāṇas. With the progress of time there were changes in ideas and beliefs, in the modes of living and thought as also in the environments and this explains why the Purāṇa-Saṁhitā was recast from time to time. It is, therefore, understandable that the Purāṇas do not possess a stable character.

Character

Extreme paucity of information leaves us in absolute darkness as to the character and contents of the ancient Paurāṇic works, none of which, it is presumed, has come down to us in its original form. The noted Sanskrit lexicographer, Amarasiṁha, gives us a definition of Purāṇas which has been repeated in some of the extant Paurāṇic texts. According to

Amarasiṁha, every Purāṇa should discuss five topics; (i) *sarga*—creation, (ii) *pratisarga*—the periodical annihilation and renewal of the world, (iii) *vaṁśa*—genealogy of gods and sages, (iv) *manvantara*—the Manu-periods of time *i.e.*, the great periods each of which has a Manu (primal ancestor of the human race) as its ruler, and (v) *vaṁśānucarita*—the history of the dynasties the origin of which is traced to the Sun and the Moon. But all these five characteristics are not present in every Purāṇa, and though in some they are partially present, we notice a wide diversity of topics in them. Thus we find many chapters dealing with the duties of the four castes and of the four *āśramas*, sections on Brāhmaṇical rites, on particular ceremonies and feasts and frequently also chapters on Sāṅkhya and Yoga philosophy. But the most striking peculiarity of all the Purāṇas is their sectarian character as they are dedicated to the cult of some deity who is treated as the principal God in the book. So we come across a Purāṇa dedicated to Viṣṇu, another to Śiva and so on.

Unique is the importance of the Purāṇas from the standpoint of history and religion. The genealogical survey of the Purāṇas is immensely helpful for the study of political history in ancient India, and yet it is a task for the scholar to glean germs of Indian history, hidden in the Purāṇas. Dr Smith says that the *Viṣṇupurāṇa* gives us invaluable informations about the Maurya dynasty. The *Matsyapurāṇa* is most dependable in so far as the Andhra dynasty is concerned, while the *Vāyupurāṇa* gives us detailed descriptions about the reign of Candragupta I. As the object of the Purāṇas was to popularize the more

Value

difficult and highly philosophical preaching of the Vedas through the medium of historical facts and tales, we naturally find in them Hinduism in a fully developed form. So the student of religion cannot pass it by. The Purāṇas are not also wanting in literary merit, and they abound in numerous passages which speak of the highly artistic talent of their makers.

Name and number

The Purāṇas or the Mahā-purāṇas, as we have them today, are eighteen in number, and there are also minor Purāṇas (Upa-purāṇas) which all again number eighteen. The eighteen Mahā-purāṇas are:—

(1) *Brahma,* (2) *Padma,* (3) *Viṣṇu,* (4) *Śiva* (5) *Bhāgavata,* (6) *Nāradīya,* (7) *Mārkaṇḍeya,* (8) *Agni,* (9) *Bhaviṣya* or *Bhaviṣyat,* (10) *Brahmavaivarta,* (11) *Liṅga,* (12) *Varāha,* (13) *Skanda,* (14) *Vāmana,* (15) *Kūrma,* (16) *Matsya,* (17) *Garuḍa* and (18) *Brahmāṇḍa.*

Classification of Purāṇas

The above-mentioned eighteen Purāṇas are classified from the standpoint of the three cosmic qualities (*guṇa*), viz., *sattva, rajas* and *tamas.* The Purāṇas generally exalting Viṣṇu are called *sāttvika,* those exalting Brahmā are called *rājasa,* while those exalting Śiva are called *tāmasa.* The Purāṇas so classified are as follows:

(*a*) Sāttvika Purāṇas: *Viṣṇu, Bhāgavata, Nāradīya, Garuḍa, Padma* and *Varāha.*

(*b*) Rājasa Purāṇas: *Brahma, Brahmāṇḍa, Brahmavaivarta, Mārkaṇḍeya, Bhaviṣya* and *Vāmana.*

(*c*) Tāmasa Purāṇas: *Śiva, Liṅga, Skanda, Agni, Matsya* and *Kūrma.*

The Bhāgavata Purāṇa is unquestionably the most famous work of Purāṇa literature. Innumerable manuscripts and prints of the text itself as well as of many commentaries thereon in addition to the many translations into Indian languages bear eloquent testimony to the popularity and reputation of the work. It is regarded by the adherents of the Vaiṣṇava cult as the 'fifth Veda'. Its artistic excellence is widely admired and it is believed by Indians that real scholarship is tested by one's proficiency in this Purāṇa.

The Bhāgavata Purāṇa

The Purāṇa which bears the stamp of a unified composition consists of 18,000 stanzas divided into twelve books (*skandhas*). The tenth book concerns itself with an account of the various activities of Lord Kṛṣṇa including the exquisite love-scenes with the milk-maids. It is quite interesting to note here that the name Rādhā, so popular among the Vaiṣṇavas of Bengal in particular, does not appear in the Bhāgavata Purāṇa.

According to Pargiter the Purāṇa was written sometime in the ninth century A.D.

The *Devīmāhātmya* which is popularly known as the '*Caṇḍī*' or the '*Saptaśatī*', is a section of the *Mārkaṇḍeyapurāṇa*. According to Dr Winternitz, its date is not later than the sixth century A.D. The book which contains thirteen chapters and seven hundred mantras, is a glorification of the Primal Energy (*Ādyā Śakti*) who descends amongst all created beings from time to time to rid the worlds of their pestilence and killed in the past the demons Madhu-Kaiṭabha, Mahiṣāsura, Śumbha and Niśumbha among others. The book is recited in many religious functions of the Hindus.

Devīmāhātmya

Name & number of Upa-purāṇas

The eighteen Upa-purāṇas which have been told by different sages are:

(1) *Sanatkumara,* (2) *Narasiṁha,* (3) *Vāyu,* (4) *Śiva-dharma,* (5) *Āścarya,* (6) *Nārada,* (7) the two *Nandi-keśvaras,* (8) *Uśanas,* (9) *Kapila,* (10) *Varuṇa,* (11) *Śāmba,* (12) *Kālikā,* (13) *Maheśvara,* (14) *Kalki,* (15) *Devī,* (16) *Parāśara,* (17) *Marīci* and (18) *Bhāskara* or *Sūrya.*[1]

REFERENCES

Bhandarkar, R. G.: *A Peep into the Early History of India* (JBRAS, Vol. XX, 1900)
Pargiter, F. E.: ERE., Vol. X, 1918
Rapson, E. J.: *Cambridge History,* Vol. I
Wilson, H. H.: *Essays on Sanskrit Literature*
Winternitz, M.: *A History of Indian Literature,* Vol. I

[1] The above list of Upa-purāṇas given by Raghunandana is taken from the *Śabdakalpadruma.* Hemādri gives a different list.

CHAPTER III

THE TANTRAS

Meaning, contents and classification

THE expression Tantra which is a generic name for works belonging to 'Āgama', 'Tantra' and 'Saṃhitā', refers to theological treatises discussing the codes of discipline and worship among different sects of religion along with their metaphysical and mystical points of view. A complete Tantra generally consists of four parts, the themes treated of being (i) knowledge (*jñāna*), (ii) meditation (*yoga*), (iii) action (*kriyā*) and (iv) conduct (*caryā*). Though it is not possible to draw any special line of demarcation among Āgama, Tantra and Saṁhitā, still it is usual to refer to the sacred books of the Śaivas by the expression Āgama,[1] while Tantra stands for the sacred literature of the Śāktas and Saṁhitā for that of the Vaiṣṇavas. The Śākta-Tantras are mainly monistic in character, while the Vaiṣṇava-Tantras generally advocate dualism, or qualified monism. The Śaiva-Tantras are divided into three schools of monism, qualified monism and dualism. It is described that under instruction from Śiva, the sage Durvāsas divided all the Śaiva-Tantras into three classes and charged his three mind-born sons, Tryambaka, Amardaka and Śrīnātha with the mission of spreading the knowledge of the Āgamas he taught them. It was Tryambaka who propagated monism.

[1] A distinction is made between Āgama and Nigama—in the former, goddess Pārvatī asks questions like a disciple while Śiva answers them like a preceptor; in the latter the reverse is the case.

Relation to Vedic literature The Tantras came to replace the Vedas when in later times it was found that performance of a sacrifice according to Vedic rites was practically impossible owing to their rigid orthodoxy. Thus the Tantras prescribe easier and less complicated methods which would suit not only the higher classes but also the Śūdras and the feminine folk of the society who had no access to Vedic ceremonies. It would, therefore, not be wise to think that Tantric literature is opposed to Vedic literature, and this point would be made abundantly clear when it is found that the rigidly orthodox Vedic scholars write original works and commentaries on Tantras.

Character The Tantras have been classified into Vedic and non-Vedic in so far as the authority of the Vedas is recognized or denied in them. The Śaiva, Śākta and Vaiṣṇava Tantras are regarded as Vedic while the Buddhist and Jain Tantras are regarded as non-Vedic. In some of the Tantras there is full-throated vilification of the Vedas. Some affinity of the Tantras with the Purāṇas is discernible in so far as the contents are concerned.

Antiquity The earliest manuscripts of Tantras date from the seventh to the ninth century A.D., and it is probable that the literature dates back to the fifth or the sixth century A.D., if not earlier. We do not find any reference to a Tantra in the *Mahābhārata*. The Chinese pilgrims also do not mention it. It is, indeed, certain that Tantric doctrine penetrated into Buddhism in the seventh and eighth centuries A.D. The worship of Durgā may be traced back even to the Vedic period.

Home The home of Āgamic literature seems to be

Kāshmir, while that of Tāntric literature is Bengal. Saṁhitā literature, as it is known, originated in different parts of India, in Bengal, South India and the Siamese country.

Works on Āgama

Among works belonging to Āgamic literature the most important are the following:—

Mālinīvijaya, Svacchanda, Vijñānabhairava, Ucchuṣmabhairava, Ānandabhairava, Mṛgendra, Mataṅga, Netra, Naiśvāsa, Svāyambhuva and *Rudrayāmala.*

Works on Pratyabhijñā

Closely associated with Āgamic literature is Pratyabhijñā literature which occupies an important place in the history of Indian philosophy. The Pratyabhijñā school is based on the Monistic Śaiva Tantras. A good account of the teachers of this school is to be found in the closing chapter of the *Śivadṛṣṭi* of Somānandanātha, the great-grand-teacher of Abhinavagupta and nineteenth descendant of Tryambaka, the founder of the Advaita Śaiva school. Somānandanātha belonged to the ninth century A.D. (A.D. 850-900). His son and pupil, Utpala (A.D. 900-950) wrote the *Pratyabhijñākārikās.* The most outstanding writer of the school was the great Abhinavagupta (A.D. 993-1015) whose *magnum opus* was the *Tantrāloka.* Abhinava was a most prolific writer and some of his other important works are the *Mālinīvijayottaravārttika, Pratyabhijñāvimarśinī, Tantrāloka, Tantrasāra* and *Paramārthasāra.* Another important work of this school is the *Pratyabhijñāhṛdaya* of Kṣemarāja, pupil of Abhinavagupta.

Works on Saṁhitā

Among works belonging to Saṁhitā literature the most important is the *Ahirbudhnyasaṁhitā* which was composed in Kāshmir in the fifth century A.D. *Īśvarasaṁhitā, Pauṣkarasaṁhitā, Paramasaṁhitā,*

Sāttvatasaṁhitā, *Bṛhadbrahmasaṁhitā* and *Jñānāmṛtasārasaṁhitā* are other well-known works of this branch of Sanskrit literature.

Works on Tantra

Among works belonging to Tantra literature, mention may be made of the following:—

Mahānirvāṇa, *Kulārṇava*, *Kulacūḍāmaṇi*, *Prapañcasāra* (ascribed to the philosopher Śaṅkara), *Tantrarāja*, *Kālīvilāsa*, *Jñānārṇava*, *Śāradātilaka*, *Varivasyārahasya* (of Bhāskara), *Tantrasāra* (of Kṛṣṇānanda) and *Prāṇatoṣiṇī*.

REFERENCES

Avalon, A.: *Tantrik Texts*
Chatterji, J. C.: *Kashmir Shaivism*
Winternitz, M.: *A History of Indian Literature*, Vol. I
Pandey, K. C.: *Abhinavagupta: An Historical and Philosophical Study*.

CHAPTER IV

POST-EPIC KĀVYA

The two Great Epics, the *Rāmāyaṇa* and the *Mahābhārata,* are undoubtedly the precursors of Sanskrit Kāvya literature and it is futile to trace back the origin of the latter to the distant Vedic hymns and discover its prototype in the Nārāśaṁsī and Dānastuti panegyrics, in the Saṁvāda hymns, in the magnificent descriptions of Vedic gods and goddesses or in the legends and gnomic stanzas occurring in the Brāhmaṇas. Some scholars have suggested that the Epics or the Kāvyas were originally composed in Prākrit and subsequently rendered into Sanskrit and their suggestion is based on the fact that all inscriptional writing in the period preceding the Christian era was done in Prākrit. But it has not been possible for these scholars to furnish any reliable evidence in support of the existence of actual Prākrit works during the period. And even if it be assumed for the sake of argument that Prākrit works were in existence at that time, the co-existence of a Sanskrit literature in some form can never be denied. Further, it is extremely difficult to prove that the Sanskrit literature was derived from the Prākrit literature, if indeed the latter preceded it. It may be quite possible that a popular secular literature in Prākrit, such as the folk-tale, existed, but we have every reason to believe that there existed a more aristocratic literature in Sanskrit which might not have been in the Bhāṣā of

Pāṇini but was certainly close to it and current among the rhapsodes and their patrons, and of this literature the two Great Epics are the most outstanding monuments. The two Epics possess such linguistic and literary peculiarities as preclude the theory of Prākrit originals and may be traced in unbroken tradition to certain aspects of Vedic language and literature. And if it can be assumed that the Epics were originally written in Sanskrit, the originality of Classical Sanskrit literature is assured once for all, for from the Epics a direct development leads to the Kāvya. As we have said before, the *Rāmāyaṇa* is the first Kāvya for it is impossible to deny to Vālmīki the command of literary art. It is worthy of notice here that though the *Rāmāyaṇa* attests the development of the Kāvya style, the other Epic affords no evidence comparable to that of the *Rāmāyaṇa*, in spite of the fact that it has afforded to later poets and dramatists almost inexhaustible material for their labours.

Direct and reliable evidence of the production of secular Sanskrit literature in its various phases is furnished by the testimony of Patañjali's *Mahābhāṣya*. Besides mentioning a *Vāraruca Kāvya* now lost to us, Patañjali refers to poetic license and appears to know various forms of Kāvya literature. Thus he knows the Bhāratan epic, refers to professional reciters (Granthikas) and mentions as many as three ākhyāyikās, *Vāsavadattā, Sumanottarā* and *Bhaimarathī*. There is also a reference to two other works, the *Kaṁsavadha* and the *Vālivadha,* probably dramatic compositions. And what is more interesting is that the *Mahābhāṣya* preserves a few quotations, mostly metrical yet fragmentary, in which one can find eulogistic, erotic or gnomic themes in the approved Kāvya-style. The allusions to such proverbial tales as that of the goat and the razor, of the crow and the palm fruit and the like are suggestive of the existence of the material which in later times gave rise to beast-fables.

The evidence of Patañjali is corroborated by Piṅgala, author of the *Chandassūtra* which though essentially a Vedāṅga is mainly confined to the exposition of secular prosody. The author is sometimes identified with Patañjali but the aspect of his work suggests considerable age. Many of the metres described in the book are certainly not derived from the Kāvya literature which has come down to us. They suggest a period of transition in which the authors of the erotic lyric were trying experiments in metrical effect. It is quite interesting to note that the names of the metres can be explained as epithets of the beloved. It needs to be said here that despite the facts stated above we have no definite knowledge of the growth and development of Kāvya during the second century B.C. and the first century A.D. as it is not possible for us to assign any of the extant Kāvyas to this period. What we can say with confidence is that the facts stated above warrant us in drawing the conclusion that a strong school of lyric poetry existed about the Christian era and probably much earlier.

CHAPTER V

KĀVYA IN INSCRIPTIONS

Renaissance theory

EARLY in the beginnings of Sanskritic studies in Europe, Professor Max Müller propounded the theory of the 'Renaissance of Sanskrit literature', which remained highly popular for a considerable length of time. This theory, set forth with much profundity, sought to establish that Brāhmaṇic culture passed through its dark age at the time when India was continuously facing foreign invasions. The earliest revival of this culture is to be found in the reign of the Guptas which is a golden page in the annals of Indian culture. In spite of all its ingenuity the theory has been generally discarded by the epigraphical and literary researches of Bühler, Kielhorn and Fleet. Bühler's detailed examination of the evidence borne out by the early inscriptions ranging from the second to the fifth century A.D. not only proved the existence during these centuries of a highly elaborate body of Sanskrit prose and verse in the Kāvya style but it also raised the presumption that most of the Praśasti writers were acquainted with some theory of poetic art. If Max Müller suggested a decline of literary activity on account of the invasions of the Śakas, it is now authoritatively gathered that the Western Kṣatrapas or Satraps of Śaka origin were not great destroyers, on the contrary they patronized Indian art and religion and Sanskrit as the epigraphical language as early as A.D. 150. It is definitely known that the study and development of Sanskrit Kāvya was never impeded.

Girnār inscription

Thus the inscription of Rudradāman at Girnār dated A.D. 150, is written in prose in the full-fledged Kāvya style in strict conformity with the rules of grammar. Though traces of epic licence can be found in the inscription, still the writer is a gifted master in the use of figures of speech. As an example of alliteration may be cited the phrase *'abhyastanāmno Rudradāmno'*. Though there are long compounds still the clearness and the lucidity of the style is nowhere forsaken. What is more significant is that the author is conversant with the science of poetics and discusses the merits attributed by Daṇḍin to the Vaidarbha style.

Nāsik inscription

Still another inscription which is derivable from a record of Siri Puḷumāyi at Nāsik is written in Prākrit prose. The date of this inscription is not far removed from the former. The author who is undoubtedly familiar with Sanskrit, uses enormous sentences with long compounds. Alliterations and even mannerisms of later Kāvyas are found in this inscription.

Allahabad inscription

Yet another inscription, the famous Allahabad Stone Pillar inscription, containing Hariṣeṇa's panegyric of Samudragupta, presents many points of close touch with the Kāvya literature and proves that court-poetry was assiduously cultivated in the fourth century A.D. The panegyric consisting of nine verses and a long prose passage is a kind of Campū. Hariṣeṇa introduces too often a change of metre in his verses, which are very simple and free from long compounds. So far as the prose passage is concerned simple words are not used and there are very long compounds.

The contrast is not accidental but intentional inasmuch as works on poetics are unanimous that the essence of good prose consists in the length of compounds. Hariṣeṇa undoubtedly follows the Vaidarbha style. He uses the simplest pattern of alliteration in the prose composition only, and that not many times. He uses figures of sense no doubt but he does not direct his attention so much to the use of poetic embellishments as to the fine execution of the pictures of the several situations described and to the selection of suitable words and their arrangement. In Hariṣeṇa's poetic imagery one comes across many a conception which is very familiar in the Kāvya literature. Thus the favourite allegory of the eternal discord between the Goddess of Learning and the Goddess of Wealth is an instance in point. The prose portion of the panegyric reveals the poet's effort at surpassing his rivals in the art of composition of Praśastis. In short, Hariṣeṇa's panegyric entitles him to be ranked with Kālidāsa and Daṇḍin.

Mandasor inscription

Vatsabhaṭṭi's wholly metrical panegyric in forty four stanzas about the Sun-temple at Mandasor is another instance to show that Kāvya literature was zealously cultivated in India in the fifth century A.D. A study of the panegyric reveals the fact that the poet has conformed to the rules of Sanskrit poetics and metre. The eagerness with which the author takes advantage of every little circumstances to bring in poetic details and descriptions cannot but suggest that he tries his best to make his composition resemble a Mahākāvya. The science of rhetoric prescribes that a Mahākāvya should contain descriptions of cities, mountains, oceans, seasons and the like. The description of the city of Daśapura in nine glorious verses and of the two seasons of winter and spring each in two verses, should be read in this connexion. And an examination of the metres and style would prove the degree of trouble the poet has taken to compose the verses. Vatsabhaṭṭi's diction bears the stamp of the poets of the Gauḍa school. He uses long compounds and allows a mixture of soft and hard-sounding syllables in the same line. It is suggested that there are sufficient traces to prove that the poet tries to imitate Kālidāsa, though it is admitted that the performance is mediocre only. Vatsabhaṭṭi is not an original genius but seeks with great care to compile a medley of the classical modes of expression. Nevertheless it is undeniable that the panegyric in form as well as in sense strictly belongs to the domain of Sanskrit artificial compositions. And it will not be wrong to conclude that in his time there existed a large number of Kāvyas which inspired his writing.

Conclusions

It may, therefore, be concluded that the works of Aśvaghoṣa, the great Buddhist poet, are not the earliest specimens of Sanskrit Kāvya. There had been a continued growth and development of Kāvya literature since the beginning of the Christian era. It may be that earlier Kāvyas are now unfortunately lost to us, or authors like Kālidāsa have completely eclipsed the glory of their predecessors. Thus of the three dramatists referred to by Kālidāsa, the dramas of only one are now known to us.

REFERENCES

Keith, A. B.: *A History of Sanskrit Literature*
Macdonell, A. A.: *A History of Sanskrit Literature*
Müller, Max: *A History of Ancient Sanskrit Literature*
Bühler, G.: *Indian Inscriptions and the Kāvya* (IA., Vol. XLII)

CHAPTER VI

EARLY BUDDHIST WORKS IN SANSKRIT

Introduction

THE paucity of authentic landmarks in the domain of early Indian history is a stupendous stumbling block in the gateway to the study of the history of Sanskrit literature. A colossal darkness that envelops the period of Sanskrit literature in the beginnings of the Christian era, makes it extremely difficult, if not hopelessly impossible, to ascertain the age in which a particular writer lived and wrote. The chronology of Indian literature is shrouded in such painful obscurity that oriental scholars were long ignorant of the vast literature produced in Sanskrit by Buddhist writers.

Buddhist Sanskrit literature includes Mahāyāna and Hīnayāna works

The thought of the Mahāyāna school of Buddhism was expressed in a language which was not Pāli, the extraordinarily rich and extensive religious literature of Ceylon and Burma, but which was partly Sanskrit and partly a dialect to which Professor Senart has given the designation Mid-Sanskrit, but which Professor Pischel prefers to call the Gāthā dialect.[1] This literature of the Mahāyāna school is called Buddhist Sanskrit literature. But it should be mentioned in this connexion that Buddhist Sanskrit literature is not synonymous with the rich literature of the Mahāyāna school alone, but it has a still wider scope including as it does the literature of the Hīnayāna school as well, inasmuch as the Sarvāstivādins, a sect of the Hīnayāna school, possess a canon and a fairly vast literature in Sanskrit. The Sanskrit canon, however, is not available in its entirety, but its existence is proved on the evidence of the several quotations from it in such works as the *Mahāvastu,* the *Divyāvadāna* and the *Lalitavistara.* This Sanskrit canon shows close affinity to the Pāli canon, and it is suggested that both of them are but translations of some original canon in Māgadhī, which is lost to us.

Mahavastu: its date

The most important work of the Hīnayāna school is the *Mahāvastu,* the book of the Great Events. This *Mahāvastu,* a book belonging to the school of the Lokottaravādins, a sub-division of the Mahāsāṅghikas, bears after the introduction the following title: *Āryamahāsāṅghikānāṁ Lokottaravādināṁ madhyadeśikānāṁ pāṭhena vinayapiṭakasya mahāvastu ādi.* This may furnish us with a clue to determine the date of its composition. In order to ascertain this it has to be found out when the Lokottaravādin sect of the Mahāsāṅghikas sprang up. In this connexion, it would be necessary to fix the date of Buddha's death. Scholars are divided in their opinions as to the exact year when Buddha died. Professors Max Müller and Cunningham make it 477 B.C., while Mr Gopala Aiyer would fix it at 483 B.C. But more probable is Dr Smith's theory according to which Buddha died in 487 B.C. It is said that Aśoka was crowned in 269 B.C., and that this coronation took place some two hundred and eighteen years after the death of Buddha. But, if the account of the Southern Buddhists is to be believed, this year was either 544 or 543 B.C. Now the opening lines of the fifth chapter of the *Mahāvaṁsa* will throw light on the age when the Mahāsāṅghikas came into being.[1] There it is stated that during the first century after the death of Buddha, there was but one schism among the Theras. After this period, other schisms took place among the preceptors. From all those sinful priests, in number ten thousand, who had been degraded by the Theras (who had held the second convocation) originated the schism among the preceptors called the Mahāsāṅghika heresy. It is recorded in this connexion that as many as eighteen schisms arose, all of them in the course of a couple of centuries after the death of Buddha. But the difficulty is that there is no mention of the Lokottaravādins in the *Mahāvaṁsa.* In the appendix of the translation of the *Mahāvaṁsa,* it has been said that the Lokottaravādins do not appear in the tradition of the Southern Buddhists. They are mentioned immediately beside the Gokulikas. In Rock hill 182, the Lokottaravādins are to be found just in the place where the Gokulikas are expected. Moreover, in two other contexts, the Gokulikas and not the Lokottaravādins are mentioned. Thus it is better to identify the two and in that case, the Lokottaravādins seem to have sprung up at least in the third century B.C. That being so, the *Mahāvastu,* which has been described as the first work of their sect, could not have been written later than that period.

Mahāvastu: its character

But a fresh difficulty makes its appearance. The *Mahāvastu* is not a composite whole. Different parts of it have been composed at different periods and

[1] Eko 'va theravādo so ādivassasate ahu | aññācariyavādā tu tato oraṁ ajāyisuṁ || Tehi saṅgītikārehi therehi dutiyehi te | niggahitā pāpabhikkhū sabbe dasasahassikā || Akaṁs'ācāriyavādaṁ Mahāsaṅghikanāmakam ||

this accounts for the unmethodical arrangement of facts and ideas in the work. Besides, the *Mahāvastu* is not a piece of artistic literature. It has rightly been called 'a labyrinth in which we can only with an effort, discover the thread of a coherent account of the life of Buddha.' The contents are not properly arranged and the reader comes across the repetition of the same story, over and over again. But the importance of the work lies in the fact that it has preserved numerous traditions of respectable antiquity and versions of texts occurring in the Pāli canon. The *Mahāvastu* has yet another claim to importance, for in it the reader discovers a storehouse of stories. It is a fact that nearly half of the book is devoted to Jātakas and stories of like nature. Most of the narratives remind us of the stories of Purāṇas and the history of Brahmadatta may be cited as an instance. To conclude, the *Mahāvastu,* though a work of the Hīnayāna school, betrays some affinity to Mahāyānism. For it mentions a number of Buddhas and describes Buddha's self-begottenness. Such ideas are undoubtedly associated with the Mahāyāna school of thought.

Lalitavistara: its character

The literature of the Mahāyāna school of Buddhism is extremely rich. Though originally a work of the Sarvāstivādin school attached to the Hīnayāna, the *Lalitavistara* is believed to be one of the most sacred Mahāyāna texts, inasmuch as it is regarded as a Vaipulyasūtra. That the work contains the Mahāyānistic faith may easily be inferred from the very title of the work which means 'the exhaustive narrative of the sport of the Buddha.' A critical study of the work reveals, however, that it is but a 'redaction of an older Hīnayāna text expanded and embellished in the sense of the Mahāyāna, a biography of the Buddha, representing the Sarvāstivādin school.' It is also a fact that the present *Lalitavistara* is not the work of a single author; it is rather 'an anonymous compilation in which both the old and the young fragments have found their places.' Such being the case, it is hardly proper to regard the work as a good ancient source for the knowledge of Buddhism. The reader finds in it the gradual development of the Buddha legend in its earliest beginnings. Hence, there is hardly any significance in the statement of Professor Vallée Poussin when he says that 'the *Lalitavistara* represents the popular Buddhism.' The book, however, is of great importance from the standpoint of literary history, inasmuch as it has supplied materials for Aśvaghoṣa's monumental epic, the *Buddhacarita*.

Date of Lalitavistara: Kern's view

To determine the date of composition of the work it would be necessary to bear in mind that the work is a Vaipulyasūtra. In the Vaipulyasūtras we find sections in a redaction of prose followed by one in verse, the latter being in substance, only a repetition of the former. The idiom of the prose portions is a kind of Sanskrit; that of the verses, Gāthās, a veiled Prākrit somewhat clumsily Sanskritized as much as the exigencies of the metre have permitted. Professor Kern thinks that the prose passages are undoubtedly translations of a Prākrit text into Sanskrit. The question, therefore, arises: why and when has the original idiom been replaced by Sanskrit? It is known that in India it has been the common fate of all Prākrits that they have become obsolete whilst the study and practice of Sanskrit have been kept up all over the country, as the common language of science and literature, and also as a bond between Aryans and Dravidians. Now it may be enquired when Sanskrit could have regained its ascendancy. Professor Kern suggests that it was in all probability shortly before or after the council in the reign of Kaniṣka, the great Indo-Scythian king.

Nariman' view and conclusions

Mr G. K. Nariman, in his Literary History of Sanskrit Buddhism, says that it is wrong to think that the *Lalitavistara* was translated into Chinese in the first Christian era. Moreover, he doubts that the Chinese biography of Buddha, called the Phuyau-king, published in A.D. 300, is the second translation of our present text of the *Lalitavistara*. On the other hand, he says that a precise rendering of the Sanskrit text was completed in Tibetan and it was produced as late as the fifth century A.D. It is, however, worthy of notice that Professor Kern has taken sufficient pains to prove that there is much that is of respectable antiquity in the work. Taking this factor into consideration the *Lalitavistara* may be assigned to some time before the Christian era.

Aśvaghoṣa: h date

The most outstanding Buddhist writer in Sanskrit is Aśvaghoṣa. Round his date hangs a veil of mystery. Dr Smith writes in his History of India: 'In literature, the memory of Kaniṣka is associated with the names of the eminent Buddhist writers Nāgārjuna, Aśvaghoṣa and Vasumitra. Aśvaghoṣa is described as having been a poet, musician, scholar, religious controversialist, and zealous Buddhist monk, orthodox in creed, and a strict observer of discipline.' Judged from all evidences it may be concluded that Kaniṣka flourished in A.D. 78. Hence Aśvaghoṣa who adorned his court, flourished in the first century of the Christian era.[1]

[1] In the chronological group generally accepted by numismatics, the Kaniṣka group succeeds the Kadphises group. But even this view has not the unanimous support of scholars. If, as some scholars hold, the group of kings comprising Kaniṣka, Vāsiṣka, Huviṣka and Vāsudeva preceded Kadphises I, the coins of the two princes last named should be found together, as they are not, and those of Khadphises II and Kaniṣka should not be associated, as they are. Chief supporters of the view stated above are Drs Fleet, Frank and Mr Kennedy. Dr Frank lays stress on the fact that Chinese historians as apart from Buddhist authors make no mention of Kaniṣka. But he himself answers the question when he holds that with the year A.D. 125, the source was dried up from which the chronicler could draw information regarding the peoples of Turkesthan. Dr Fleet connects Kaniṣka's accession to the throne with the traditional Vikrama Saṁvat, beginning with the year 57 B.C. This view has been ably controverted by Dr Thomas and discoveries of Professor Marshall totally belie its truth. Inscriptions, coins and the records of Hiuen Tsang point out that Kaniṣka's dominion included Gandhāra. According to Chinese evidence, Kipin or Kāpiśa-Gandhāra was not under the Kuṣāṇa kings in the second half of the first century B.C. Professors Marshall, Sten Konow, Smith and other scholars think that Kaniṣka's rule begins about A.D. 125. The evidence of Sue Vihār inscriptions proves that Kaniṣka's empire extended as far as the Lower Indus valley; but the Junāgaḍh inscription of Rudradāman tells us that the dominions of the Emperor included Sindhu and Sauvīra. It is known that Rudradāman lived from A.D. 130 to A.D. 150. Under the circumstances, it is almost impossible to reconcile the suzerainty of the Kuṣāṇa King with the independence of this powerful satrap (cf. *Svayamadhigataṁ mahākṣtrapanāma*). From Kaniṣka's dates 3—23, Vāsiṣka's dates 24—28, Huviṣka's dates 31—60, and Vāsudeva's dates 74—98 it is almost evident that Kaniṣka was the originator of an era. But according to our evidence, no new era began about the beginning of the second century A.D. Dr R. C. Mazumdar is of opinion that the era started by Kaniṣka was the Kalachuri era of A.D. 248-49. But Professor Jouveau Dubreuil contends that it is not likely that Vāsudeva's reign terminated after 100 years from Kaniṣka's date of accession; for Mathurā where Vāsudeva reigned, came under the Nāgas about A.D. 350. It may be further mentioned that for the reason stated above we can hardly accept the theory of Sir R. G. Bhandarkar who accepts A.D. 278, as the date of Kaniṣka's accession. According to Professors Ferguson, Oldenberg, Thomas, R. D. Banerjee, Rapson and others, Kaniṣka started the Śaka era commencing from A.D. 78. Professor Dubreuil does not accept the view on the following grounds. First, if the view that Kujula-kara-Kadphises and Hermaois reigned about A.D. 50 and that Kaniṣka founded the era in A.D. 78 is accepted, there remains only twenty-eight years for the end of the reign of Kadphises I and the entire reign of Kadphises II. But Kadphises II succeeded an octoge-

Personal history

But very little is known of Aśvaghoṣa's personal history except what is available to us from legends and what can be gathered from his works themselves. It appears from the colophons to his works that he was a Buddhist monk of Sāketa and his mother's name was Suvarṇākṣī.

Buddhacarita

The masterpiece of Aśvaghoṣa is his *Buddhacarita*, the life-history of Buddha. From the account of I-tsing it appears that the *Buddhacarita* with which he was acquainted, consisted of twenty-eight cantos. The Tibetan translation, too, contains the same number of cantos. But unluckily the Sanskrit text comprises seventeen cantos only, of which, again, the last four are of dubious origin. It is said that one Amṛtānanda of the ninth century A.D. added those four cantos. Even the manuscript discovered by MM Haraprasāda Śāstriṇ, goes as far as the middle of the fourteenth canto.

nerian and it is not impossible that his reign was one of short duration. Professor Marshall says that Professor Dubreuil has discovered at Taxila a document which can be placed in A.D. 79 and the king it mentions was certainly not Kaniṣka. But Professor H. C. Ray Chaudhuri has shown that the title Devaputra was applicable to the Kaniṣka group and not to the earlier group. The omission of a personal name does not prove that the first Kuṣāṇa king was meant. Secondly, Professor Dubreuil says that Professor Sten Konow has shown that Tibetan and Chinese documents prove that Kaniṣka lived in the second century A.D. But it is not improbable that this Kaniṣka is the Kaniṣka of the Āra inscription of the year 41 which, if referred to the Śaka era, would give a date that would fall in the second century A.D. Po-t'iao may be one of the successors of Vāsudeva I. Professors Banerjee and Smith recognize the existence of more than one Vāsudeva. Finally, Professor Konow has shown that inscriptions of the Kaniṣka era and the Śaka era are not dated in the same manner. The learned scholar shows that the inscriptions of Kaniṣka are dated in different fashions. In the Kharoṣṭhī inscriptions, Kaniṣka follows the method of his Śaka-Pallava predecessors. On the other hand, in the Brāhmi inscriptions he follows the ancient Indian method. Is it then impossible that he adopted a third method to suit the local conditions in Western India?

5

A critical appreciation

The *Buddhacarita* is really a work of art. Unlike the *Mahāvastu* and the *Lalitavistara*, it is a systematic treatment of the subject matter. The reader seldom comes across a confused or incoherent description. The poet is very cautious about the use of figures of speech, and abstinence from a super-abundant employment of figures of speech has lent special charm to the poem. Besides, the presentment of the miraculous in the Buddha legend has been done with equal moderation. Thus, in short, the poem is an artistic creation. An account of the assemblage of fair and young ladies watching from gabled windows of high mansions the exit of the royal prince from the capital, is followed by a vivid description of how he came in contact with the hateful spectacle of senility. As the ladies came to know that the prince was going out of the city, they rushed to the window, careless of girdles falling off from their bodies and the poet describes their faces as so many full-blown lotuses with which the palace was decorated. The poet shows very artistic craftsmanship when he depicts how the prince overcame the lures of sweet ladies when they attempted to win him away from his firm resolve to deny the privileges of this world. And the description of the famous scene in which the prince, gazing on the undecked bodies of fair women, locked in the sweet embrace of sleep, resolved to abandon the palace, is yet another instance of rare poetic excellence. No less artistically pathetic is the scene in which the prince takes leave of his charioteer after a conversation with him which reveals his spirit of absolute disinterestedness towards worldly happiness. The poet is also gifted with the power of description and no one can forget the spirited picture of the contest of Buddha against Māra and his monstrous hosts. Evidences are also discernible in the poem to show that the poet was familiar with the doctrine of statecraft.

Saundarananda

Aśvaghoṣa is the author of another epic, the *Saundarananda,* which has been discovered and edited by MM Haraprasāda Śāstrin. This work in eighteen cantos also turns upon the history of Buddha's life, but the central theme is the history of the reciprocal love of Sundarī and Nanda, the half-brother of Buddha, who is initiated into the order against his will by the latter.

Gaṇḍīstotragāthā

The third work of the poet is a lyrical poem of twenty-nine stanzas, the *Gaṇḍīstotragāthā,* reconstructed in the Sanskrit original from the Chinese by A. von Staël-Holstein. It is in praise of the Gaṇḍī, the Buddhist monastery gong, consisting of a long symmetrical piece of wood, and of the religious message which its sound is supposed to carry when beaten with a short wooden club.

Sūtrālaṅkāra

Another work of the poet is the *Sūtrālaṅkāra,*[1] which undoubtedly is a later production than the *Buddhacarita,* inasmuch as it quotes the latter. It is to be regretted that the Sanskrit original is not yet available ; what we have is only the Chinese translation of the work. This *Sūtrālaṅkāra* is a collection of pious legends after the model of Jātakas and Avadānas. This work, however, has furnished us with a clue to the existence of dramatic literature even at the time of Aśvaghoṣa. In the piece relating to Māra we have the recapitulation of a drama.

[1] Dr Winternitz is of opinion that this work was written by Kumāralāta, a junior contemporary of Aśvaghoṣa. The work bears the title *Kalpanāmaṇḍitikā* or *Kalpanālaṅkṛtikā.*

Śāriputra-prakaraṇa

There is positive evidence to show that Aśvaghoṣa was a dramatist as well and in this connexion reference may be made to the momentous discovery of the concluding portion of a nine-act drama entitled the *Śāriputraprakaraṇa* which treats of the conversion of Śāriputra and his friend Maudgalyāyana. Among the valuable manuscript treasures in palm-leaf recovered from Turfan there is a fragmentary manuscript in which Professor Lüders found this drama which bore the name of Aśvaghoṣa as its author.

Mahāyāna-śraddhot-pādasūtra

One more work attributed to the poet is the *Mahāyānaśraddhotpādasūtra*, a philosophical treatise on the basis of the Mahāyāna doctrine.[1] Herein, as Professor Lévi remarks that the author shows himself as a profound metaphysician, as an intrepid reviver of a doctrine which was intended to regenerate Buddhism. It is believed that the author came of a Brāhmaṇa family and that he was later initiated into the doctrine of Buddhism. At first he joined the Sarvāstivādin school, and then prepared for the Mahāyāna. It was at one time believed that Aśvaghoṣa was a pioneer in the field of Mahāyānism. It would, however, be wiser to suppose that he was not the first to write a treatise on the subject, but was a strong exponent of it. For it is an undeniable fact that the Mahāyāna school grew and developed long before Aśvaghoṣa.

Vajrasucī

Another work attributed to Aśvaghoṣa, is the *Vajrasūcī*. Here the author takes up the Brāhmaṇic standpoint and disputes the authority of sacred texts and the claims of caste, and advocates the doctrine of

[1] According to Dr Winternitz this work has been wrongly ascribed to Aśvaghoṣa.

equality. In the Chinese *Tipiṭaka* Catalogue the work has been ascribed to Dharmakīrti.[1]

Mātṛcetā: his works

Mātṛcetā is the mystical name of a Buddhist-Sanskrit poet who, according to the Tibetan historian Tārānātha, is none other than Aśvaghoṣa. According to I-tsing, Mātṛcetā is the author of the *Catuśśatakastotra* and the *Śatapañcāśatikanāmastotra*, two poems in four hundred and one hundred and fifty verses respectively. Fragments of the Sanskrit original of the former have been discovered in Central Asia. The poems show some artistic excellence. Another work attributed to him is the *Mahārāja-Kanikalekha*.[2]

Āryacandra: *Maitreya-vyākaraṇa*

Āryacandra belonging probably to the same period as that of Mātṛcetā, is known as the author of the *Maitreyavyākaraṇa* or the *Maitreyasamiti* which is in the form of a dialogue between Gotama Buddha and Śāriputra. The work, translated into various languages, seems to have been very popular.

Āryaśūra: *Jātaka-mālā*

Very well-known is the name of the poet Āryaśūra, the author of the popular *Jātakamālā*, written after the model of the *Sūtrālaṅkāra*. Among the frescoes in the caves of Ajantā, there are scenes from the *Jātakamālā* with inscribed strophes from Āryaśūra. The inscriptions belong to the sixth century A.D.; but as another work of the poet was translated into Chinese in A.D. 434, he must have lived in the fourth century A.D.

Saddharmapuṇḍarīka,

The Buddhist Sanskrit literature belonging purely to the Mahāyāna school has preserved a number of books called the Mahāyānasūtras which are mainly

[1] Vide Bunyiu Nanjio, *Catalogue of the Chinese Translation of the Buddhist Tipiṭaka*, No. 1303.

[2] F. W. Thomas: *Mātṛcetā and the Mahārāja—Kanikalekha* (I. A. Vol. XXXII).

devoted to the glorification of Buddhas and Bodhisattvas. The most important of them is the *Saddharmapuṇḍarīka* written in the manner of the Purāṇas. The book which is a glorification of Buddha Śākyamuni, contains elements of quite different periods ; for it is believed that Sanskrit prose and Gāthās in mixed Sanskrit could not have developed at the same time. The book was translated into Chinese between A.D. 225 and A.D. 316. The original, therefore, must have been composed not later than the second century A.D. Some scholars, however, like to give it an early date. But even Professor Kern has not been able to find out passages which may show any ancient thought.

Kāraṇḍavyūha,

Another work is the *Kāraṇḍavyūha* preserved in two versions and betraying a theistic tendency. It contains a glorification of the Bodhisattva Avalokiteśvara. It was translated into Chinese as early as A.D. 270.

Sukhāvatīvyūha and Akṣobhyavyūha

The *Sukhāvatīvyūha* in which is glorified the Buddha Amitābha, is one more important book in which the reader finds a longing for spiritual liberation. The *Akṣobhyavyūha* which was translated into Chinese between A.D. 385 and A.D. 433, contains an account of the Buddha Akṣobhya.

Philosophical literature

The philosophical writings of Buddhist poets constitute no mean contribution to early Sanskrit literature. Among philosophical works belonging to the earliest Mahāyānasūtras mention should be made of the *Prajñāpāramitās* which occupy a unique place from the point of view of the history of religion. The Chinese translation of a *Prajñāpāramitā* was made as early as A.D. 179. Other philosophical Mahāyānasūtras are the *Buddhāvataṁsaka*, the *Gaṇḍavyūha*, the *Daśabhūmaka*, the *Ratnakūṭa*, the *Rāṣṭrapāla*, the

Laṅkāvatāra, the *Samādhirāja* and the *Suvarṇa-prabhāsa*.

Nāgārjuna: his works

The *Mādhyamikakārikā* which is a systematic philosophical work of the class with which we are familiar in the Brāhmaṇic philosophical literature was written in a metrical form in four hundred verses by Nāgārjuna whose name is associated with the Kuṣāṇa King Kaniṣka.[1] Nāgārjuna is also known as the author of the *Akutobhaya*, a commentary on his own work, which is preserved in a Tibetan translation. The *Yuktiṣaṣṭikā*, the *Śūnyatāsaptati*, the *Pratītyasamutpādahṛdaya*, the *Mahāyānaviṁśaka*, the *Vigrahavyāvartanī*, the *Ekaślokaśāstra*, the *Prajñādaṇḍa* and a few commentaries are his other works. There is another work the *Dharmasaṁgraha*, which passes as his composition. The *Suhṛllekha* is also ascribed to Nāgārjuna but it contains no Mādhyamika doctrine.

Āryadeva, Maitreyanātha, Ārya Asaṅga and Vasubandhu Asaṅga: their works

In the Chinese translations (A.D. 404) of the biographies of Aśvaghoṣa and Nāgārjuna, there occurs the name of one Āryadeva. His *Catuśśataka* is a work on the Mādhyamika system and is a polemic directed against the Brāhmaṇic ritual. His other works are the *Dvādaśanikāyaśāstra* and the *Cittaviśuddhiprakaraṇa*. Maitreyanātha, the real founder of the Yogācāra school, is the author of the *Abhisamayālaṅkārakārikās*, translated into Chinese probably in the fourth century A.D. Ārya Asaṅga, the famous student of Maitreyanātha, wrote the *Yogācārabhūmiśāstra* besides a few works all preserved in Chinese translations. Vasubandhu Asaṅga, a strong adherent of the Sarvāstivādin

[1] Some think that Nāgārjuna lived at the close of the second century A.D.

school, whom Professor Takakusu places between A.D. 420 and A.D. 500 and to whom Professor Wogihara assigns a date between A.D. 390 and A.D. 470, wrote the *Abhidharmakoṣa* and the *Paramārthasaptati* to combat the Sāṅkhya philosophy. In his later life, when he is believed to have been converted to Mahāyāna, he wrote the *Vijñaptimātratāsiddhi*.

Diṅnāga: his works

Diṅnāga is the chief of the early philosophers who made a valuable contribution through his masterpieces, the *Pramāṇasamuccaya* and the *Nyāyapraveśa*. He lived probably in the fifth century A.D. To the same century probably belonged Sthiramati and Dharmapālā who wrote valuable commentaries on the Mādhyamika system.[1]

Avadāna literature

The vast field of Avadāna literature presents a good and sufficient example of Sanskrit writing by Buddhist poets. The word 'avadāna' signifies a 'great religious or moral achievement as well as the history of a great achievement'. Such a great act may consist in the sacrifice of one's own life or the founding of an institution for the supply of incense, flowers, gold and jewels to, or the building of, sanctuaries. Avadāna stories are designed to inculcate that dark (ignoble) deeds bear dark (ignoble) fruits while white (noble) acts beget white (noble) fruits. Thus they are also tales of 'karman'.

Avadānaśataka and Karmaśataka

The *Avadānaśataka* heads the list of works on Avadāna literature. It consists of ten decades each having a theme of its own. Another work, the *Karma-*

[1] Later philosophical works, belonging to definitely identified schools of Buddhism, e.g., the works of Yaśomitra. Candrakīrti, Śāntideva, Dharmakīrti, Dharmottara and others, will be treated in detail in a subsequent chapter on Philosophy.

śataka, preserved only in the Tibetan translation, bears close affinity to the former. Yet another collection of stories in Tibetan (translated, of course, from original Sanskrit) is known as 'Dsanglun'.

Divyāvadāna

A well-known collection of Avadāna literature is the *Divyāvadāna.* The book belongs broadly to the Hīnayāna school; but traces of Mahāyānistic influence may yet be discovered in it. The collection is composed of many materials and consequently there is no uniformity of language. But the language is lucid, and true poetry is not wanting. The book has great importance from the standpoint of Indian sociology. As regards the time of redaction, it may be said that as Aśoka's successors down to Puṣyamitra are mentioned and the word 'dīnāra' is frequently used, a date prior to the second century A.D., can hardly be assigned to it.

Aśokāvadāna, Kalpadrumāvadānamālā, Ratnāvadānamālā, Dvāviṁśatyavadāna and minor avadānas

Mention may be made of the *Aśokāvadāna,* the cycle of stories having for its central theme the history of Aśoka. Historically, these stories have little value. The work was translated into Chinese as early as the third century A.D. A passing reference may be made to the *Kalpadrumāvadānamālā,* the *Ratnāvadānamālā* and the *Dvāviṁśatyavadāna,* the materials of which are drawn from the *Avadānaśataka.* Three more works, the *Bhadrakalpāvadāna,* the *Vratāvadānamālā* and the *Vicitrakarṇikāvadāna* are known to us in manuscripts only.

Avadānakalpalatā

A most extensive work on Avadāna literature is the *Avadānakalpalatā* of Kṣemendra of the eleventh century A.D. The work has been written in the style of ornate Court-epics.

REFERENCES

Keith, A. B.: *A History of Sanskrit Literature*
Kern, H.: *Manual of Buddhism*
Nariman, G. K.: *Literary History of Sanskrit Buddhism*
Raychaudhuri, H. C.: *Political History of Ancient India*
Smith, V. A.: *Oxford History of India*
Winternitz, M.: *A History of Indian Literature*. Vol. II

CHAPTER VII

COURT-EPICS

A. INTRODUCTION

Characteristics: essential

Authoritative writers on Sanskrit rhetoric have given an exhaustive list of the characteristics of epic poems in Classical Sanskrit. These characteristics may be divided under two heads—essential or important and non-essential or formal. Of them the essential characteristics are based on the conception of the three constituents of poetry, viz., the plot (*vastu*), the hero (*netṛ*) and the sentiment (*rasa*).[1] First, the plot of an epic must have a historical basis and should not be fictitious. Secondly, the hero must be an accomplished person of high lineage and should be of the type technically called Dhīrodātta. Delineation of various sentiments and emotions is the third important characteristic.

Characteristics: non-essential

The non-essential characteristics which are formal and apply only to technique, are many in number. They demand (i) that the epic should begin with a benediction, salutation or statement of facts, (ii) that

[1] Generally the sentiments are eight in number, viz., *śṛṅgāra* (erotic), *hāsya* (comic), *karuṇa* (pathetic), *raudra* (furious), *vīra* (heroic), *bhayānaka* (terrible), *bībhatsa* (disgustful) and *adbhuta* (marvellous). It is held by some that *śānta* (quietistic) was added later on by Abhinavagupta, the erudite commentator on Bharata's *Nāṭyaśāstra*. This was perhaps added to represent the spirit of *mahāprasthāna* in the *Mahābhārata*. It is even argued that Bharata has enumerated the eight sentiments for the drama only, and not for the epic.

chapters or sections should bear the appellation 'sarga', (iii) that the number of cantos should not exceed thirty and should not be less than eight, (iv) that the number of verses in each canto should not generally be less than thirty and should not exceed two hundred, (v) that there should be descriptions of sunrise and sunset, pools and gardens, amorous sports and pleasure-trips and the like, (vi) that the development of the plot should be natural and the five junctures of the plot (sandhi) should be well-arranged, and (vii) that the last two or three stanzas of each canto should be composed in a different metre or metres.[1]

B. GROWTH AND DEVELOPMENT OF COURT-EPICS

Aśvaghoṣa

The name of Aśvaghoṣa has come down to us as one of the earliest known epic poets. An account of his two great epics the *Buddhacarita* and the *Saundarananda* has already been given in a preceding chapter.

Kālidāsa: his age

The prince of epic poets is Kālidāsa. But it is difficult, if not impossible, to identify the age in which he flourished. The most popular theory of the day states that the poet flourished during the reign of Chandragupta II (A.D. 380-A.D. 415), that his powers were at their highest during the reign of Kumāra-

[1] It is easy to find that these characteristics are not always present in every epic. The *Haravijaya* in fifty cantos, some cantos of the *Naiṣadhīyacarita* containing more than two hundred verses and the first canto of the *Bhaṭṭikāvya* having only twenty-seven verses, are examples to the point.

gupta I (A.D. 415-A.D. 455) and that he lived to see the reign of Skandagupta (A.D. 455-A.D. 480).[1]

[1] The date of Kālidāsa is one of the most perplexing questions in the history of Sanskrit literature and the opinions of scholars, however ingeniously conceived, fail to give us definiteness and certainty. It is a fact to be regretted that India has not preserved the history of her greatest poet and dramatist. Tradition has been busy in weaving round the name of Kālidāsa many fictitious stories and it is almost impossible to separate at such a distant date the historical fact from its rich colouring of fables. The traditional theory makes Kālidāsa a contemporary of the Vikrama Saṁvat, the initial year of which is 57 B.C. Among the chief supporters of this theory are the late Sir William Jones, Dr Peterson, Principal S. Roy, and Mr I. R. Bālasubrahmaṇyam. Principal Roy has argued that 'the Bhītā medallion found near Allahabad by Dr Marshall in 1909-10 pictures a scene which looks exactly like the opening scene of the *Śākuntala*. The medallion belongs to the Śuṅga period 185-73 B.C. Moreover, the diction and style of Kālidāsa definitely establishes him as a predecessor of Aśvaghoṣa who has made use of the description of Aja's entry to the capital found in the *Raghuvaṁśa*, and has borrowed Kālidāsa's words and style. But archæologists are of opinion that the scene found in the Allahabad Bhītā medallion cannot be definitely proved to be identical with the scene in the *Sākuntala*. Professor Cowell in his edition of the *Buddhacarita* remarks that it is Kālidāsa who imitates Aśvaghoṣa and not vice versa. Mr Bālasubrahmaṇyam has based his theory on the internal evidences found in Kālidāsa's dramas. Thus the epilogue of the *Mālavikāgnimitra* supports the view that Kālidāsa lived in the reign of Agnimitra, the son of Puṣyamitra, of the first century B.C. The system of law, specially that of inheritance, as found in the *Śākuntala*, points to the fact that the poet must have lived before the beginning of the Christian era. Moreover, there was one Vikramāditya in Ujjayinī in the first century B.C., and Kālidāsa's works indirectly allude to him, as the poet lived in his court.

Dr Peterson has no particular argument to take his stand upon. He simply writes, 'Kālidāsa stands near the beginning of the Christian era if indeed he does not overtop it.' Sir William Jones in his introduction to the *Śākuntala* advances no argument but accepts the B.C. theory.

Another theory places Kālidāsa in the sixth century A.D. The late MM Haraprasāda Śāstrin, one of the supporters of this theory, has pointed out that the defeat of Hūṇas by Raghu in course of his world-conquest, refers to the conquest of Hūṇas by Skandagupta (A.D. 455-A.D. 480). And the terms Diṅnāga and Nicula, occurring in the *Meghadūta*, refer to the great teachers who lived before Kālidāsa. Professor Max Müller, another adherent of this doctrine, has based his theory on the suggestions of Professor Fergusson who points out that the era of the Mālavas was put back to 56 B.C., and Yaśodharmadeva Viṣṇuvardhana Vikramāditya who conquered the Hūṇas in A.D. 544, commemorated his victory by starting the Mālava era. But in doing so, he deliberately antedated it by 600 years.

Kumāra-sambhava

The *Kumārasambhava* of Kālidāsa is an epic in seventeen cantos of which the first eight are believed to be genuine. Mallinātha writes his commentary on the first eight cantos alone. There is also difference of opinion regarding the propriety of the theme of the later cantos. The theme of the epic is the marriage of Lord Śiva and Umā, daughter of the Himalayas, and the birth of Kārttikeya who vanquished Tāraka, the demon. Scholars are of opinion that the work is one of the first compositions of the poet. But it should be borne in mind that the *Kumārasambhava* appeals to modern taste more than the *Meghadūta* because of its rich variety, the brilliance of its fancy and the greater warmth of its feeling. The poem varies from the loveliness of the vernal season and the delights of married love to the grim tragedy of the death of the beloved. The theme is indeed a daring one inasmuch as it seeks to express the love of the highest deities. The appearance of the young hermit in Umā's hermitage and

Fergusson's theory (known as the Korur theory), however, has been exploded by Dr Fleet who pointed out by his researches that there was no Vikramāditya who achieved a victory over the Hūṇas in A.D. 544, and furthermore, that there was in existence an era known as the Mālava era long before A.D. 544. Thus the theory of Professor Max Müller is without any historical value. In this connexion, mention may be made of his once popular and now discarded 'Renaissance Theory of Classical Sanskrit Literature', which states that there was a revival of Sanskrit learning and literature in the wake of the Gupta civilization and culture and that Kālidāsa was the best flower of this age.

It is, however, generally believed that Kālidāsa flourished in the reign of Chandragupta II of the Imperial Gupta dynasty (A.D. 380—A.D. 515). But it has been argued that his best works were written during the reign of Kumāragupta I (A.D. 415-A.D. 455). But some would like to suggest that the poet lived to see the reign of Skandagupta (A.D. 455-A.D. 480). It should be noted, however, that both Candragupta and Skandagupta held the title of 'Vikramāditya', while Kumāragupta had the title of 'Mahendrāditya'.

his depreciation of Śiva followed by a strong and angry rebuke from Umā leading to the discovery of the identity of the hermit is a fine specimen of charming fancy and gentle humour. Kālidāsa's poetic powers are best revealed in his delineation of Śiva's temptation in canto iii and the touchingly pathetic picture of the lament of Rati for her dead husband in canto iv. It has been suggested that the model of this poem is the *Rāmāyaṇa*. There is indeed a very beautiful description of the spring in the Kiṣkindhyā forest which may have influenced Kālidāsa to draw the wonderful picture of spring's advent and the revival of life of the world. There is also a close parallel to Rati's lamentations. When Vālin is killed Tāra addresses him with words equally sincere and bearing the stamp of classical style.

Raghuvaṁśa

The *Raghuvaṁśa*, which is undoubtedly a production of a mature hand, deals with the life-history of the kings of the Ikṣvāku family in general and of Rāma in particular. The epic which is composed in nineteen cantos, is the tale of Vālmīki retold with the mastery of a finished poet. It is said that the work fulfils to a considerable extent the conditions of Sanskrit epic poetry. It has been rightly said that the *Raghuvaṁśa* has given full scope to the poet's extraordinarily artistic imagination. It is true that out of its nineteen cantos there is none that does not succeed in presenting some pleasing picture. Throughout the long poem the poet has maintained a fairly uniform excellence of style and expression. Kālidāsa seems to be at his best when he prepares his reader through Rāma's passionate clinging to the melancholy but sweet memories of the past for the grim tragedy in Sītā's banishment. The picture of the later history of Rāma which is more heroic in its silent suffering than the earlier has received unequivocal admiration from discerning critics.

Bhāravi: Kirātārjunīya

It is not difficult to surmise the date of Bhāravi as his name is mentioned along with Kālidāsa in the famous Aihole inscription of Pulakeśin II, dated A.D. 634. Bhāravi has to his credit only one epic, viz., the *Kirātārjunīya* which is based on the *Mahābhārata*. The poem describes how Arjuna obtained the Pāśupata weapon from Śiva. The work in nineteen cantos is written in an ornate style, though full of profundity of thought (*arthagaurava*) with occasional jingling of words. Though Bhāravi is not as great as Kālidāsa, yet he is never mediocre. His poetry is more sedate, more weighted with learning and technique but he is seldom fantastic. Bhāravi excels in descriptions—in the observation and record of the beauties of nature and of maidens. His poetry lacks the lyrical touch but his expressions give a pleasing surprise as they are invariably characterized by the qualities of brevity and propriety.

Bhaṭṭi: Rāvaṇavadha

Nowhere in the literature of the world can be found a single instance where poetry has been written with the sole object of illustrating the rules and principles of grammar. The *Bhaṭṭikāvya* or *Rāvaṇavadha* which is written in twenty-two cantos, is divided into four sections, viz., *Prakīrṇakāṇḍa*, *Prasannakāṇḍa*, *Alaṅkārakāṇḍa* and *Tiṅantakāṇḍa*. The poem is an epic depicting the life-history of Rāma from his birth up to the time of Rāvaṇa's death. The author of this epic, Bhaṭṭi, must be distinguished from the great grammarian-philosopher Bhartṛhari, popularly known as Hari. The author writes in his own work that he lived in Valabhī under one Śrīdharasena. History gives us four Dharasenas, the last of whom died in A.D. 651. It is, therefore, probable that Bhaṭṭi flourished in the latter half of the sixth and the first quarter of the seventh century A.D. It may be mentioned in this connexion that Bhaṭṭi lived before Bhāmaha, the great rhetorician who decries the poetic excellence of the *Rāvaṇavadha*.[1] Though the work is a grammatical poem, still in more places than one the poet has given ample proof of his artistic talents. The second, eleventh and twelfth cantos of the poem may be cited as instances.

Kumāradāsa: Jānakīharaṇa

Kumāradāsa, said to be the King of Ceylon from A.D. 517 to A.D. 526, is mentioned as a poet of remarkable talent by Rājaśekhara. It is maintained by Dr Keith that the poet knew the *Kāśikāvṛtti* (A.D. 650), and was known to Vāmana (A.D. 800). The theme of his poem, the *Jānakīharaṇa*, in twenty-five cantos, is taken from the *Rāmāyaṇa*, as the title indicates. The poet follows in the footsteps of Kālidāsa. Though he does not display imagination of a high order, he may still be called a vigorous descriptive poet. He is fond of alliteration, but careful enough not to carry it to the point of affectation.

Māgha: Śiśupālavadha

Ānandavardhana, the great rhetorician of the ninth century A.D., mentions Māgha who must have flourished in the eighth century A.D. He was the son of Ḍattakasarvāśraya and mentions Jinendrabuddhi, the author of the famous grammatical work, the *Nyāsa*, whose date is believed to be A.D. 700.[2] Māgha's

[1] *Kl.* II. 20
[2] *Sv.* ii. 112

Śiśupālavadha is a work in twenty cantos based on a legend of the *Mahābhārata*. His style is extremely ornate, and he often sacrifices sense for jugglery in words. He imitates Bhāravi, but his style is without the dignity of the latter. But it must be admitted on all hands that he commands much luxuriance of expression and thought. His admirers often refer to his rare gift of poetic fancy which has earned for him the appellation, 'Ghaṇṭā-Māgha'. A hill towering between sunset and moon-rise is compared to an elephant on whose two sides two bells are hung.

Śrīharṣa: Naiṣadhacarita

The fascinating story of Nala and Damayantī in the *Mahābhārata* forms the central theme of Śrīharṣa's masterpiece the *Naiṣadhacarita* or *Naiṣadhīyacarita* which was written in the latter half of the twelfth century A.D. The work is written in twenty-two cantos. The poet is a scholar of repute in the different systems of Indian philosophy and possesses a unique command over grammar, rhetoric and lexicon. Though he does not show that power of poetical suggestion which distinguishes the writings of great Indian poets like Kālidāsa, his power of expression is singularly captivating. What strikes us as his defect is that he has an especial liking for exaggerated statements in the form of poetic conceit. The importance of the *Naiṣadhacarita* does not lie in its poetic character—the poem is a repository of traditional learning and the reader is expected to be equipped with such learning in order that he may fully appreciate its value. The modern reader often lacks this equipment and this accounts for his lack of interest in the poem.

C. LESSER EPIC POEMS

Jāmbavatīvijaya and *Pātāla-vijaya*: ascribed to Pāṇini—it is not known whether they are two different works or different names of the same book—not free from grammatical errors—the authorship is much disputed.

Vāraruca-kāvya: mentioned by Patañjali but lost to us.

Padyacūḍāmaṇi: ascribed to Buddhaghoṣa (not later than the fifth century A.D.)—a poem in ten cantos describing the life of the Buddha up to the defeat of Māra differing in some details from the versions of the *Lalitavistara* and the *Buddhacarita*.

Kunteśvaradautya: ascribed to Kālidāsa by Kṣemendra—describing an embassy to the court of Kuntala.

Hayagrīvavadha: a lost work by Bhartṛmeṇṭha who flourished under Mātṛgupta of the sixth century A.D.

Padmapurāṇa: by Raviṣeṇa of the seventh century A.D.—containing a glorification of Ṛṣabha, the first Tīrthaṅkara.

Rāvaṇārjunīya or, *Ārjunarāvaṇīya*: by Bhaumaka—written in twenty-seven cantos in the fashion of Bhaṭṭi—based on the strife between Kārtavīrya and Rāvaṇa.

Harivaṁśapurāṇa: by Jinasena of the eighth century A.D.—in sixty-six cantos—describing the story of the *Mahābhārata* in a Jinistic setting.

Kapphaṇābhyudaya: by Śivasvāmin, a Kāshmirian Buddhist, during the reign of Avantivarman of the ninth century A.D.—written in twenty cantos—based on a tale in the *Avadānaśataka*.

Haravijaya: by Ratnākara, a Kāshmirian of the ninth century A.D.—based on the slaying of the demon Andhaka by Śiva—written in fifty cantos—influenced by Bāṇa and Māgha.

Rāghavapāṇḍavīya: by Kavirāja who flourished under Kādamba Kāmadeva of Jayantapurī (twelfth century A.D.) giving us in thirteen cantos the two stories of the *Rāmāyaṇa* and the *Mahābhārata* simultaneously through *double entendre*.

Mahāpurāṇa: by Jinasena and Guṇabhadra of the ninth century A.D.—containing two parts, the *Ādipurāṇa* and the *Uttarapurāṇa*.

Pārśvābhyudaya: by Jinasena of the ninth century A.D. who has incorporated the entire *Meghadūta* while relating the story of Pārśvanātha.

Kādambarīkathāsāra: by Abhinanda, son of the logician Jayantabhaṭṭa of the tenth century A.D. describing in eight cantos the story of Bāṇa's *Kādambarī*.

Yaśodharacarita: written in four cantos by Vādirāja in the first quarter of the eleventh century A.D. describing the legend of King Yaśodhara. Another work of the same name written by Māṇikyacandra of unknown date.

Kavirahasya: by Halāyudha of the tenth century A.D.—containing an eulogy of the Rāṣṭrakūṭa King Kṛṣṇa III—written after the style of Bhaṭṭi.

Rāmacarita: by Abhinanda, son of Śatānanda of unknown date.

Rāmāyaṇamañjarī and *Bhāratamañjarī*: by polymath Kṣemendra of Kāshmir of the eleventh century A.D.

Harivilāsa: by Lolimbarāja of the eleventh century A.D.—describing the Kṛṣṇa legend in five cantos.

Śrīkaṇṭhacarita: by Maṅkha—a Kāshmirian and a pupil of Ruyyaka of the twelfth century A.D.—written in twenty-five cantos—based on the tale of the destruction of the demon Tripura by Śiva—possessing some historical interest as an assembly of learned men, thirty in number, held under the patronage of the poet's brother Alaṅkāra, a minister of Jayasiṁha of Kāshmir (A.D. 1127—A.D. 1150) is mentioned—written in a highly ornate style which lacks lucidity.

Śatruñjayamāhātmya: by Dhaneśvara of the twelfth century A.D.—written in fourteen cantos—containing a glorification of the sacred mountain Śatruñjaya.

Triṣaṣṭiśalākāpuruṣacarita: by Hemacandra of A.D. 1088-1172—a very important work, its seventh book being called the *Jaina-Rāmāyaṇa*, the tenth entitled the *Mahāvīracarita*, containing the life-story of Mahāvīra, and its appendix-section, the *Pariśiṣṭa-parvan*, being a mine of fairy tales and stories.

Dharmaśarmābhyudaya: by Haricandra of unknown date—written in twenty-one cantos devoting the life of Dharmanātha, the fifteenth Tīrthaṅkara.

Neminirvāṇa: by Vāgbhaṭa of the twelfth century A.D. written in fifteen cantos—dealing with Neminātha's life.

Bālabhārata: by Amaracandra of the thirteenth century A.D.—narrating the story of the *Mahābhārata* in the order of the *parvans*.

Pāṇḍavacaritra and *Mṛgavatīcaritra*: by Devaprabhasūri of the thirteenth century A.D.—the former is in eighteen cantos and the latter is based on the Udayana legend.

Pārśvanāthacarita: by Bhāvadevasūri of the thirteenth century A.D.

Sahṛdayānanda: by Kṛṣṇānanda of the fourteenth century A.D.—narrating the Nala-legend in fifteen cantos.

Nalābhyudaya: by Vāmanabhaṭṭa Bāṇa of the fourteenth century A.D.—dealing with the story of Nala in eight cantos.

Harivaṁśa: by Sakalakīrti and his pupil Jinadāsa of the fifteenth century A.D.

Rasikāñjana: by Rāmacandra of the sixteenth century A.D.—describing the two sentiments of love and asceticism through *double entendre*.

Pāṇḍavapurāṇa: by Śubhacandra of the sixteenth century A.D.—also called the *Jaina-Mahābhārata*.

Rāghavanaiṣadhīya: by Haradattasūri of unknown date—describing the tales of Rāma and Nala through *double entendre*.

Rāghavapāṇḍavīyayādavīya: by Cidambara, protégé of Veṅkaṭa I of Vijayanagara (A.D. 1586—A.D. 1614)—describing the tales of the *Rāmāyaṇa*, the *Mahābhārata* and the *Bhāgavata* through treble punning.

REFERENCES

Keith, A. B.: *A History of Sanskrit Literature*

Macdonell, A. A.: *A History of Sanskrit Literature*

Winternitz, M: *A History of Indian Literature*, Vol. II

Dasgupta, S. N. and De, S.K.: *History of Sanskrit Literature*, Vol. I

Krishnamachariar, M.: *Classical Sanskrit Literature*

CHAPTER VIII

DRAMA

A. ORIGIN OF SANSKRIT DRAMA

THE origin of Sanskrit drama is a most interesting study in the history of Sanskrit literature and divergent views are found amongst scholars which can hardly be reconciled. It is an undeniable fact that Bharata's *Nāṭyaśāstra* is the earliest known book on Sanskrit dramaturgy. The third century A.D. is the generally accepted date of the *Nāṭyaśāstra*, and some scholars hold that the book is a compilation on the basis of an original work of the Sūtra-type. According to a legend found in this book, Brahmā created drama by taking passages for recitation from the *Ṛgveda*, songs from the *Sāmaveda*, gestures from the *Yajurveda* and emotions from the *Atharvaveda*. Thus a drama is known as the fifth Veda. From Śiva and Pārvatī, Tāṇḍava and Lāsya dances were obtained and Viṣṇu gave the Rīti. The same book also informs us that the dramas were enacted during the Indradhvaja festival where the sons and disciples of the same Bharata together with Gandharvas and Apsarases took part in the play. The first two plays enacted were the *Amṛtamanthana* and the *Tripuradāha* both written by Brahmā himself. Orthodox view

There was a time when the theory of the Greek origin of Indian drama found its adherents amongst

Theory of Greek origin

scholars.[1] The chief exponent was Professor Windisch (1882) who found many striking similarities between Greek and Sanskrit plays and based his theory on the ground that Indians were in touch with Greeks for a considerable period after the invasion of Alexander and that none of the extant Sanskrit plays belongs to a pre-Christian date. Thus to him the very classification into acts, the prologues and the epilogues. the way in which the actors make their entrance and exit, the term *yavanikā*, the theme and its manipulation, the variety of stage-directions, the typical characters like the Vidūṣaka, Pratināyaka, etc.,—all smell of Greek origin. This theory was further corroborated by the discovery in the Sītābeṅgā cave, of an Indian version of a Greek theatre.[2] But this theory has been rejected as the points of contrast are far too many. The absence of the three unities of time, space and action in a Sanskrit drama brings it nearer to an Elizabethan drama than to a Greek drama where the three unities are essential. The difference in time between two acts in a Sanskrit drama may be several years (e.g., the *Uttararāmacarita* of Bhavabhūti where twelve years intervene between the incidents of the first two acts). Moreover, it is only in a particular act of a Sanskrit drama that the actions which happen in a single place are usually represented. Thus while the sixth act of the *Śākuntala* represents the scene at King Duṣyanta's palace, the seventh act shows the scene at sage Mārīca's hermitage on the top of the Himālayas and the first part of it represents the

[1] The suggestion came from Professor Weber, but Professor Pischel vehemently repudiated it.

[2] On the antiquities of Ramgarh Hill, District of Sargujā—IA. Vol. II.

king's aerial journey. As for the term *yavanikā*, most scholars think that it is of later introduction and it refers to Persian tapestries and not to anything Greek.

Origin of Sanskrit drama connected with vernal festivities

On the other hand, there are some scholars who want to determine the origin of Sanskrit dramas in the same manner in which Western scholars seek to explain the origin of European plays. So it has been argued that as the first Sanskrit play is stated to have been produced at the Indradhvaja festival (which has a parallel in the May-pole dance in Europe), the origin of Sanskrit dramas is to be connected with the festivities of the spring after the passing away of the winter. But this theory is rejected as MM Haraprasāda Śāstrin has pointed out that the aforesaid Indradhvaja festival comes off at the end of the rains.

Ridgeway's theory

Professor Ridgeway has connected the origin of Indian drama with the worshipping of dead ancestors. But the theory is inapplicable to the case of Indian Aryans whose ritual of the disposing of the dead has the minimum ostentation.

Kṛṣṇa-cult origin

The Kṛṣṇa-worship is thought by some scholars to be the origin of Sanskrit plays. Thus the role which the Śaurasenī Prākrit plays in a Sanskrit drama is easily explained. But this theory involves anachronism, as it remains to be proved that Kṛṣṇa dramas are the earliest Sanskrit dramas.[1]

Pischel's theory

Professor Pischel has set forth the theory that Sanskrit drama in its origin was a puppet-play. The stage-manager in a Sanskrit drama is called Sūtradhāra (the holder of the string) and his assistant Sthāpaka is to enter immediately after the stage-manager and is

[1] It may be proved in the same way that the theories of the Viṣṇu-cult, Śiva-cult and Rāma-cult origin of Indian drama cannot be accepted.

expected to place in proper position, the plot, the hero or the germ of the play. The puppets also are frequently mentioned in Sanskrit literature; they could be made to dance or move about and they could even be made to talk. Such a talking puppet, impersonating Sītā, is found in one of Rājaśekhara's plays. The episode of the Shadow-Sītā in Bhavabhūti's *Uttararāmacarita* is reminiscent of the old shadow-play in ancient India. But this theory cannot furnish sufficient explanation of many points about Sanskrit drama such as the mixture of prose and verse, as also the varieties of language and the like.[1]

Origin to be traced to the Vedic period

Another theory on this subject states that the origin of Sanskrit drama should be sought in the Saṁvāda-hymns of the *Ṛgveda*. These ballad hymns which are nearly twenty in number, are markedly dramatic in spirit.[2] These Saṁvāda hymns have no specific ritualistic applications and they seem to have been recited between the intervals of long sacrificial sessions (pāriplava) for the satisfaction of the patrons of sacrifices. But whether the hymns were treated as ballads (as Professors Pischel and Geldner thought); or as regular ritualistic dramas with actual stage-directions and action including singing and dancing (as held by Professor von Schroeder); or, finally as narrative stories with an admixture of prose to connect the poems into one whole, with a preponderance of dialogue (as maintained by Professor Oldenberg)—is still keenly disputed amongst scholars.[3]

[1] Professor Hillebrandt has argued that Professor Pischel's theory cannot be accepted as the puppet-play assumes the pre-existence of the drama.

[2] *RV*. I. 165, 170 and 179, III. 33, IV. 18, VII. 33, VIII. 100, X. 11, 28, 51—53, 86, 95 and 108, etc.

[3] Professor Hertel has found a full drama in the *Suparṇādhyāya*.

Conclusion

It has been universally found that the growth of drama is intimately connected with royal patronage. And India is no exception. Bearing in our mind the existence of the ritualistic drama which marks the early beginnings of Indian plays we can boldly assert that Sanskrit drama is a product of the Indian mind which viewed life in all its various aspects and passed through many stages of development, being influenced by Jainism and Buddhism in its allegorical sphere or by any other foreign factor and yet maintaining its own peculiarity. No one theory, therefore, can adequately explain all its features and accordingly one should refrain from making a choice of any one of them.

B. CHARACTERISTICS OF SANSKRIT DRAMA

Predominance of sentimei

According to Indian thinkers, the best of poets is a dramatist. Sanskrit drama evolved in all its aspects in a particularly Indian atmosphere. Sanskrit dramatists with their inherent aesthetic sense gave more importance to the portrayal of sentiment than to character or plot. Sanskrit dramas were, therefore, very idealistic and romantic in their character. The breath of poetry and romance vivified the Sanskrit drama and its higher and more poetic naturalness was attractive in revealing the beauty and the depth of human character. The predominance of sentiment in Sanskrit dramas has been responsible for the creation of typical characters rather than individualized figures. It is said that the characters are often conventional and not original. But though in the hands of lesser dramatists idealistic creation overshadowed action and characterization, still the best Sanskrit dramatists have been able to create outstanding characters which are not fantastic creations. Thus Cārudatta in the *Mṛcchakaṭika* and Duṣyanta in the *Abhijñāna Śakuntalam* are not mere typical characters. Similarly the Śakāra and the Vīṭa in Śūdraka's drama are finely characterized. Though the best of Sanskrit dramas glow with occasional touches of realism, still the fact cannot be denied that the poetic value has never been sacrificed for direct delineation of action or character. Judged by modern standards most of the Sanskrit dramas would, however, be regarded as dramatic poems. In some authors the sense of the dramatic seems to have been hopelessly lost in their ever-increasing effort at depicting the sentimental and the poetic, and it is a fact that the choice of lyric or epic subjects which are scarcely capable of dramatic treatment is responsible for the lack of dramatic quality in the plays of some of the well-known dramatists. Nevertheless we cannot say that Sanskrit dramatists were totally indifferent to the action of a drama, and it has been said clearly that drama must have five critical junctures of plot (*sandhi*), viz., *mukha* (opening or *protasis*), *pratimukha* (progression or *epitasis*), *garbha* (development or *catastasis*), *vimarśa* (pause or *peripeteia*) and *nirvahaṇa* (conclusion or *catastrophe*). Further, Sanskrit dramaturgists have laid it down as a rule that there should be perfect fusion of sentiment and theme or plot in a drama. Over delineation of sentiment at the cost of gradual and systematic development of plot and too much elaboration of details in the plot hampering the flow of sentiment must be carefully avoided. It was the usual convention with Sanskrit poets to select the erotic, the heroic or the quietistic as the principal sentiment in a nāṭaka (the type of major dramas) which is assisted by every other sentiment according to propriety. It needs to be added here that in the opinion of some thinkers, the aforesaid convention should not command any respect and any one of the nine sentiments may be the predominant sentiment in a nāṭaka.

Absence of tragedy

A charge is often levelled by critics that Sanskrit drama is marked by an absence of tragedy ; but it may be answered by saying that what is known as *vipra-lambha-śṛṅgāra* (love-in-separation) more than compensates for the comparatively rare 'pathetic' which is the prominent sentiment in only one class of minor dramas. But it is a fact that Sanskrit dramas have never a tragic catastrophe, and the reason is to be found in the conception that it mars the sentiment. Hence the representation of death, murder, war, revolution and anything indecorous which is a hiatus in aesthetic pleasure, has been prohibited on the stage. The Sanskrit drama generally keeps to the high road of life and believes that grim realism cannot exalt the mind, rather it tends to disturb the romantic atmosphere. It has, therefore, subordinated tragedy to finer sentiments and tragedy as such has remained comparatively undeveloped. And there is truth in the statement that the imposition of the condition of happy union in the Sanskrit drama has in some cases tended to weaken the value of tragedy in it.

Hero

As the main interest in Sanskrit dramas lies in the creation of the sentiment, it is convenient for a dramatist to take a plot with a popular theme. The hero of the drama (nāṭaka) must be an accomplished person of high lineage belonging to the *dhīrodātta* type. He must be a hero either of the earth or of heaven, and sometimes we even find in a Sanskrit drama gods side by side with mortal men, and thus ample scope is given to the dramatist's imagination to create the appropriate romantic atmosphere.

Morality and drama

Like every other branch of Indian literature, the Sanskrit drama has a religious basis and nothing violating the moral and religious code has been represented in Sanskrit dramas.

Satire and farce

It should be mentioned in this connexion that Sanskrit dramatic literature is not poor in farcical compositions. The discovery of the four one-act monologue plays under the title of *Caturbhāṇī*[1] has brought to light the talent of Sanskrit dramatists in the domain of humorous and farcical writing. The four plays which are of the same type present variety, satire, comic-relief and free colloquial style. The plot of such plays is slight but within its limited scope there is much of variety. The satirical and comic pictures of various classes of people—the sky-gazing poet, the penniless impotent, the dried-up mistress, the mendicant consoling a courtezan with the words of the Buddha, the grammarian with his affectations, the hypocritical Buddhist—are indeed enjoyable. The Viṭa, the central character in such plays, whose origin may be traced back to the earlier dramas such as *Cāru-*

[1] The four plays discovered and published in 1922 are the *Ubhayābhisārikā*, the *Padmaprābhṛtaka*, the *Dhūrtaviṭasaṁvāda* and the *Pādatāḍitaka* respectively ascribed to Vararuci, Śudraka, Īśvaradatta and Śyāmilaka. The plays exhibit common characteristics and it is presumed that considerable time intervened between these plays and the later specimens of the bhāṇas. It is quite likely that these bhāṇas belonged to the age of the Classical dramatists.

datta and *Mṛcchakaṭika*, enjoys an important status of his own. It is true that in the later bhāṇas he has lost much of his glamour and appears as a gallant in the worst sense of the term. The later bhāṇas are merely literary exercises lacking in variety and the natural human and polite banter which characterize the earlier bhāṇas are absent in them. Besides the bhāṇas there is another species of farcical literature in Sanskrit which is closely related to them. It is the prahasanas which like the bhāṇas are undoubtedly artistic productions. The difference between the prahasana and the bhāṇa is that whereas there is greater scope for comedy and satire in the former, there is a preponderance of the erotic sentiment in the latter.

C. CLASSIFICATION OF SANSKRIT DRAMAS

Rūpaka & Uparūpaka

It must be said at the outset that the Sanskrit synonym for drama is rūpaka and not nāṭaka, the latter being a variety of the former which has a more comprehensive import. Writers on Sanskrit dramaturgy have classified Sanskrit dramas into two types: (1) the major (rūpaka) and (2) the minor (uparūpaka). The varieties of each type differ according to different authorities. The following is the list given by Viśvanātha in his *Sāhityadarpaṇa* of the varieties of the two types of Sanskrit dramas:

1. The major type: (i) nāṭaka (e.g., *Abhijñānaśakuntala* of Kālidāsa), (ii) prakaraṇa (e.g., *Mālatīmādhava* of Bhavabhūti), (iii) bhāṇa (e.g., *Karpūracarita* of Vatsarāja), (iv) vyāyoga (e.g., *Madhyamavyāyoga* of Bhāsa), (v) samavakāra (e.g., *Samudrama-*

thana of Vatsarāja), (vi) ḍima (e.g., *Tripuradāha* of Vatsarāja), (vii) īhāmṛga (e.g., *Rukmiṇīharaṇa* of Vatsarāja), (viii) aṅka or Utsṛṣṭikāṅka (e.g., *Śarmiṣṭhā-yayāti*), (ix) vīthī (e.g., *Mālavikā*) and (x) prahasana (e.g., *Mattavilāsa* of Mahendravikramavarman).

2. The minor type: (i) nāṭikā (e.g., *Ratnāvalī* of Śrī-Harṣa), (ii) troṭaka (e.g., *Vikramorvaśīya* of Kālidāsa), (iii) goṣṭhī (e.g., *Raivatamadanikā*), (iv) saṭṭaka (e.g., *Karpūramañjarī* of Rājaśekhara), (v) nāṭyarāsaka (e.g., *Vilāsavatī*), (vi) prasthāna (e.g., *Śṛṅgāratilaka*), (vii) ullāpya (e.g., *Devīmahādeva*), (viii) kāvya (e.g., *Yādavodaya*), (ix) preṅkhaṇa (e.g., *Vālivadha*), (x) rāsaka (e.g., *Menakāhita*), (xi) saṁlāpaka (e.g., *Māyākāpālika*), (xii) śrīgadita (e.g., *Krīḍārasātala*), (xiii) śilpaka (e.g., *Kanakāvatīmādhava*), (xiv) vilāsikā (no work mentioned in *Sd.*), (xv) durmallikā (e.g., *Bindumatī*), (xvi) prakaraṇikā (no work mentioned in *Sd.*), (xvii) hallīśa (e.g., *Keliraivataka*) and (xviii) bhāṇikā (e.g., *Kāmadattā*).[1]

D. GROWTH AND DEVELOPMENT OF SANSKRIT DRAMA

Introduction

The Indian drama can be traced to the fifth or the fourth century B.C. Pāṇini refers to dramatic aphorisms[2] and the *Arthaśāstra* of Kauṭilya, which is a work of the fourth century B.C., contains reference to the term *Kuśīlava*, which may have an allusion to the twin sons of Rāma or to the proverbially bad character of

[1] The works, against which authors are mentioned, have now been published and are all available. The other works are only mentioned by the author of the *Sāhityadarpaṇa* and are not actually known to exist at present.

[2] *Aṣṭ* IV. iii. 110.

actors. The *Mahābhāṣya*, beside its reference to the dramas, *Kaṁsavadha* and *Balibandha*, speaks of the painting of actors and of the three kinds of artists. In the *Rāmāyaṇa* we find the mention of nāṭaka and the *Mahābhārata* refers to a wooden feminine figure[1] In the *Harivaṁśa*, however, we find unmistakable reference to a full-fledged drama acted by Kṛṣṇa's descendants. But Dr Keith looks upon all these evidences as mere references to pantomimes and not to pure dramas. He, however, admits that the dramas of Aśvaghoṣa and Bhāsa, the first extant dramas, are not the earliest specimens of Indian plays, inasmuch as they show much polish and exquisite finish.[2] The earliest extant Sanskrit drama according to European scholars is the *Śāriputraprakaraṇa* of Aśvaghoṣa which was discovered sometime ago in Turfan in Central Asia.

Bhāsa: age and authorship

The Bhāsa-problem has in recent years been a most interesting topic for discussion in the history of Sanskrit drama.[3] It has drawn the attention of many

[1] *Mbh.* III. xxx, 23.

[2] Aśvaghoṣa has followed the rules of Sanskrit dramaturgy; the higher characters use Sanskrit, while others speak Prākrit.

[3] The discovery of the Trivandrum plays is a most important event in the domain of Indology comparable only to the discovery of Kauṭilya's *Arthaśāstra*. The community of technique, language, style, ideas, treatment and identity of names of dramatis personae, prose and metrical passages and scenes are so remarkable that the conclusion of their common authorship is inevitable. Considering the superior and manifold merits of the plays in question it may be said that if the author of these plays is not Bhāsa, he may without doubt be given a position as high as that which the real Bhāsa used to occupy.

References to Bhāsa or quotations from his works are found in later literature. MM G. Sāstri, the fortunate discoverer of the plays ascribed them to Bhāsa and attempted to assign a very early date to the celebrated dramatist on the strength of the following arguments: (i) The close resemblance of the thirteen plays to one another in language and mode of expression, (ii) The Prologue in each play begins with the entrance of the Sūtradhāra, a peculiarity ascribed to

scholars widely differing in their opinions on the authenticity and authorship of the plays of Bhāsa.

Bhāsa by Bāṇabhaṭṭa. (iii) The naming of the Prologue as Sthāpanā instead of Prastāvanā—a remarkable departure from the Classical dramas. (iv) The opening verses of some of the plays (e.g. *Pratimā*, *Svapnavāsavadattā*, etc.) string together the principal characters—an uncommon peculiarity of the plays. (v) The omission of the name of the work and the author in the Sthāpanā proving that the dramatist lived in an age before the convention of mentioning the name of the author in his work came in vogue. (vi) The Bharatavākya in all the dramas ends with the same prayer—a pre-classical peculiarity. (vii) The plays reveal a poetic elegance which is comparable only to the writings of Vālmīki and Vyāsa. (viii) Kālidāsa's reference to Bhāsa is suggestive of his hoary antiquity. (ix) The violation in many cases of the rules of the extant *Nāṭyaśāstra* leads us to presume that he followed in all probability another work on dramaturgy different from the present *Nāṭyaśāstra*. (x) The evidence of language employed by Bhāsa would suggest that he was anterior to Pāṇini, Kātyāyana and Patañjali—Bhāsa's language makes us think that he lived in an age when Sanskrit was a spoken language, but Sanskrit ceased to be a spoken language during the time of Patañjali. (xi) Cāṇakya probably quotes from the *Pratijñāyaugandharāyaṇa* and is, therefore, posterior to Bhāsa.

The ante-Bhāsites put forward the following as counter-arguments: (i) As the title of the plays and the name of their author are not mentioned in the Prologue they are adaptations. (ii) As to the reference to the entrance of the Sūtradhāra, it is pointed out that the same is a peculiarity of South Indian manuscripts in general and not a characteristic of the thriteen plays alone. (iii) The dramatic technique has been shared by all South Indian plays and is not the monopoly of the plays of Bhāsa. (iv) The deviations from Bharata's *Nāṭyaśāstra* do not point to the pre-Classical age of Bhāsa's dramas—they have been usually introduced in the later plays with a view to securing a more arresting stage-effect. (v) Regarding the linguistic grounds it is pointed out that too much importance cannot be placed on this argument as similar grammatical anomalies occur also in the Epic-legendary literature and in very late texts. Further the Prākṛta archaisms are the characteristics of the Malayalam mss. And the Prākrit of the dramas is a factor depending more on the provenance and age of the mss. than on the provenance and age of the dramatist. (vi) The verses cited in later works are never associated with the name of Bhāsa. (vii) Some verses found in different anthologies are not found in the Trivandrum plays. (viii) The possibilitiy of Kerala influence has been advanced as the final argument.

MM K. Sāstri and others have tried to attribute the authorship of the Trivandrum dramas to Śaktibhadra on the strength of the fact that the mss. of *Āścareyacūḍāmaṇi*, *Pratimā* and *Abhiṣeka* were found combined together in one ms of Malabar. On the basis of this curious combination as also structural and verbal similarities, it was attempted to attribute some of the plays to the authorship of Śaktibhadra; but it may be pointed out that the views of the Anti-

Credit goes to MM Ganapati Śāstrin who first published the thirteen plays of Bhāsa in 1912. But for

Bhasites are confused on this point. Rightly does Keith remark: The attribution of Trivandrum dramas to Śaktibhadra evinces the same curious lack of discrimination which ascribes to Daṇḍin the *Avantīsundarīkathā,* credits Bāṇa with the *Pārvatīpariṇaya* and would rob Kālidāsa of the *Ṛtusaṁhāra.*

An attempt has been made to establish the identity of Śūdraka with Bhāsa and to ascribe that some of the dramas, *Mṛcchakaṭika, Bālacarita, Avimāraka* and *Vatsarājacarita* to Śūdraka. In the opinion of some scholars *Cārudatta* is a stage-abridgment of the *Mṛcchakaṭika* but it has been found that the two dramas do not belong to the same age and are not written by the same author. The *Mṛcchakaṭika* is a later, revised and enlarged version of the *Cārudatta.*

The genealogy of Raghu's dynasty as found in the *Pratimā* follows the same order as described in Kālidāsa's *Raghuvaṁśa* and does not tally with the order given in the *Rāmāyaṇa.* This fact has led the Piṣhraotis to conclude that Bhāsa was indebted to Kālidāsa. In reply to this argument it is pointed out that it is quite probable that both Bhāsa and Kālidāsa have drawn this genealogy from common sources such as, the *Viṣṇupurāṇa,* the *Padmapurāṇa* and the *Harivaṁśa.*

Dr Raja has referred to Kerala influence in the Trivandrum plays. He has picked up three words of Kerala origin in the *Cārudatta.* Dr Thomas and H. Sastri controvert his views. Kuppuswami Sastri finds a reference to the 'Sambandha' marriages of Malabar on the strength of the word 'Sambandha'. This view has been controverted by R. Kavi. K. R. Pishraoti bases his arguments on some minor details and comes to the conclusion that the plays are from Kerala. But the details can be found all over India and are not confined to Kerala alone. The absence of Sītā in the coronation, reference to Statue houses and the manner of worshipping the statutes exhibit a local colouring in the opinion of Pishraoti, but G. Sastri's reply on this point appears to be quite satisfactory. It has been argued again that the Trivandrum plays form a part of repertoire of the Cākyārs, the traditional actors of Kerala. It has been shown that the peculiar practice of the Cākyārs is that they never act a drama in full but selected scenes only, that for every act they stage they have the set introduction. The Pishraotis maintain that the Prologues of the plays are later additions while the main scenes have preserved the original plays, abridged or modelled in parts, to suit the exigencies of local theatres. In their opinion much of the relative uniformity of style, dramatic method and formal technique may have been the result of local editing. It is by no means certain that these plays are the production of one writer, they are a heterogeneous group—the product of a class of writers who belonged to one school and worked under its convention. Against this argument it can be said that the stage-reform in Kerala is not earlier than the 8th century A.D. while the existence of the *Svapnavāsavadatta* and other plays in their present form much before that period is definitely proved. So it is only possible that the Kerala dramatists and actors

his editorship, the plays of Bhāsa would have remained mere fictitious names. Bhāsa is mentioned by Kālidāsa, Bāṇa, Rājaśekhara and others. MM G. Śāstrin, the editor, fixed the third century B.C. or earlier as the date for Bhāsa ; but European scholars would not agree on the evidence of Prākrit. They would like to place the author of these plays in the third century A.D.

Appreciation

Bhāsa's myriad-mindedness is well reflected in the number of his plays and the variety of their themes. The style of Bhāsa is simple, at the same time forceful, and conforms to what is known as the Vaidarbha style. The initial characteristic of the dramas of Bhāsa is action which has never been sacrificed for poetry and poetic charm. In fact, the plays of Bhāsa are really of dramatic value and have qualities of a very high order. On the other hand, there are scholars who hold that the dramas in their present

impressed by the manifold devices and technique of these old plays copied these peculiarities and embodied them in their own manuals. Though the Pishraotis assert that Cākyārs are Sanskrit scholars, Professor O. Stein raises doubt how far they were literary men capable of recasting classical dramas by shortening them and working them up into stage-plays. It has also been suggested that the plays are not the original compositions of the Cākyārs but later compilations or adaptations. Dr Barnett holds that the plays were worked over by the court-poets of the Pāṇḍya kings while others take them to be from the Pallava kings. The compilation or adaptation theory has been set aside by Winternitz.

Scholars are divided into two groups, one accepting and another refusing to accept the discovery:

Abhyankar, A. Banerjee-Sastri, S. K. Belvalkar, K. H. Dhruva, J. C. Ghatak, H. Jacobi, K. P. Jayaswal, J. Jolly, M. R. Kale, A. B Keith, S. Konow, F. Lacote, V. Lesny, M. Lindanam, A. M. Murwarth, G. Morgenstierne, S. M. Parajpe, W. Printz, A. D. Pusalker, L. Sarup, MM H. Sastri, H. Sastri, V S. Sukthankar, F. W. Thomas, H. Weller, M. Winternitz and others belong to the first group, while L. D. Barnett, J. Charpentier, C. R. Devadhara, P. V. Kane, R. Kavi, A. K. Pishraoti, K. R. Pishraoti, C. K. Raja, MM. R. Sarma, Hirananda Sastri, MM K. Sastri, S. Levi, A. C. Woolner belong to the second group.

forms are not the composition of one and the same poet, but they are the composite product of the plagiarism of many scribes. Some scholars have even gone so far as to surmise the existence of a genuine Bhāsa of whose works the extant plays are mere abridgements by the traditional players of Southern India (especially Kerala).

Classification of Bhāsa's dramas

The thirteen plays of Bhāsa may be arranged under three heads according to the sources from which the plots have been taken:—(a) plots taken from the *Rāmāyaṇa*, (b) plots taken from the *Mahābhārata*, the *Harivaṁśa* and the Purāṇas, and (c) plots taken probably from the *Bṛhatkathā* of Guṇāḍhya and other popular sources.

Rāmāyaṇa-plays

The *Pratimā* (nāṭaka) which is the most popular of the *Rāmāyaṇa*-plays, is written in seven acts. The story starts from the death of King Daśaratha and ends with Rāma's return to Ayodhyā from Laṅkā. The second play, based on the *Rāmāyaṇa*, is the *Abhiṣeka* (nāṭaka) in six acts. It takes up the story of the epic at the point of the slaying of Vālin and consecration of Sugrīva and ends with the ordeal of Sītā and the consecration of Rāma. It may be that the drama is so named because it starts and ends with a consecration. Compared with the *Pratimā* its dramatic value appears to be somewhat inferior. It is said that the play contains a series of situations only but one misses a sequence of incidents gradually developed.

Mahābhārata-plays

The *Madhyama-vyāyoga* deserves mention first amongst the *Mahābhārata*-plays. This drama (vyāyoga) in one act amply testifies to the skill of the dramatist in characterization. The play is based on the tale of Hiḍimbā's love for Bhīma, for which there is no hint in the epic. It is said that the possibilities of the theme have not been fully developed. The *Dūtaghaṭotkaca* is also a drama (vyāyoga) in one act which describes Ghatotkaca appearing before the Kauravas immediately after the death of Abhimanyu, with the news that Arjuna is preparing for their punishment. There is not much of action in the play which presents a somewhat sketchy scene. The *Karṇabhāra* (vyāyoga) also contains one act, the story being how the armour and ear-rings of Karṇa are stolen by Indra. Though the dramatic value of the work is not universally acknowledged still the characterization of the hero appeals to our imagination. It has been rightly said that the *Karṇabhāra* is 'not only a one-act play but really a one-character play'. The story of *Ūrubhaṅga* (probably of the aṅka type) in one act depicts the fight between Bhīma and Duryodhana ending in the breaking of the latter's thigh. The play reveals in an abundant measure the dramatic power of the writer and the scene which introduces the blind king and his consort and depicts the young son attempting to climb on his father's broken thigh produces the maximum pathos. The *Dūtavākya* is also a drama (vyāyoga) in one act where Kṛṣṇa appears as an ambassador to bring about reconciliation between the contending parties, the Kauravas and the Pāṇḍavas, and is ill-treated by Duryodhana who tries to entrap him without success. The *Pañcarātra* is a play (samavakāra) in three acts. There the story is how Droṇa undertakes a sacrifice for Duryodhana and seeks as fee the grant of half the kingdom to the Pāṇḍavas and Duryodhana promises on the condition that the Pāṇḍavas who are living *incognito*, shall be found out within five nights. The story-value of the drama is not striking—rather it is definitely inferior to that of the original. But it must be admitted that the drama possesses remarkable interest and that there are effective dramatic scenes. The *Bālacarita* is a drama (nāṭaka) in five acts depicting various loosely-joined incidents in the early life of Kṛṣṇa up to the death of Kaṁsa. Its plot seems to be derived from the *Harivaṁśa* and the Purāṇas describing Kṛṣṇa's life. Critics have found fault with the amount of killing in the drama. It is a fact that there is a good deal of killing in almost all the epic dramas but the *Bālacarita* seems to have surpassed them all in this respect. The drama, however, depicts a series of exciting incidents which are very attractive.

Bṛhatkathā-plays

Indian critics claim that *Svapnavāsavadatta* is the best of Bhāsa's dramas where the poet has displayed his skill of characterization and a fine manipulation of the plot which has made the drama interesting up to the last. The play (nāṭaka) contains six acts. Its theme is the marriage between Vatsarāja Udayana and Padmāvatī, the sister of King Darśaka, which was effected by Yaugandharāyaṇa, Udayana's minister, to serve a political purpose. To gain the end in view, Yaugandharāyaṇa spread the rumour that Vāsavadattā, the former queen of Udayana, had been burnt in a conflagration : but he actually kept her as a hostage to Padmāvatī. The plot of the drama has been effectively devised. The motif of the drama in Act V has been finely conceived. The characters of the two heroines, Vāsavadattā and Padmāvatī have been ably differentiated and the psychological study of the feelings of the former is wonderful indeed. 'It is a drama of fine sentiments and is entirely free from the intrusion of melodrama.' The *Pratijñāyaugandharāyaṇa* (nāṭaka) in four acts is the prelude to *Svapnavāsavadatta* which depicts Yaugandharāyaṇa coming to Ujjayinī and causing Vāsavadattā to escape with Udayana who was taken captive by Pradyota Mahāsena while the former was out hunting. It is really a drama of political intrigue but achieves a more diversified interest than the *Mudrārākṣasa* by interweaving a most colourful romance. The drama, which is characterized by simplicity and rapidity of action, is a skilful composition as the main interest of political strategy is enhanced by the erotic sub-plot the principal characters of which have not been allowed to appear. The portrayal of Yaugandharāyaṇa is perfect and the manner of treatment of some of the episodes bears the stamp of a careful dramatist. The *Cārudatta* is an incomplete drama (prakaraṇa) in four acts on which Śūdraka seems to have based his *Mṛcchakaṭika*. The theme is the love-story of Brāhmaṇa Cārudatta and courtezan Vasantasenā. The material for this drama was taken from popular stories. The *Avimāraka* is a play (nāṭaka) in six acts, having for its theme the union of Princess Kuraṅgī with Prince Viṣṇuṣeṇa *alias* Avimāraka. The drama is interesting for its refreshing theme but is not entirely free from a sentimental and melodramatic atmosphere in which the hero seeks suicide twice and the heroine once. The dialogue of the hero with the nurse and the episode of the jester and the maid are quite enjoyable. The plots of all the four dramas are said to have been taken from the *Bṛhatkathā*, and they can be traced to the *Kathāsaritsāgara*.

Śūdraka: age and authorship

The date and authorship of the *Mṛcchakaṭika* (prakaraṇa) in ten acts is still a disputed point in the history of Sanskrit literature.[1] According to some scholars, the drama was written by the poet Daṇḍin who quotes a verse of the *Mṛcchakaṭika* in his *Kāvyādarśa*.[2] But the discovery of the thirteen dramas of Bhāsa shows that the verse is found in the *Cārudatta* and the *Bālacarita* also, and it is highly probable that the drama was written just after the *Cārudatta*, near about the first century A.D. It is a point to be noted that though Kālidāsa mentions Bhāsa, Saumilla and Kaviputra, he does not say a word about Śūdraka. In the prologue of the *Mṛcchakaṭika* the royal author has been described as master of various Śāstras. He performed a horse-sacrifice and in the one hundred and tenth year of his life entered into fire having made over the kingdom to his son. From this it is evident that either this portion of the text is an interpolation or that the real author was some one else. The name of King Śūdraka is found in the *Rājataraṅgiṇī*, the *Kathāsaritsāgara* and the *Skanda-purāṇa*. In some of the manuscripts, Śūdraka has been described as a minister of Śālivāhana who subsequently became the ruler of Pratiṣṭhāna. According to Professor Konow, Śūdraka is to be identified with the Ābhīra prince, Śivadatta. According to Dr Fleet, Śūdraka's

[1] Vāmana is the earliest known writer to quote from the drama of Śūdraka.

[2] Professor Pischel first ascribes this play to Bhāsa and next to Daṇḍin. According to the orthodox tradition, Daṇḍin is the author of three works, the other two being, the *Kāvyādarśa* and the *Daśakumāracarita*.

son Īśvarasena defeated the Andhras and established the Cedī era of A.D. 248-49. The play which is universally acclaimed as unrivalled among similar works in Sanskrit both for its execution as well as design, is a prakaraṇa in ten acts having the love-story of Cārudatta and Vasantasenā for its central theme. It is a social drama with magnificient touches of realism. Here we have a refreshing plot of every-day life and find ourselves coming down from the heights of refined poetry and sentiment which characterize the writings of Kālidāsa and Bhavabhūti to 'the firm rock of grim reality'. Here we move about in the company of thieves and gamblers, rogues and idlers, courtezans and their associates, police constables and mendicants. The characterization is of a high standard. The drama is written in a simple yet dignified style and the dramatist knows the art of employing humour in all its aspects.

Use of obscure words, extensive employment of Prākrits, violation of the dramatic rules laid down by Bharata in his *Nāṭyaśāstra*, the flourishing state of Buddhism as depicted and the attitude of tolerance towards it, the reference to the promulgators of the science of theft, the custom of self-immolation, all these and other facts are evidence of the play's comparative antiquity.[1]

Kālidāsa

Kālidāsa is acclaimed as the best of Indian dramatists, whom Goethe has praised in the most fascinating

[1] Wilford assigns a date between first and third century B.C. while J. C. Ghatak places him in the third century B.C. on the strength of astronomical data. According to Fergusson his date is 31 B.C. while Prinsep makes it 21 B.C. M. Williams places him in the first century A.D. while Lassen thinks that his age is A.D. 150. According to Wilson he belonged to A.D. 190 while Macdonell, Pischel and Mahendale would place him as late as the sixth century A.D.

terms. Superb characterization, study of human nature and wonderful mastery over the Sanskrit language have placed him in the forefront of Indian dramatists. Kālidāsa is not verbose like later Sanskrit dramatists, economy being the most remarkable feature of his technique. Though Kālidāsa is pre-eminently a poet of love, he can rise occasionally to a tragic elevation. Every character of Kālidāsa's dramas has a core of personality which is sharply individualized. Though it is said that the dramas of Kālidāsa lack action to some extent, yet they have a moral purity and a peculiar charm unsurpassed by any other Indian dramatist.

Mālavikāgnimitra

The *Mālavikāgnimitra* (nāṭaka), undoubtedly an earlier writing of the dramatist, is written in five acts. It describes the love-story of Mālavikā and Agnimitra, King of Vidiśā and founder of the Śuṅga dynasty. This drama, unlike the two others, is characterized by quick action. The jester is a veritable rogue and is far more intelligent than the jester in the *Śākuntala*. The female characters and the dancing masters are all creations of genuine and great merit.

Vikramorvaśīya

The second drama, the *Vikramorvaśīya* shows a remarkable advance upon the former in the manipulation of the plot, characterization and language, and there are scholars who think that it is the last of the three dramatic compositions of the poet. The materials for this drama, preserved in two recensions, northern and southern, have been taken from a Saṁvāda-hymn (X. 95) of the *Ṛgveda*. This drama (troṭaka) which is written in five acts, has for its theme the union of the earthly King Purūravas and the celestial nymph Urvaśī. The fourth act of this drama which is a soliloquy of the love-stricken and frenzied Purūravas, is a novel conception of the dramatist. Though the scene is hardly dramatic and lacks action still it scales a lyric height in course of the description of the tumultuous ardour of undisciplined passion.

Śākuntala

The *Abhijñānaśakuntala* or *Śākuntala* is the production of Kālidāsa's maturer hand, which has gained world-wide recognition and the play has been translated into many European languages. The drama (nāṭaka) which is in seven acts, describes the union of Duṣyanta and Śakuntalā culminating in the birth of Bharata or Sarvadamana which is the final result in the drama. According to the dramatist 'love to be in divine form needs to be in three' i.e., conjugal love reaches its perfection with the birth of a child. The plot of this drama has been taken from the *Mahābhārata,* but the dramatist has introduced many noble innovations. One important innovation is the curse of Durvāsas, a highly irritable sage to whom Śakuntalā fails to extend rites of hospitality. The story of the drama hinges on this supernatural event. The curse produces a chastening influence on both the hero and the heroine whose love which was more of the flesh in the beginning turned out to be spiritual in the end. The character of the foster-father of the heroine, Kaṇva, is also another innovation. Kaṇva does not appear as an austere ascetic uninterested in the affairs of the world. He is full of the milk of human kindness—he is not only sympathetic towards his loving daughter and forgives her but he is also anxious on her account. He loves his daughter and appreciates her ways of life. It is, therefore, that he has not taught her the duties of ascetic life but has allowed her to grow independently in the company of her loving friends, Anasūyā and Priyaṁvadā. Not only the woodland, the flowing Mālinī, the antelope and the jessamine creeper formed the background of the growth and development of the heroine but it was the loving and large-hearted father, the sage, who contributed much towards the fruition of her career as the consort of an admiring husband. The story is also to be found in the *Padma-purāṇa* and the Pāli Jātaka collections. There are four different recensions of this drama, viz., Bengal, North-western, Kāshmirian and South Indian. According to Professor Pischel, the Bengal recension fully represents the original.

Harṣa

Three dramas are ascribed to Harṣa, King of Kānyakubja, who reigned from A.D. 606 to A.D. 647.[1] He was the reputed patron of Bāṇabhaṭṭa who has glorified him in his *Harṣacarita*. Harṣa comes after Kālidāsa and has been able to improve upon the pattern supplied by his predecessor. It is a fact that he has 'succeeded in establishing the comedy of court-intrigue as a distinct type in Sanskrit drama'. There is an unmistakable trace of delicate workmanship in all his dramas and though he does not possess a transcendent genius his writings are noted for grace and perspicuity. Though a contemporary of Bāṇa his style is simple and his prose is never ornate.

Ratnāvalī

The *Ratnāvalī* which is Harṣa's masterpiece, is a drama (nāṭikā) in four acts which deals with the story

[1] It is believed by some scholars that the author of these plays was Bāṇa and not Harṣa. Thus Professor Weber attributes *Ratnāvalī* to Bāṇabhaṭṭa while Professors Konow, Winternitz, Lévi and others accept Harṣa's authorship.

of the union of King Udayana and Ratnāvalī, daughter of the King of Ceylon. Later dramaturgists seem to regard it as a standard Sanskrit drama.

Priyadarśikā

The *Priyadarśikā* is also a drama (nāṭikā) in four acts having for its theme the union of Udayana and Priyadarśikā, daughter of King Dṛḍhavarman. In both these dramas we have not only a similarity of subject-matter and form but also a reminiscence of Kālidāsa's *Mālavikāgnimitra*. The only original feature of the *Priyadarśikā* is the effective introduction of a play within a play which is technically called *garbhāṅka,* as an integral part of the action.

Nāgānanda

The *Nāgānanda* is a drama (nāṭaka) in five acts which describes the self-sacrifice of Jīmūtavāhana, Prince of Vidyādharas. Besides the main theme there is an interesting sub-plot in the drama in which the hero's love for Malayavatī has been depicted. But this sub-plot has not been made essential to the development of the principal story. In a sense the two are not well co-ordinated. It is not Malayavatī's love which prompts the hero to perform the great act of sacrifice. But the ideal of self-sacrificing magnanimity is in itself an ennobling theme which cannot but catch the imagination of a discerning critic.

Mahendravikrama: Mattavilāsa

Mahendravikrama flourished in the first quarter of the seventh century A.D. His *Mattavilāsa* is a farce (prahasana) in one act which describes the moral degradations of the dramatist's contemporary society. The play shows the same technique of stage-craft and other peculiarities as the plays of Bhāsa, except that the author is mentioned in the Prologue.

Bhavabhūti

Bhavabhūti is the next great name after Kālidāsa who is mentioned by Kalhaṇa in his *Rājataraṅgiṇī* as a poet in the court of Yaśovarman, King of Kānyakubja whose probable date is A.D. 736. Vākpati also refers to Bhavabhūti in his *Gauḍavaho*. As is evident from the prologue of the *Mālatīmādhava*, Bhavabhūti could not enjoy any popularity in his life-time. Nevertheless, Bhavabhūti displays a masterly skill in characterization, and his language is forceful. Though he is pre-eminently a poet of the pathetic sentiment, he has excelled his great predecessor in the delineation of the heroic and the wonderful. Bhavabhūti is a follower of the Gauḍa style, while Kālidāsa is an advocate of the Vaidarbha. Bhavabhūti amplifies his theme, while Kālidāsa suggests it.

Three dramas are ascribed to Bhavabhūti of which the *Mahāvīracarita* is the earliest. The drama (nāṭaka) is written in seven acts, depicting the heroic achievements of Rāma's early life. The plot is based on the *Rāmāyaṇa*, but the dramatist has introduced several significant innovations. Though the characterization is not always very happy and perfect, still the play betrays a clear conception of dramatic technique and workmanship. Mahāvīracarita

The *Mālatīmādhava* is a prakaraṇa in ten acts which deals with the love-story of Mālatī and Mādhava. But there is a by-plot as well which concerns itself with the love of Makaranda and Madayantikā. It is the genius of the dramatist which has skilfully blended together these two parallel love stories. In spite of the length of the drama the dramatist has been successful in sustaining the interest of his audience by a careful interplay of the two parallel but contrasted plots. It has been maintained by critics that the play lacks restraint and a tendency Mālatīmādhava to over-emphasize and an inability to stop at the right moment sometimes characterize his composition. There is an exuberance of descriptive and emotional stanzas as also elaborate prose passages. It is, however, admitted that the drama possesses a unique interest in the sense that it furnishes an attractive description of certain aspects of ordinary middle-class life.

Uttara-rāmacarita

The *Uttararāmacarita* is regarded as the best product of Bhavabhūti's virile pen, where the dramatist has shown his wonderful skill in delineating genuine pathos and describing the sublime and awful aspects of nature. The plot of this drama (nāṭaka), which is written in seven acts, covers the later life of Rāma, beginning from the banishment of Sītā and ending in their happy re-union. The drama 'idealizes conjugal love and affection through the chastening influence of sorrow'. The third act, known as the *Chāyā-aṅka*, the best in the drama, brings the hero and the heroine nearer each other and thus prepares the ground for the reunion in the final act. The conception of the picture-gallery scene in Act I, the fight between Lava and Candraketu in Act V, the visit of Vaśiṣṭha and the party to the hermitage of Vālmīki in Act IV and the like are skilful details which have been invented by the creative genius of the dramatist for the development of the theme. Likewise the characters of Ātreyī, Vāsantī and others bear eloquent testimony to the excelling genius of the dramatist. But in spite of Bhavabhūti's dramatic skill his poetry appears more as an exceedingly human story of love and suffering steeped in the charm of poetry and sentiment.

The date of Viśākhadatta may be placed about A.D. 860, as the lunar eclipse mentioned in his drama *Mudrārākṣasa* is taken by some to refer to the phenomenon of that date. The drama (nāṭaka) in seven acts may have the *Bṛhatkathā* of Guṇāḍhya as the source of its plot. The theme is a political intrigue between Rākṣasa, the minister of the Nandas and Cāṇakya, the great politician, who succeeded in overthrowing the Nandas and winning Rākṣasa to the side of Candragupta. The drama occupies a unique place in the history of Sanskrit dramatic literature inasmuch as unlike almost all Sanskrit dramas it avoids not only the erotic feeling but also the erotic atmosphere. The only interest in the drama is political intrigue which has been delineated with such mastery that it can absorb the mind of the audience. The difference between this drama and the *Pratijñāyaugandharāyaṇa* of Bhāsa which is also a drama of political intrigue lies in this that whereas in the latter the plotting centres round a romantic episode the former breaks away from the subject of love. It has been rightly pointed out that the *Mudrārākṣasa* is a drama without a heroine. **Viśākhadatta: Mudrārākṣasa**

Viśākhadatta's power of characterization is indeed commendable. A study in contrast lends vividness to the distinctive traits. The characters of Cāṇakya and Rākṣasa as also of Candragupta and Malayaketu are illustrations of this point. The dramatist does not follow the conventional mode of technique; yet his work betrays a considerable mastery over dramatic presentation. His style is forceful but not affected. It is free from unnecessary embellishments. But it cannot be denied that it marks a distinct falling off from the lucid diction of Kālidāsa and the grandeur of Bhavabhūti.

Bhaṭṭa-nārāyaṇa: Veṇīsaṁhāra

Vāmana and Ānandavardhana quote from the work of Bhaṭṭanārāyaṇa who probably flourished in the eighth century A.D. His only drama (nāṭaka) *Veṇīsaṁhāra,* written in six acts, is based on the story of the *Mahābhārata.* Bhīma kills Duśśāsana and ties the braid of Draupadī with his blood. Ultimately he succeeds in killing Duryodhana also. Bhaṭṭa-nārāyaṇa is undoubtedly a remarkable craftsman among later Sanskrit dramatists; he is particularly adept in describing the heroic sentiment. The first three acts of the *Veṇīsaṁhāra* are full of action, and the predominant emotion is enthusiasm (*utsāha*). The poet has also very successfully illustrated the manifold technicalities of Sanskrit dramaturgy in his drama and it is for this reason that later dramaturgists have profusely quoted from his work.

Critics, however, have not spared Bhaṭṭanārāyaṇa for some of his glaring defects. It has been pointed out that the drama is not a unified work. It is rather a panoramic presentation of a large number of incidents which cannot be held together by a gradually developed sequence. Further, the preponderance of long compounds and high-sounding expressions makes his diction a highly unsuitable vehicle for drama.

Murāri: Anargha-rāghava

No other later dramatist was able to dramatize successfully the Rāma-episode, after Bhavabhūti had written his masterpieces. Murāri who is no exception wrote his *Anargharāghava* somewhere about the beginning of the ninth century A.D. The drama (nāṭaka) is written in seven acts. Murāri is more an elegant poet than a dramatist in the true sense and it may be said of him that he is typical of the decadent Sanskrit dramatists. The play has been considered a standard for poetic criticism and grammatical learning.

Rājaśekhara: his plays

Rājaśekhara was the reputed teacher of King Mahendrapāla of Kanauj (A.D. 893-907). Among his many works, Rājaśekhara has written four dramas. The *Bālarāmāyaṇa* is a drama (nāṭaka) in ten acts, dealing with the life-history of Rāma. The *Bālabhārata* is an incomplete drama (nāṭaka) of which two acts only are available. The *Karpūramañjarī*, a play (saṭṭaka) in four acts, is written in Prākrit. It describes the vicissitudes of the love of king Candrapāla for a princess of Kuntala, the jealousy of the queen with the consequent impediments, the secret meetings of the lovers and the final marriage. The *Viddhaśālabhañjikā* also is a drama (nāṭaka) in four acts depicting the secret marriage between King Vidyādhara and Princess Mṛgāṅkavatī, daughter of King Candravarman of Lāṭa who sends her in the guise of a boy to King Vidyādhara's queen. Rājaśekhara's style is highly artificial, but the dramatist himself claims to be a great poet.

Kṣemīśvara: Caṇḍakauśika

The *Caṇḍakauśika* of Kṣemīśvara is a drama (nāṭaka) in five acts. The author wrote this play for King Mahīpāla of Kanauj whose accession to the throne took place in A.D. 914. The plot of this drama is the famous story of King Hariścandra and sage Viśvāmitra. The style of this drama also is highly artificial.

Dāmodaramiśra: Mahānāṭaka

Dāmodaramiśra wrote his *Mahānāṭaka* or *Hanumannāṭaka* in the eleventh century A.D. The drama is found in three recensions separately containing nine, ten and fourteen acts. The plot is based on the *Rāmāyaṇa*, and the dramatist shows considerable skill in versification. It is a voluminous work, more a poem than a play and we often discover verses of other authors freely introduced into it.

According to Lüders it is a specimen of shadow-plays in Sanskrit in the sense that it is written mainly in verse with little of prose, that the verse is not of the dramatic type but narrative in character, that there is complete absence of Prākrit and that the dramatis personae though large do not include the Vidūṣaka.

Kṛṣṇa-miśra: Prabodha-candro-daya

The date of the *Prabodhacandrodaya*, an early allegorical drama, written by Kṛṣṇamiśra is approximately the latter half of the eleventh century A.D. In the Prologue there is a reference to one Gopāla at whose command the play was written to commemorate the victory of King Kīrtivarman over the Cedi King Karṇa. As the Cedi King is mentioned in an inscription dated A.D. 1042 and as an inscription of Candella King Kīrtivarman is also dated A.D. 1098 it is concluded that Kṛṣṇamiśra belongs to the second half of the eleventh century A.D. The characters of this drama are Viveka, Manas, Buddhi, etc. This drama is a solitary instance where the quietistic sentiment has been represented on the stage. The drama (nāṭaka) contains six acts, and the style is simple.

The history of the origin of allegorical dramas in Sanskrit is little known and it is difficult to say whether Kṛṣṇamiśra has revived an old tradition or the credit belongs to him of attempting to produce a symbolical drama by means of personified abstractions. Philosophical allegories may be traced in the story of Purañjaya in the *Śrīmad Bhāgavata* (chap. 25-28) which may have inspired later writers in turning a dogma into a drama. It is obvious that such allegorical dramas by reason of their remoteness from real life and their concern with abstract ideas and symbols are hardly expected to create the maximum interest. Kṛṣṇamiśra has, however, succeeded in presenting a vivid picture of the spiritual struggle of the human mind in the dramatic form of a lively conflict in which the erotic, comic and devotional interests are cleverly utilized. In form the work is a regular comedy and its dialogue is lively. The author shows considerable power of introducing satire of the purest type. His power of characterization is bold and the interest is not allowed to flag. Though Kṛṣṇamiśra's work possesses a permanent value of its own, still the works of later writers inspired by him are of little importance. Thus *Mohaparājaya* of Yaśaḥpāla (thirteenth century), a play in five acts, written in the interest of Jainism, the *Caitanyacandrodaya* of Paramānandadāsasena Kavikarṇapūra (sixteenth century) depicting a dramatized form of Śrī Caitanya's life at the command of Pratāparudra of Orissa, the *Dharmavijaya* of Bhūdeva Śukla (sixteenth century) in five acts, the *Vidyāpariṇaya* and the *Jīvānanda* of Vedakavi each in seven acts (the (seventeenth-eighteenth century), the *Amṛtodaya* of Gokulanātha in five acts (seventeenth century), the *Śrīdāmacarita* of Sāmarājadīkṣita in five acts (seventeenth century), the *Saṅkalpasūryodaya* of Veṅkaṭanātha Vedāntadeśika Kavitārkikasiṁha in ten acts and the *Yatirājavijaya* of Varadācārya in six acts are some of the allegorical dramas.

E. LESS IMPORTANT DRAMAS

Bhagavadajjukīya: by Bodhāyanakavi—sometime between the first and the fourth century A.D.—written with the purpose of ridiculing the doctrine of Buddhism—a prahasana in two acts, so named because the principal characters are Bhagavān, a mendicant and Ajjukā, a *hataera*.

Tāpasavatsarājacarita: by Anaṅgaharṣa Mātrarāja—Dr Keith fixes the age of the *Ratnāvalī* as the upper limit of the work—based on a variation of the theme of Vatsarāja, Padmāvatī and Vāsavadattā.

Lokānanda: a Buddhist drama in Tibetan version ascribed to Candra or Candraka(?) who is identified with Candragomin, the grammarian, of the seventh century A.D.

Udāttarāghava: a lost Rāma-drama by Māyurāja—quoted five times in the *Daśarūpaka* and is known to Abhinavagupta and Kuntaka.

Svapnadaśānana: by Bhīmaṭa who wrote five dramas in all—mentioned by Rājaśekhara.

Dharmābhyudaya: a play in one act by Meghaprabhācārya—a shadow-drama of unknown date—the stage-direction mentioning clearly a puppet (*putraka*) and calling itself a *chāyānāṭyaprabandha*.

Karṇasundarī: by Bilhaṇa of the eleventh century A.D.—a nāṭikā.

Citrabhārata: by Kṣemendra of the eleventh century A.D.—a lost drama.

Prabuddharauhiṇeya: by Rāmabhadra Muni of the twelfth century A.D.—in six acts.

Kaumudīmitrānanda: by Rāmacandra of the twelfth century A.D.—a prakaraṇa in ten acts.

Laṭakamelaka: by Śaṅkhadhara Kavirāja of the twelfth century A.D.—a prahasana in two acts describing the assemblage of different kinds of roguish people at the house of Danturā for winning the favour of her daughter. Madanamañjarī.

Mudritakumudacandra: by Yaśaścandra of the twelfth century A.D.—a Jinistic drama.

Nirbhayabhīmavyāyoga: by Rāmacandra, a prolific Jaina dramatist, belonging to the twelfth century A.D.

Kirātārjunīya, Rukmiṇīharaṇa, Tripuradāha, Samudramathana, Karpūracarita and Hāsyacuḍāmaṇi: by Vatsarāja of the twelfth century A.D.—the first, a vyāyoga; the second, an īhāmṛgā in four acts; the third, a ḍima in four acts; the fourth, a samavakāra in three acts, the fifth, a bhāṇa and the sixth, a farce (prahasana) in one act.

Pārthaparākrama: by Prahlādanadeva of the twelfth century A.D.—a vyāyoga.

Prasannarāghava: by Jayadeva (of Berar) of the twelfth century A.D.—based on the *Rāmāyaṇa*—a nāṭaka in seven acts.

Harakelināṭaka: by Viśāladeva Vigraharāja of the twelfth century A.D.—partially preserved in stone.

Kundamālā: ascribed to Diṅnāga or Dhīranāga—quoted in the *Sāhityadarpaṇa*—not later than the thirteenth century A.D.
Dūtāṅgada: by Subhaṭa of the thirteenth century A.D. a shadow-play.
Hammīramadamardana: by Jayasiṁha of the thirteenth century A.D. —in five acts.
Vikrāntakaurava and Maithilīkalyāṇa: by Hastimalla of the thirteenth century A.D.—in six and five acts respectively.
Pārvatīpariṇaya: attributed to Bāṇa, but allotted to Vāmana Bhaṭṭa Bāṇa of the fourteenth century A.D.
Saugandhikāharaṇa: by Viśvanātha of the fourteenth century A.D.—a vyāyoga.
Dhūrtasamāgama: by Kaviśekhara of the fourteenth century A.D.—a prahasana in one act.
Vidagdhamādhava and *Lalitamādhava*: by Rūpagosvāmin of the sixteenth century A.D.—dealing with the attractive Kṛṣṇa legend—in seven and ten acts respectively.
Kaṁsavadha: by Śeṣakṛṣṇa of the seventeenth century A.D.—in seven acts.
Jānakīpariṇaya: by Rāmabhadra Dīkṣita of the seventeenth century A.D.
Mallikāmāruta: by Uddaṇḍin of the seventeenth century A.D.—a prakaraṇa.
Dhūrtanartaka: by Sāmarāja Dīkṣita of the seventeenth century A.D.—a prahasana in one act but with two sandhis.
Kautukaratnākara: by Kavitārkika, son of Bāṇīnātha of the sixteenth century A.D.—a prahasana.
Adbhutadarpaṇa: by Mahādeva, contemporary of Rāmabhadra—in ten acts.
Hāsyārṇava: by Jagadīśvara of unknown date—a highly popular prahasana in two acts.
Kautukasarvasva: by Gopīnātha of unknown date—a prahasana written for the Durgā pujā in Bengal—more amusing and less vulgar than other prahasanas.
Unmattarāghava: by Bhāskara of unknown date—an aṅka.
Mukundānanda: by Kāśīpati Kavirāja who flourished at the Court of Nañjarāja of Mysore of the eighteenth century A.D.—a mixed bhāṇa.
Mādhavasādhana: by Nṛtyagopāla Kaviratna of the nineteenth century A.D.
Amaramaṅgala: by Pañcānana Tarkaratna of the latter half of the nineteenth century A.D. and the first half of the twentieth century A.D.—in eight acts.

REFERENCES

Ayyar. A. S. P.: *Two plays of Bhāsa*
Barooah, A.: *Bhavabhūti—His Place in Sanskrit Literature*
Basu, Chandranath: *Śakuntalātattva*
Basu, Devendranath: *Śakuntalāy Nāṭyakalā*
Belvalkar, S. K.: (i) *Origin of Indian Drama* (*The Calcutta Review*, May, 1922) (ii) *Uttararāmacarita* (HOS)
Bhandarkar, R. G.: *Mālatīmādhava*

Bühler, G.: *On the Authorship of the Ratnāvalī* (IA. Vol. II)
Chatterjee, Bankim Chandra: *Vividhaprabandha*
Chatterjee, N.: *Mṛcchakaṭika: A Study*
Devadhar, C. R.: *Plays Ascribed to Bhāsa: Their Authenticity and Merits*
Gajendragadkar, A. B.: *The Veṇīsaṁhāra—A Critical Study*
Horrwitz, E. P.: *The Indian Theatre*
Kāle, M. R.: (i) *Abhijjñānaśakuntala,* (ii) *Uttararāmacarita*
Keith, A. B.: (i) *The Sanskrit Drama,* (ii) JRAS. 1909.
Kulkarni, K. P.: *Sanskrit Drama and Dramatists*
Konow, S.: IA. Vol. XLIII (on Viśākhādatta)
Konow, S. & Lanmann, C. R.: *Karpūramañjarī* (HOS)
Lévī, S.: *Le Theatre Indien*
Macdonell, A. A.: *A History of Sanskrit Literature*
Mankad, D. R.: *The Types of Sanskrit Drama*
Nariman, G. K. & & Jackson, A. V. W.: *Priyadarśikā*
Pishraoti, A. K.: *Bhāsa's Works—a Criticism*
Pusalker. A. D.: *Bhāsa: a Study*
Rapson, E.: IRAS. 1900, (on Viśākhadatta)
Ridgeway: (i) *The Origin of Tragedy,* (ii) *Dramas and Dramatic Dances of Non-European Races*
Śāstrin, Ashokanath: (i) *Prācīnbhārate Dṛśyakāvyotpattir Itihāsa* (*Bhāratavarṣa,* B.S. 1333-34), (ii) *Bhāratīyanāṭyer Vedamūlakatā,* (iii) *Bharatīyanāṭyer Pracīnatā* (*Māsik Vasumatī,* B.S. 1345-46), (iv) *Abhinayadarpaṇa of Nandikeśvara*
Śāstrin, T. G.: *Bhāsa's Works—a Critical Study*
Tagore, Rabindranath: *Prācīn Sāhitya*
Vidyābhūṣaṇa, S. C.: *Date of Ratnāvalī*
Weber, A.: *The History of Indian Literature*
Wilson, H. H.: *Theatre of the Hindus*
Winternitz, M.: *Some Problems of Indian Literature*
Yajnik, R. K.: *The Indian Theatre*

CHAPTER IX

LYRIC POETRY

A. INTRODUCTION

Classical Sanskrit literature is very rich in lyrical poetry. Though it is a fact that Classical lyric poetry has not produced many works of considerable length and size, yet none would deny that its merit is usually of a high order. Lyrical poets have often been successful in depicting the amorous feeling with a few artistic strokes, and their compositions can very well stand comparison with those of foreign poets The range of lyrical literature in Sanskrit is very wide. It is not confined to the theme of love and amorous feeling only. It includes secular, religious, gnomic and didactic poems and thus offers a variety which is sufficient to prevent monotony. Extent of Sanskrit lyrics

In all lyrical poems dealing with love, Nature plays a very important part. The intimate relation between Nature and Man has not in all probability found a more charming expression in any other branch of literature. The Lotus and the Lily, the Cakora, the Cakravāka and the Cātaka, all are inseparably connected with human life and love in its different phases. Nature in Sanskrit lyrics

It is further to be noted that Prākrit literature is also very rich in lyrical poetry. The *Sattasai* or *Gāthāsaptaśatī* attributed to Sātavāhana is an outstanding work of this type. The book is a collection Prākrit lyrics of seven hundred verses in Prākrit dealing with various phases of the sentiment of love. Bāṇa refers to this work in his *Harṣacarita*. Professor Macdonell wants to place it before 1000 A.D. If, on the other hand, Hāla or Sātavāhana, to whom the work is attributed, is taken as a king of that name of the Andhra dynasty, the work must be placed early in the Christian era.

B. GROWTH AND DEVELOPMENT OF LYRIC POETRY

Megha-dūta

The name of Kālidāsa stands high in the realm of Sanskrit lyrical poetry. There is no gainsaying the fact that his *Meghadūta* which has been unsuccessfully imitated times without number by later poets,[1] is the finest flower of Classical lyric poetry. The lyric has inspired poets like Goethe and Rabindranath who have lavishly bestowed their praise upon this magic personality in literature. Fancifully the poet makes a cloud the messenger of the message of love and admiration to the beloved of a banished Yakṣa, who had been pining for her during the rainy season at Alakā. The work is divided into two sections

[1] No less than fifty Dūta-kāvyas on the model of Kālidāsa's *Meghadūta* are extant in Sanskrit literature. It is true that their poetical worth is not much. Their chief interest lies in the utilization of the original form and motive in diverse ways and for different purposes. Not only inanimate objects but beasts and birds as well as mythological personalities and even abstract things have been chosen as messengers for imaginary journeys over different places in India. Metres other than Mandākrāntā have been employed. Jaina and Vaiṣṇava writers have used such poems as the vehicle of religious instruction.

Vedāntadeśika's *Haṁsasandeśa* (thirteenth century A.D.), Rūpagosvāmin's *Haṁsadūta* (sixteenth century A.D.), Kṛṣṇānanda's *Padāṅkadūta* (seventeenth century A.D.) are some of the more well-known Dūtakāvyas.

known as the *Pūrvamegha* and the *Uttaramegha*. The poem is written in Mandākrāntā metre of gorgeous rhythm like the roar of a July cloud weary under the burden of its water. This is also quite in keeping with the sublime conception of love which, tinged with the burning colour of separation, resembles a black cloud with a silver lining. The stanzas containing the words of message are the most poignant and beautiful in literature, and the lyric will ever stand impressed on our memory like a rainbow springing from the earth. The book has been translated into various European languages, and Schiller's *Maria Stuart* owes its origin to it.

Ṛtusaṁhāra

The *Ṛtusaṁhāra* is the second lyric of Kālidāsa. It is a short poem in six cantos describing all the six seasons of the year. It is undoubtedly an earlier production of the poet and though Kālidāsa's authorship of this poem is doubted by many scholars,[1] still we can find in it the aspirations of a budding poet.[2]

Ghaṭakarpara: Ghaṭakarpara-kāvya

Tradition makes Ghaṭakarpara one of the nine gems in the court of King Vikramāditya. The *Ghaṭakarpara-kāvya* after the name of the poet is written in twenty-two stanzas. It describes how a young wife in the beginning of the rains sends a cloud-messenger to her absent husband. The poem abounds in *yamakas* (figures of speech) of which the author feels proud.

Bhartṛhari: three Śatakas

Bhartṛhari has to his credit the three *Śatakas* (collections, of a hundred verses), viz., (a) the *Śṛṅgāraśataka* (b) the *Nītiśataka* and (c) the *Vairāgyaśataka*.

[1] Professors Kielhorn, Bühler, Macdonell, Schroeder and others accept the authorship of Kālidāsa while other scholars entertain a different view.

[2] See, Aurobinda Ghosh, Kālidāsa; Gajendragadkar, *Ṛtusaṁhāra*.

The single authorship of these three poems is doubted by some scholars, but Indian tradition accepts Bhartṛhari as their author. Bhartṛhari is said to have died in A.D. 651.[1] All the three poems are written in a very lucid style, and they have the greatest interest to those for whom they are intended.

Mayūra: Sūrya-śataka

Mayūra was a contemporary of Bāṇabhaṭṭa of the seventh century A.D., and is reported to be his father-in-law. His *Sūryaśataka*[2] is a religious lyric in one hundred verses written in honour of the Sun. Tradition says that the poet was cured of leprosy by composing this eulogy of the Sun.[3]

Amaru: Amaru-śataka

It is impossible to ascertain the date of Amaru. Vāmana (A.D. 800) is the earliest writer who quotes three verses from the *Amaruśataka*, a lyrical poem in one hundred stanzas[4] describing the conditions of women at different stages of life and love. The poet is really gifted and his delineation of sentiments and emotions, especially of love, is superb in character. The love which Amaru likes is gay and high-spirited, and unlike Bhartṛhari he paints the relation of lovers and takes no thought of other aspects of life. According to the commentator Ravicandra Amaru's stanzas have double meanings, one erotic and the other philosophical. But another commentator Vemabhūpāla takes it to be a purely rhetorical textbook meant for

[1] It is yet to be decided whether the author of the Śatakas is the same person as the famous grammarian of that name who wrote the *Vākyapadīya*.

[2] There are other *Sūryaśatakas* by different poets which do not deserve any special mention.

[3] Vajradatta, a Buddhist poet of the ninth century A.D. composed his *Lokeśvaraśataka* and was cured of leprosy.

[4] The text of the poem has come down to us in four recensions which vary widely among themselves.

illustrating the various classes of heroines and the diversity of their modes of love. His style is difficult, but certainly graceful. Amaru's poem has found the widest recognition in the hands of Sanskrit rhetoricians and he is quoted by great thinkers on poetry like Ānandavardhana. The poem has been commented on by more than a dozen writers including Arjunavarman (A.D. 1215).

Bilhaṇa: Caurapañcāśikā

The *Caurapañcāśikā* or *Bilhaṇakāvya* of Bilhaṇa is a lover's recollections of the sweet company of his beloved. The poem contains fifty stanzas. The date of the poet is A.D. 1076-A.D. 1127. Bhāratacandra, a Bengali poet of the eighteenth century A.D., drew the inspiration of his popular poem '*Vidyāsundara*' from this work of Bilhaṇa.

Jayadeva: Gītagovinda

The Kṛṣṇa-legend found a poetical interpreter in Jayadeva, the last great name in Sanskrit poetry, who flourished in Bengal during the reign of King Lakṣmaṇasena of the twelfth century A.D. He was the son of Bhojadeva of Kendubilva. His poem, the *Gītagovinda,* ranks high amongst Sanskrit lyrics, and the poet is a gifted master of poetry. According to Professor Macdonell the poem marks a transitional period between pure lyric and pure drama.[1] Sir William Jones calls it a small pastoral drama while Professor Lassen regards it as a lyrical drama. Leopold von Schroeder would look upon it as a refined yātrā. Both Professors Pischel and Lévi place it in the category between song and drama. Some Indian scholars maintain that the poem is a court-epic.

[1] It is probable that the poet took as his model popular plays representing incidents from the life of Kṛṣṇa as the modern yātrās in Bengal still do.

Dhoyī: Pavana-dūta

Dhoyī, a contemporary of Jayadeva, graced the court of King Lakṣmaṇasena. Like other Dūtakāvyas, his poem, the *Pavanadūta*, is written in imitation of the *Meghadūta*. The poet makes Kuvalayavatī, a Gandharva maiden of the Malaya hills, fall in love with the hero (the poet's patron, King Lakṣmaṇasena) during the latter's career of conquest in the south and send the south-easterly wind as a messenger.

C. LESSER LYRIC POEMS AND ANTHOLOGIES

Śṛṅgāratilaka: attributed to Kālidāsa—containing attractive pictures of love in twenty-three stanzas.

Bhaktāmarastotra: by Mānatuṅga, probably a contemporary of Bāṇa or earlier—written in honour of the Jaina saint Ṛṣabha in forty-four verses.

Kalyāṇamandirastotra: by Siddhasena Divākara, probably of the seventh century A.D.—written in imitation of Mānatuṅga—containing forty-four stanzas.

Suprabhātastotra and *Aṣṭamahāśrīcaityastotra*: by King Harṣavardhana—the first being a morning hymn in twenty-four verses in praise of Buddha and the second, a hymn in five verses in praise of the eight great shrines.

Caṇḍīśataka: by Bāṇabhaṭṭa of the seventh century A.D.—a collection of one hundred and two verses written in honour of the goddess Pārvatī.

Sragdharāstotra: by Sarvajñamitra, a Buddhist of the eighth century A.D.—dedicated to Tārā, the Buddhist goddess—containing thirty-seven stanzas.

Kuṭṭanīmata: by Dāmodaragupta, minister of King Jayāpīḍa of Kāshmir (A.D. 772-A.D. 813) an interesting treatise on Indian pornography showing how a young girl wins gold by making use of all the arts of flattery and feigned love—possessing historical interest as it depicts a representation of Harṣa's *Ratnāvalī*.

Ānandalaharī or *Saundaryalaharī* and *Mohamudgara*: attributed to Śaṅkara, the great teacher of monistic Vedānta.

Devīśataka: by Ānandavardhana, the famous rhetorician of the ninth century A.D.

Bhallaṭa-Śataka: by Bhallaṭa, a junior contemporary of Ānandavardhana—a gnomic poem.

Mahimnasstotra: by Puṣpadanta, not later than the ninth century A.D.—a religious lyric.

Subhāṣitaratnasandoha, *Dharmaparīkṣā* & *Yogasāra*: by Amitagati of the tenth century A.D.—all didactic poems.

Kṛṣṇakarṇāmṛta & *Vṛndāvanastuti*: by Bilvamaṅgala or Līlāśuka of the eleventh century A.D.—very popular and graceful in style.

amayamātṛkā, Kalāvilāsa, Darpadalana, Sevyasevakopadeśa, Caturvargasaṁgraha & *Cārucaryāśataka*: by Kṣemendra of Kāshmir—all didactic poems.

:avīndravacanasamuccaya: an anthology in 525 stanzas—of the eleventh century A.D.

.nyoktimuktālatāśataka: by Śambhu who wrote under Harṣa of Kāshmir (A.D. 1089-A.D. 1101)—a gnomic poem.

ryāsaptaśatī: by Govardhana, a contemporary of Jayadeva—containing seven hundred erotic stanzas—written after the *Sattasai* of Hāla.

'ogaśāstra, Vītarāgastotra & *Mahāvīrastotra*: by Hemacandra of the twelfth century A.D.—very good didactic lyric poems, sometimes reminding us of the poems of Bhartṛhari.

aduktikarṇāmṛta: an anthology by Śrīdhara of the twelfth century A.D.—including excerpts from 446 poets, largely of Bengal.

āntiśataka: by Śilhaṇa, of Kāshmir who lived before A.D. 1205—written in the style of Bhartṛhari's poems.

3haktiśataka: by Rāmacandra of Bengal who came to Ceylon with King Parākramabāhu (thirteenth century A.D.).

ṛṅgāravairāgyataraṅgiṇī: by Somaprabha of the thirteenth century A.D.—a didactic poem in forty-six stanzas written in perfect Kāvya style.

ubhāṣitamuktāvalī: an anthology by Jalhaṇa of the thirteenth century A.D.

ārṅgadharapaddhati: an anthology by Śārṅgadhara of the fourteenth century A.D.—arranged in 163 sections and containing 4689 stanzas.

Subhāṣitāvalī: an anthology by Śrīvara of the fifteenth century A.D.

Padyāvalī: an anthology by Rūpagosvāmin of the fifteenth century A.D.—containing verses in honour of Kṛṣṇa from a wide range of authors.

Bhāminīvilāsa & *Gaṅgālaharī*: by Jagannātha, the famous rhetorician of the seventeenth century A.D.

[*N.B.* Names of some lyrical poetesses and their stray verses are found in some anthologies. The more important among them are Śīlābhaṭṭārikā, Vijjakā, Vikaṭanitambā, Priyaṁvadā etc.]

REFERENCES

Keith, A. B.: *A History of Sanskrit Literature*

Krishnamachariar, M: *Classical Sanskrit Literature*

Macdonnell, A. A.: *A History of Sanskrit Literature*

Weber, A.: *The History of Indian Literature*

CHAPTER X

HISTORICAL WRITINGS

A. INTRODUCTION

Paucity of Historical works: causes

Nobody denies the antiquity and greatness of Indian civilization but it is rather unfortunate that in the wide range of early or medieval Sanskrit literature, one seldom comes across a useful work of history. The paucity of authoritative historical books bewilders all students of Classical Sanskrit literature, and it is a pity that India has failed to produce even one outstanding historian noted for his critical insight and scientific presentation of facts. It is, however, admitted on all hands that Kalhaṇa is the most successful of all Indian historians and that the history of Kāshmir would have remained obscure without his immortal work, the *Rājataraṅgiṇī*. But even Kalhaṇa's writings are not without exaggerated and confusing statements, and poetic fancy has often been allowed to dominate the genuine spirit of a historian. The causes of the paucity of historical works may be traced to the peculiarities of Indian psychology aided by environment and the course of events. The popular Indian view on worldly life and the teachings of Indian philosophical and religious works are surely responsible for fostering a feeling of apathy towards making any serious attempt at recording facts and dwelling on them.

The beginnings of Indian history are to be traced to the Purāṇas which contain amidst vast masses of religious and social matters, accounts of genealogies which are the very germs of history.

Earliest Historical works

In Prākrit, however, there is a very important historical work called the *Gauḍavaho* which was written by Vākpati. It celebrates the defeat of one Gauḍa king by Yaśovarman, king of Kanauj, the poet's patron, who was again overthrown by Lalitāditya Muktāpīḍa, king of Kāshmir. Vākpati is a follower of the Gauḍa style and uses long compounds. His date has approximately been fixed in the eighth century A.D., and he is mentioned along with Bhavabhūti.

Vākpati: Gauḍavaho

B. GROWTH AND DEVELOPMENT OF HISTORICAL WORKS

Padmagupta also known as Parimala, wrote his *Navasāhasāṅkacarita* in A.D. 1050. The book contains eighteen cantos and describes the winning of Princess Śaśiprabhā and also alludes to the history of Sindhurāja Navasāhasāṅka of Mālava.

Padmagupta: Navasāhasāṅkacarita

Sandhyākaranandin's *Rāmapālacarita* describes through double entendre the story of Rāma and also the history of King Rāmapāla of Bengal who recovered his ancestral home from Bhīma, a Kaivarta chief, and conquered Mithilā. Sandhyākaranandin flourished during A.D. 1057-A.D. 1087.

Sandhyākaranandin: Rāmapālacarita

Billhaṇa's patron was Vikramāditya VI, a Cālukya king of Kalyāṇa who flourished during A.D. 1076-A.D. 1127. Bilhaṇa glorified his patron by writing his *Vikramāṅkadevacarita* in eighteen cantos. Bilhaṇa

Bilhaṇa: Vikramāṅkadevacarita

was more a poet than a historian and his work abounds in numerous imaginary and fanciful descriptions.

Kalhaṇa: Rājataraṅgiṇī

Kalhaṇa is the best of Indian historians. He wrote his *Rājataraṅgiṇī* in A.D. 1100. Kalhaṇa has derived materials for his book from older sources including the *Nīlamata-purāṇa*. The *Rājataraṅgiṇī* is the only reliable book on the history of Kāshmir after the death of King Harṣa when the country passed through stormy bloody days. Though a historian, Kalhaṇa has the rare gifts of a poet, and his book is a wonderful admixture of poetic fancy and historical facts. According to European scholars, it is the only work in Sanskrit literature which approaches history to a certain extent.

Hemacandra: Kumārapālacarita

Hemacandra who flourished during A.D. 1088-A.D. 1172 wrote his *Kumārapālacarita* or *Dvyāśrayakāvya* in honour of Kumārapāla, king of the Cālukyas.

Pṛthvīrājavijaya

The anonymous *Pṛthvīrājavijaya* celebrates the victories of King Pṛthvīrāja over Shihāb-ud-din Ghorī in A.D. 1191.

C. MINOR HISTORICAL WORKS

Prabhāvakacaritra: by Prabhācandra and revised by Pradyumnasūri (A.D. 1277)—regarded as a continuation of Hemacandra's *Pariśiṣṭa-parvan*—containing the life-history of twenty-two Jaina teachers —a semi-historical work.

Rājendrakarṇapūra: by Śambhu who wrote in honour of Harṣadeva of Kāshmir (A.D. 1089-A.D. 1101).

Kīrtikaumudī & *Surathotsava*: by Someśvaradatta (A.D. 1179-A.D. 1262) —more in the form of panegyrics—the latter, written in fifteen cantos.

Sukṛtasaṅkīrtana: by Arisiṁha of the thirteenth century A.D.—a panegyric in eleven cantos.

Jagaḍūcarita: by Sarvānanda of unknown date—a panegyric of a Jaina who rendered help to his townsfolk at the time of the famine of A.D. 1256-8 in Gujarāt.

Prabandhacintāmaṇi: by Merutuṅga of the fourteenth century A.D.—a quasi-historical-biographical work.
Prabandhakośa: by Rājaśekhara of the fourteenth century A.D.—containing the life-stories of Jaina teachers, poets, kings and other personages.
Kīrtilatā: by Vidyāpati of the fourteenth century A.D.

REFERENCES

Keith, A. B.: *A History of Sanskrit Literature*
Macdonell, A. A.: *A History of Sanskrit Literature*
Weber, A.: *The History of Indian Literature*
Winternitz, M.: *A History of Indian Literature*, Vol. II.

CHAPTER XI

PROSE LITERATURE

A. INTRODUCTION

History of Sanskrit Prose literature

In matters of expression the Indian mind has always preferred poetry to prose. Commentaries and lexicons were written in verse, and sometimes even conversation was carried on in metre. The major portion of Vedic literature is in metre. So this peculiarity of the Indian mind is the cause of the dearth of prose literature in Sanskrit. In the *Kṛṣṇa-Yajurveda*, however, we come across the earliest specimen of prose-writing. The prose of the *Atharvaveda* should also be considered in connexion with the study of the history and development of prose-writing in ancient India. The prose of the Brāhmaṇas is simple yet elegant, and the prose of the Sūtra literature is more or less in the form of a message such as we usually send in a telegram. None of these, however, can give us any standard of writing which may be imitated with profit. The prose portions of the *Mahābhārata*, and of the Pūraṇas such as the *Viṣṇu* and the *Bhāgavata*, and of the medical compilations of Caraka and Suśruta should also be mentioned. The earliest standard of prose-writing is to be found in Patañjali's *Mahābhāṣya* which is noted for its grace, vigour and elegance, and in it we find the perfection of Brāhmaṇical prose. The prose of explanatory treatises or commentaries offers a good example of Sanskrit composition. Thus the writings of Śabarasvāmin on the *Mīmāṁsāsūtras*, of Vātsyāyana on the *Nyāyasūtras*, the commentaries of Śaṅkara on the *Brahmasūtras* and the Upaniṣads and the explanatory work of Medhātithi on *Manusmṛti* are instances to the point. Besides all these, there is the prose of the early dramatic literature which necessarily demands a careful study. In fact, the extent of prose-writing is not very small, but by comparison with the greater quantity of poetic composition it is considered insignificant.

Romance and Fable

Though the beginnings of Sanskrit prose-writings may be traced to a very dim antiquity, the extant works of prose literature are of a comparatively late date. The extant prose literature may be divided into two broad classes: romance and fable.

Ākhyāyikā & Kathā

It appears that in early Classical Sanskrit there were numerous types of prose romances, the two most important among them being Ākhyāyikā and Kathā. But as early as the seventh century A.D., Daṇḍin writes in his *Kāvyādarśa* that there is no vital point of difference in the nature of these two types of prose compositions and he regards them as the different names of one and the same species. Amarasiṁha, the lexicographer, however, distinguishes between the two, Ākhyāyikā having a historical basis and Kathā being a purely poetic creation.

Origin of Fable literature

The origin of Indian fable literature must be traced back to the earliest times in the life of Vedic Indians. The tales current among the people were later on used for a definite purpose, and the didactic fable became a mode of inculcating useful knowledge.

B. ROMANCE

There is a great difference of opinion amongst scholars regarding the age of Daṇḍin. It is held on

Daṇḍin: age and home

the evidence of the *Kāvyādarśa*, a well-known work on rhetorical canons by the poet, that he flourished after Pravarasena. According to the *Rājataraṅgiṇī*, Pravarasena ruled Kāshmir in the sixth century A.D. This Pravarasena was probably the author of the poem *Setubandha*. The relation between Daṇḍin and Bhāmaha, another rhetorician, has created a great controversy. Some scholars are inclined to believe that Daṇḍin has criticized the views of Bhāmaha while others entertain the opposite view. There is some controversy again with regard to the relation of Daṇḍin to Bhaṭṭi, the grammarian-poet. Some scholars are definitely of opinion that Daṇḍin used the *Bhaṭṭikāvya*. It is, however, presumed that he flourished in the seventh century A.D. From the internal evidence furnished by both the *Daśakumāracarita* and the *Kāvyādarśa*, it appears that Daṇḍin was an inhabitant of South India. He was fairly acquainted with the Kāverī, the Andhras and the Colas.

Daśakumāracarita: contents & character

Daṇḍin's *Daśakumāracarita*, a work of the Akhyāyikā type, describes the exploits of eight princes, Rājavāhana and others. As the name of the work implies, it should have contained accounts of ten princes. The stories of the other two princes are given in the prelude (*Pūrvapīṭikā*), and the incomplete story of one of the princes (Viśruta) has been incorporated in the sequel (*Uttarapīṭikā*), which two chapters seem to be the work of a different hand. The romance reflects admirably the social conditions in which the author lived and where the standard of morality was markedly poor. Daṇḍin's writings usually conform to the Vaidarbha style.

Subandhu: age and work

Subandhu appears to have been earlier than Bāṇabhaṭṭa who has referred to the former's *Vāsavadattā* in his introduction to the *Kādambarī*. In a passage in the *Vāsavadattā* Subandhu laments over the death of Vikramāditya. This has led scholars to surmise that after the death of Candragupta II of the Gupta dynasty who assumed the title of Vikramāditya, there was a civil war in the country, and Subandhu suffered from upholding the losing cause. This theory, however, is not generally accepted. From two passages in the *Vāsavadattā*, European scholars find references to Uddyotakara, the great writer on Nyāya, and the *Bauddhasaṅgatyalaṅkāra* of Dharmakīrti. If the allusions are correct, Subandhu may be placed in the beginning of the seventh century A.D.

Story of Vāsavadattā

The theme of Subandhu's *Vāsavadattā* is the love-story of Prince Kandarpaketu and Princess Vāsavadattā. The playful imagination of the poet conceives how on one night, the prince dreams about a beautiful princess and starts in quest of her. Meanwhile, the princess having dreamt of Prince Kandarpaketu sends one of her personal attendants in search of him. Kandarpaketu in course of his travels comes to learn about Vāsavadattā from the conversation of a pair of birds. He arrives at Pāṭaliputra and is united with Vāsavadattā. But the king, Vāsavadattā's father, wants to give her away to another prince. Thereupon the two leave the palace on a magic steed and go to the Vindhyas. One night they fall asleep but in the morning the prince gets up and is surprised not to find Vāsavadattā by his side. He commences a vigorous search and at last discovers her in the hermitage of a sage. She is turned into a stone, and the prince revives her by his touch

Style

The poet is a master of a style which is marked by a preponderant use of alliteration. Subandhu claims that he is a storehouse of cleverness in the composition of works in which there is a pun in every syllable. But even though his style lacks artistic grace his writings reveal the poetic genius in him.

Bāṇa: age & works

Bāṇabhaṭṭa is undoubtedly the greatest of Indian prose-writers. Fortunately, the date of Bāṇa is one of the surest planks in the tottering edifice of ancient Indian chronology. Bāṇa has to his credit the *Harṣacarita* and the *Kādambarī* which are respectively an Akhyāyikā and a Kathā.

Harṣacarita

In his *Harṣacarita,* Bāṇa glorifies his patron, King Harṣa who flourished during A.D. 606-A.D. 647. In the first and second chapters of this incomplete book Bāṇa gives an account of his genealogy and early life which reveals him as a great traveller.

Kādambarī

Bāṇa makes lavish use of his poetic imagination in relating the story of *Kādambarī* which also he could not complete. The theme of this book is the fascinating love-story of Candrāpīḍa and Kādambarī in their several births. Running parallel with the main story we also find the love-episode of Puṇḍarīka and Mahāśvetā. The romance relates how the Moon-god being cursed by Puṇḍarīka who was pining for Mahāśvetā, was born on earth as Candrāpīḍa and fell in love with Kādambarī, the Gandharva princess. Puṇḍarīka also cursed by the Moon-god was born on earth as Vaiśampāyana, the friend of Candrāpīḍa. In this birth also both Candrāpīḍa and Vaiśampāyana gave up their lives and were again born as King Sūdraka and the parrot respectively. Happily in this birth they were all reunited.

Much has been said of Bāṇa's style. Western Style critics describe it as a big forest where all access is prohibited because of the luxuriant undergrowth of words. But Indian scholars have the highest admiration for Bāṇa and his style, and it would not be an exaggeration to say that his style has been regarded by Indian scholars as the standard style of prose. Superb is Bāṇa's power of description and he wields the language with the greatest ease. With regard to the theme European scholars have frankly admitted that they find no interest in it in view of the fact that they have no belief in rebirth or even in a reunion after this mortal life. The whole romance, therefore, seems to be fantastic with uninteresting characters living in an unreal atmosphere. But be this as it may, they have also the highest admiration for Bāṇa's treatment of love, which they think, is refined and graceful. They also pay him the compliment for possessing a wonderful insight into the currents of youthful passion and virgin modesty which sway a girl's mind when she is moved to love for the first time. Bāṇa is praised also on account of his awareness of the advantage of contrast and his dramatic sense. And the Indian critic recognizes and appreciates the extraordinarily rich creative talent of the poet, when he says that he has touched upon all the different topics of description.

C. FABLE

The short stories in Indian literature may be classed under three different heads, viz., the popular tales,

Classification of fables

the beast-fables and the fairy tales. The popular tales again may be broadly sub-divided into Buddhistic and non-Buddhistic.[1]

Buddhist popular tales

The Buddhist popular tales are the Pāli Jātakas which were current among the Buddhists from the earliest times. Apart from these Jātaka stories there are some Buddhist Sanskrit popular stories.

Guṇāḍhya's Bṛhatkathā & works based on it

Guṇāḍhya's *Bṛhatkathā* is an outstanding work among non-Buddhistic popular tales. It was written in Paiśācī Prākrit, a dialect spoken in the north western parts of India. The work is now unfortunately lost to us, but the story has been preserved in three Sanskrit works, viz., (1) Budhasvāmin's *Ślokasaṁgraha* (composed between the eighth and the ninth century A.D.), (2) Kṣemendra's *Bṛhatkathāmañjarī* (A.D. 1037) and (3) Somadeva's *Kathāsaritsāgara* (A.D. 1063-81). According to Dr Keith the *Ślokasaṁgraha* (which is found only in a fragment of twenty-eight chapters and some 4539 verses) is a genuine translation of Guṇāḍhya's work and he holds that neither Somadeva's *Kathāsaritsāgara* (containing 21,388 verses) nor Kṣemendra's *Bṛhatkathāmañjarī* (containing about 7,500 verses) is from the original *Bṛhatkathā*. Nevertheless, the *Bṛhatkathā* is mentioned as early as the seventh century A.D. in Daṇḍin's *Kāvyādarśa,* and Dr Bühler has placed the work in the first or the second century A.D. Dr Keith suggests that it was written not later than the fourth century A.D. The importance of the *Bṛhatkathā* can never be overestimated. As a perpetual source of inspiration the

[1] The fable literature of the Jainas is extremely rich. But only a few works are written in pure Sanskrit.

Bṛhatkathā occupies in ancient Indian literature, a place next only to that of the two Great Epics, the *Rāmāyaṇa* and the *Mahābhārata*.

Viṣṇuśarman: Pañcatantra

The *Pañcatantra* attributed to Viṣṇuśarman is an important piece of beast-fable literature and it is said that the book has an earlier basis called the *Tantrākhyāyikā* now lost to us. The work is written in five books in clear lucid style with a mixture of prose and verse. It appears to allude to Cāṇakya and follow Kauṭilya's *Arthaśāstra*. It is suggested by Hertel that it was originally conceived as a work for teaching political wisdom but it must be admitted that its character as a political textbook is never glaring. It is essentially a story-book 'in which the story-teller and the political teacher are unified in one personality'. The importance of this work may be judged from the fact that it was translated into Pahlavi and Syriac in the sixth century A.D., into Arabic in the eighth century A.D., into Hebrew in the eleventh century A.D., into Spanish in the thirteenth century A.D., and into Latin and English in the sixteenth century A.D.

Nārāyaṇa: Hitopadeśa

The *Hitopadeśa* is another beast-fable literature written by one Nārāyaṇa Paṇḍita. The author imitates the style of Viṣṇuśarman and the method of arrangement is entirely the same in both works. The author lived in the court of King Dhavalacandra of whom we know little. A manuscript of this work dates from the fourteenth century A.D. According to Dr Keith its date cannot be later than the eleventh century A.D., as a verse of Rudrabhaṭṭa is cited in the book. Moreover a Jaina scholar made use of it in A.D. 1199 in order to produce a new version.

Śrīvara: Kathākautuka

Another work of the beast-fable class is Śrīvara's *Kathākautuka* written in the fifteenth century A.D.

Vetālapañcaviṁśati, Siṁhāsanadvātriṁśikā & Śukasaptati

Under fairy-tale literature we may class the following three books of unknown date. The *Vetālapañcaviṁśati* attributed to Śivadāsa and the *Siṁhāsanadvātriṁśikā* are probably of the Buddhist origin. Both books are based on the character of a fictitious king named Vikrama. The *Śukasaptati* of unknown origin and date is a collection of seventy tales which the parrot narrates to the mistress who was about to play her husband false.

D. LESSER PROSE TALES

Upamitibhavaprapañca-kathā: by Siddha or Siddharṣi, a Jaina monk, of A.D. 906—written in prose interspersed with verses—a didactic tale.

Kathārṇava: by Śivadāsa—containing thirty-five tales chiefly of fools and thieves—of unknown date but appearing as a late work.

Puruṣaparīkṣā: by Vidyāpati belonging to the latter part of the fourteenth century A.D.—containing forty-four stories.

Bhojaprabandha: by Ballālasena of the sixteenth century A.D.—containing legends of the court of King Bhoja.

Campakaśreṣṭhikathānaka & *Pālagopālakathānaka*: by Jinakīrti of the fifteenth century A.D.

Kathākośa: collection of tales of unknown date—written in bad Sanskrit.

Samyaktvakaumudī: by an unknown author, probably of a later date—having a propagandist character.

Kathāratnākara: by Hemavijaya-gaṇi of the seventeenth century A.D. —containing 258 different short tales, fables and anecdotes.

REFERENCES

Keith, A. B.: *A History of Sanskrit Literature*
Macdonell, A. A.: *A History of Sanskrit Literature*
Weber, A.: *The History of Indian Literature*

CHAPTER XII

CAMPU LITERATURE

A. INTRODUCTION

Campū: character and age

COMPOSITION in mixed prose and verse in Sanskrit is called Campū.[1] Though the admixture of prose and verse can be traced even in Vedic literature, specially in the Brāhmaṇas, still the origin of Campū is to be sought in its immediate predecessors, the fables and the romances. Already in the writings of Subandhu and Bāṇa and in some inscriptions we find stray verses, until much later the mingling of prose and verse became a singular characteristic of a different section of literature. In the literature of Kathā and Akhyāyikā, which makes prose its exclusive medium, one invariably comes across a number of verses and in order to distinguish the Campū from this type of prose literature it becomes necessary to presume that the mingling of prose and verse in the Campū must not be disproportionate. And it should be carefully remembered that the employment of prose and verse in the Campū need not follow any fixed principle. Authors of the Campū use prose and verse quite indifferently for the same purpose. The use of verse is not restricted to passages of poetic description or impressive speech or sentimental outburst. Prose is as much the medium in a Campū as verse. It is worthy of notice in this connexion that the history

[1] *Kāvyādarśa*, i. 31.

of the Campū does not possess any great literary interest and we refrain from giving a detailed account of the available Campū literature on this ground. Suffice it to note that the Campū form of composition flourished in Southern India and the Bengal Vaiṣṇava school and the Jaina writers made use of this kind of literature for religious propaganda. It is a curious fact that no Campū older than the tenth century A.D. is extant, though Professor Oldenberg has discovered something like Campū in the *Jātakamālā* of *Āryaśūra*.

B. SOME IMPORTANT WORKS

Nalacampū & *Madālasācampū*: by Trivikramabhaṭṭa of the tenth century A.D.
Yaśastilaka: by Somadeva, a Digambara Jaina, in A.D. 959—describing the conversion of King Māridatta.
Tilakamañjarī: by Dhanapāla, a Jaina, who wrote about A.D. 970.
Jīvandharacampū: by Haricandra, not earlier than A.D. 900 in eleven *lambhakas* (sections).
Rāmāyaṇacampū: attributed to Bhojarāja and Lakṣaṇabhaṭṭa.
Bhāratacampū: by Ananta of unknown date in twelve sections.
Udayasundarīkathā: by Soḍḍhala of A.D. 1040—strongly influenced by Bāṇa.
Gopālacampū: by Jīvagosvāmin of the sixteenth century A.D.
Pārijātaharaṇacampū: by Śeṣakṛṣṇa in the second half of the sixth century.
Ānanda-Vṛndāvanacampū: by Kavikarṇapūra dealing with the early life of Kṛṣṇa.
Svāhāsudhākaracampū: by Nārāyaṇa of the seventeenth century A.D.
Śaṅkaracetovilāsacampū: by Śaṅkara—a very late work.

REFERENCES

Keith, A. B.: *A History of Sanskrit Literature*
Winternitz, M.: *A History of Indian Literature*, Vol. II
Dasgupta, S. N. & De, S. K.: *History of Sanskrit Literature*, Vol. I

CHAPTER XIII

GRAMMAR

A. INTRODUCTION

Importance of Sanskrit grammar

GRAMMAR is one of the most important branches of Sanskrit literature. From very early times till most recently, grammar has held a unique place, and its study has been continued through centuries with deepest reverence and consummate application. Patañjali, the author of the *Vyākaraṇamahābhāṣya*, has dwelt at length on the various uses of the study of grammar. It is a fact that grammar as a branch of literature had a peculiar appeal to the early Indians, and it is worthy of notice that it is in India alone that the study of grammar has ultimately led to the discovery of a system of philosophy.[1]

Pāṇini & his predecessors

The most popular of all the schools of grammar is that of Pāṇini who has mentioned no less than sixty-four names of previous grammarians among which Kāśyapa, Āpiśali, Gārgya, Gālava, Śākaṭayana, Senaka and Sphoṭāyana may be cited.

[1] The high degree of popularity enjoyed by Sanskrit grāmmar is corroborated by the existence of nearly a dozen schools of grammar each of which is represented by writers of established reputation and following. Indra is, however, mentioned in the *Taittirīyasaṁhitā* as the first of grammarians. The *Kathāsaritsāgara* informs us that the Aindra school was supplanted by Pāṇini, the author of the *Aṣṭādhyāyī*. This has led Dr Burnell to conclude that the Aindra school of grammar is the oldest in India. It should be noted, however, that neither Pāṇini nor Patañjali mentions Indra as a grammarian. It is, therefore, argued by some that the Aindra school is post-Pāṇinīya in date, though pre-Pāṇinīya in substance.

B. THE PĀṆINI SCHOOL

Pāṇini: Aṣṭādhyāyī

Scholars vary widely among themselves in determining the age of Pāṇini. Professor Goldstücker places him in the eighth century B.C., while Professors Max Müller and Weber are of opinion that he belonged to the fourth century B.C. His grammar, the *Aṣṭādhyāyī*, is a work in eight chapters each of which contains four sections. The arrangement of the rules is highly scientific, economy being the most outstanding characteristic.

Kātyāyana: Vārttika

Kātyāyana who is known as the Vārttikakāra came after Pāṇini and he is usually assigned to the third century B.C. The Vārttikas are undoubtedly 'supplementary rules' which were framed by Kātyāyana to justify certain new forms which crept into the language after Pāṇini had written his Sūtras. But Kātyāyana did not only supplement the rules of Pāṇini but also rejected some of them which were deemed unnecessary. In some cases again he improved upon the text of the *Aṣṭādhyāyī* to meet the demands of a living language.

Patañjali: Mahābhāsya: 150 B.C.

Patañjali who is regarded as the last of the 'three great sages', lived during the reign of King Puṣyamitra (or Puṣpamitra) of the Śuṅga dynasty. His date is one of the few definite landmarks in the whole range of early Indian literature. Patañjali earned for himself a rare reputation and his views were referred to by later schools of rival philosophers with the utmost respect and reverence. Patañjali used some technical devices whereby he could effectively extend the scope of the original Sūtras of Pāṇini and did not on that account venture any addition like Kātyāyana.

It must, however, be said that he, too, rejected quite a large number of the Sūtras of Pāṇini. The prose of Patañjali's *Mahābhāṣya,* is inimitable and marked by the qualities of grace, brevity and perspicuity.

Bhartṛhari: Vākyapadīya and other works

After the three great sages mentioned above, one must remember the name of Bhartṛhari who is often wrongly identified with Bhaṭṭi, the grammarian-poet, and who is in all probability referred to by I-tsing when he says that a great grammarian died in A.D. 651. Bhartṛhari is known as the author of the *Vākyapadīya* (in two chapters), the *Prakīrṇaka* and a commentary on Patañjali's *Mahābhāsya,* fragments of which are preserved in the Berlin Library. It may be proved on the strength of the internal evidence furnished by the *Vākyapadīya* that the grammarian lived earlier than the seventh century A.D. The opening chapter of the *Vākyapadīya* discusses the philosophy of Sanskrit grammar. In the second chapter and the *Prakīrṇaka,* he discusses various topics of Sanskrit grammar.

Vāmana & Jayāditya: Kāśikā

Vāmana and Jayāditya are the two Buddhist writers who wrote the *Kāśikā,* a commentary on the Sūtras of Pāṇini. I-tsing informs us that Jayāditya died about A.D. 660. The object of Vāmana and Jayāditya was to incorporate in the system of Pāṇini all the improvements made by Candragomin. The *Kāśikā* is usually known as the *Vṛtti.*

Jinendrabuddhi: Nyāsa

Jinendrabuddhi, a Bengali Buddhist, wrote an excellent and exhaustive commentary called the *Nyāsa* or the *Kāśikāvivaraṇa-pañjikā,* on the *Kāśikā* of Vāmana and Jayāditya. Jinendrabuddhi is referred to by Bhāmaha, the rhetorician, and accordingly he cannot be later than the eighth century A.D.

Kaiyaṭa: Pradīpa

Kaiyaṭa is one of the most authoritative writers affiliated to the school of Pāṇini. His commentary, the *Pradīpa*, on the *Mahābhāṣya* of Patañjali, is an invaluable treatise. It is believed that Kaiyaṭa wrote in the eleventh century A.D.

Haradatta: Padamañjarī

Haradatta, the author of the *Padamañjarī*, a commentary on the *Kāśikā*, is well-known for his independent views which more often than not contradict the statements of Patañjali. Haradatta is quoted by Mallinātha while he himself quotes Māgha. It is assumed that Haradatta flourished in the twelfth century A.D.

Rāmacandra: Prakriyākaumudī

The *Aṣṭādhyāyī* of Pāṇini was remoulded by later grammarians who arranged the Sūtras according to the topics selected for discussion. Rāmacandra who flourished in the first half of the fifteenth century A.D., wrote his *Prakriyākaumudī* which is supposed to be the model for Bhaṭṭoji's *Siddhāntakaumudī*. The most famous commentary, the *Prasāda*, on the *Prakriyākaumudī* was written by Viṭṭhalācārya in the first half of the sixteenth century A.D.

Bhaṭṭoji: Siddhāntakaumudī & other works

The *Siddhāntakaumudī* of Bhaṭṭoji is a recast of the Sūtras of Pāṇini in the topical method. Bhaṭṭoji flourished in seventeenth century A.D. Bhaṭṭoji himself wrote a commentary on his *Siddhāntakaumudī* which is called the *Prauḍhamanoramā*. His *Śabdakaustubha* is an authoritative commentary on Pāṇini's *Aṣṭādhyāyī*. Bhaṭṭoji's reputation as an authority on Sanskrit grammar is enviable. The most famous commentary on the *Siddhāntakaumudī* is the *Tattvabodhinī* by Jñānendra Sarasvatī of the eighteenth century A.D. The *Bālamanoramā* of Vāsudeva is an easy commentary on the *Siddhāntakaumudī*.

Nāgeśabhaṭṭa was a versatile genius of the eighteenth century A.D. who wrote treatises not only on grammar but also on Yoga, Alaṅkāra and other subjects. Among his important works in grammar are the *Uddyota*, a commentary on Kaiyaṭa's *Pradīpa*, the *Bṛhacchabdenduśekhara* and the *Laghuśabdenduśekhara* (both commentaries on Bhaṭṭoji's *Siddhāntakaumudī*) and the *Paribhāṣenduśekhara*, a collection of Paribhāṣās in connexion with Pāṇini's grammar. The *Vaiyākaraṇasiddhāntamañjūṣā* (*Bṛhat* and *Laghu*) is another outstanding work which discusses various topics of Sanskrit grammar.[1] Nāgeśa: his works

Varadarāja, a very recent writer popularized his name by making abridgements of the *Siddhāntakaumudī*. His two books, the *Laghusiddhāntakaumudī* and the *Madhyasiddhāntakaumudī* are widely read by all beginners of Sanskrit grammar. Varadarāja: his works

C. OTHER IMPORTANT SCHOOLS OF GRAMMAR

Candragomin flourished in the middle of the fifth century A.D. Bhartṛhari in his *Vākyapadīya* refers to the Cāndra school of grammarians. The object of Candragomin was to rearrange with marked brevity the system of Pāṇini. The Cāndra grammar, however, gained much popularity and was widely commented upon. The commentaries are now preserved mostly in Tibetan translations. Cāndra school

Jinendra flourished in the latter part of the fifth century A.D. and condensed the Sūtras of Pāṇini and Jinendra school

[1] According to the tradition which we have been privileged to inherit and which comes down uninterruptedly from Nāgeśabhaṭṭa, the *Paramalaghumañjūṣā* is not the work of Nāgeśa.

the Vārttikas. Two main commentaries on his grammar have been preserved—one by Abhayanandī (A.D. 750) and another called *Śabdārṇavacandrikā* by Somadeva.

Śākaṭāyana school

Śākaṭāyana, the founder of a school after his name, should not be confused with the ancient Śākaṭāyana mentioned by Pāṇini. Śākaṭāyana wrote his *Śabdānuśāsana* in the first quarter of the ninth century A.D. *Amoghavṛtti* is another work of this author. Śākaṭāyana has based his work on Pāṇini, Kātyāyana and Jinendra. Śākaṭāyana is also credited with the authorship of (i) the *Paribhāṣāsūtras* (ii) the *Gaṇapāṭha* (iii) the *Dhātupāṭha* (iv) the *Uṇādisūtras* and (v) the *Liṅgānuśāsana*.

Hemacandra school

Hemacandra, the prolific Jaina writer, wrote his *Śabdānuśāsana* in the eleventh century A.D. The book consists of more than four thousand Sūtras, and is a compilation rather than an original work. Hemacandra himself wrote a commentary on his book known as *Śabdānuśāsanabṛhadvṛtti*.

Kātantra school

Sarvavarman is the author of the *Kātantrasūtras* otherwise known as the Kaumāra and the Kālāpa. The beginnings of this school belong to the early centuries of the Christian era. There are, however, evidences of later interpolations in the *Kātantrasūtras*. Sarvavarman's views are in many places different from those of Pāṇini. Durgasiṁha wrote his famous *Vṛtti* on this grammar not later than the ninth century A.D. Durgasiṁha's *Vṛtti* was commented by Vardhamāna in the eleventh century A.D. Pṛthvīdhara wrote a subcommentary on Vardhamāna's work. The Kātantra school has been very popular in Bengal and Kāshmir.

Anubhūtisvarūpācārya, the author of the *Sārasvata-prakriyā*, flourished in the middle of the fourteenth century A.D. Brevity of expression is a characteristic of this school. Some of the many commentators on the *Sārasvataprakriyā*, are Puñjarāja, Amṛtabhāratī, Kṣemendra and others. Sārasvata school

Vopadeva wrote his *Mugdhabodha* in the thirteenth century A.D. Vopadeva's style is brief and simple. His technical terms in many places differ from those of Pāṇini. Rāma Tarkavāgīśa is the most celebrated commentator of this grammar. Mugdha-bodha school

Kramadīśvara wrote his *Saṁkṣiptasāra* in the thirteenth century A.D. The work has eight sections and the illustrations have been taken from the *Bhaṭṭikāvya*. The *Saṁkṣiptasāra* underwent a thorough revision in the hand of Jumaranandin who wrote a commentary called the *Rasavatī*. This grammar is widely read in Western Bengal. Jaumara school

The author of the *Supadma* is Padmanābha who flourished in the fourteenth century A.D. This system of grammar, like many other systems, is based on Pāṇini. Padmanābha himself wrote a commentary known as the *Supadmapañjikā*. Saupadma school

D. SECTARIAN SCHOOLS OF GRAMMAR

In recent centuries there flourished some grammarians who wanted to make grammar the vehicle of religion. This tendency was already present in Vopadeva. Rūpagosvāmin wrote his *Harināmāmṛta* in the sixteenth century A.D. The names of Kṛṣṇa and Rādhā are used as actual technical terms of grammar. Jīvagosvāmin wrote a grammar of the same name. Harināmāmṛta & Caitanyāmṛta

A third Vaiṣṇava grammar named *Caitanyāmṛta* is mentioned by Professor Colebrooke.

E. SOME IMPORTANT WORKS ON GRAMMAR

Durghaṭavṛtti: by Śaraṇadeva, a Bengali Buddhist of the twelfth century A.D.—dealing with derivations of difficult words.

Bhāṣāvṛtti: by Puruṣottamadeva of the twelfth century A.D.—a commentary on the *Aṣṭādhyāyī* (sections on Vedic accent are left out).

Gaṇaratnamahodadhi: by Vardhamāna in A.D. 1140.

Paribhāṣāvṛtti: by Sīradeva—a collection of *paribhāṣās* with their explanation.

Dhātupradīpa: by Maitreyarakṣita who is later than Hemacandra—containing a list of roots and their uses.

Dhātuvṛtti: by Mādhava, son of Sāyaṇa—written after the model of the *Dhātupradīpa*.

Vaiyākaraṇabhūṣaṇa & *Vaiyākaraṇabhūṣaṇasāra*: by Koṇḍabhaṭṭa, nephew of Bhaṭṭoji—dealing with philosophical and other points of Sanskrit grammar.

Śabdaratna: by Haridīkṣita, grandson of Bhaṭṭoji and teacher of Nāgeśa—a commentary on the *Prauḍhamanoramā*.

Prauḍhamanoramākucamardinī: by Paṇḍitarāja Jagannātha, the great rhetorician—a criticism of the *Prauḍhamanoramā*.

REFERENCES

Belvalkar, S. K.: *Systems of Sanskrit Grammar*
Keith, A. B.: *A History of Sanskrit Literature*

CHAPTER XIV

POETICS AND DRAMATURGY

A. INTRODUCTION

Bharata: Nāṭya-śāstra

History of Sanskrit Poetics

TRACES of early poetic efforts may be seen in the *Ṛgveda*, the *Śātapatha Brāhmaṇa*, the Upaniṣads and the *Mahābhāṣya* of Patañjali. Many of the Vedic hymns exhibit fine specimens of poetry. It is true that unlike Classical poets Vedic poets did not employ figures of sense like *dīpaka* and *utprekṣā* but that they had some idea about the embellishing factors underlying different kinds of literary compositions can be ascertained from the repetitions of the same letters or words which approach an *anuprāsa* or a *yamaka*. The two great Epics contain gems of poetical expressions which are undoubtedly instances of very common figures of speech and sense. The term *alaṅkāra* in the technical sense does not occur in the *Nirukta* but Yāska uses it in the sense of 'one that adorns'. In the *Nighaṇṭu* iii. 13 a list of twelve varieties of particles of comparison is given. Six of such varieties are indicated by the particles, *iva, yathā, na, cit, nu* and *ā*. Yāska also mentions *bhūtopamā, siddhopamā, rūpopamā* and *luptopamā* among other varieties of comparison. The rules of Pāṇini, however, illustrate that the technical words like *upamā, upamāna,* etc. had gathered a fixed meaning long before Pāṇini wrote his grammar. Reference to a science of poetics, however, cannot be found in the works of Yājñavalkya and Āpastamba or the *Viṣṇupurāṇa* and the

Arthaśāstra and it is extremely doubtful whether any science of Poetics really evolved in India before Patañjali. As we have said before the origin may be traced with certainty from the time of Bharata who in the *Nāṭyaśāstra* mentions four *alaṅkāras,* ten *guṇas* and thirty-six *lakṣaṇas* of a good Kāvya.

The literature on poetics and dramaturgy is conspicuously rich in Classical Sanskrit. Many able thinkers have written important works both on poetics and dramaturgy. These allied subjects have been treated by one and the same author. Bharata's *Nāṭyaśāstra* is the earliest known treatise on poetics and dramaturgy. The date of this monumental composition has been variously assigned by scholars to the period between the second century B.C. and third century A.D. The *Nāṭyaśāstra* shows unmistakable proofs of a systematic tradition which has preceded it by at least a century. Bharata has been held in high esteem by all later writers on poetics and his work has continued to be a source of inspiration to them.

Four schools of poetics

With the progress of years there arose four main schools of poetics which maintain different views with regard to the essential characteristics of poetry. Thus from time to time, alaṅkāra (figure), rīti (style), rasa (aesthetic pleasure) and dhvani (suggestion) have been declared to be the essential factors of poetry. The Dhvani school, however, has grown to be the most important of all schools of Alaṅkāra literature. Ānandavardhana, the author of the *Dhvanyāloka* is known to be the pioneer of this school and it has been for his commentator Abhinavagupta to bring out the importance of the doctrine of Dhvani through his lasting contributions.[1]

(i) Alaṅkāra school

Bhāmaha is one of the earliest rhetoricians to take up a systematic discussion of poetic embellishments after Bharata's treatment of figures. Bhāmaha flourished in all probability in the seventh century A.D. His only work, the *Kāvyālaṅkāra*, contains six chapters. In his definition of poetry Bhāmaha has accorded equal status to 'word' and 'import', though he has devoted more attention to the former.

Bhāmaha: Kāvyālaṅkāra

Udbhaṭa wrote his *Alaṅkārasaṁgraha* in the latter half of the eighth century A.D. The work is a collection of verses defining forty-one figures and contains six chapters. In his treatment of figures Udbhaṭa has followed in the line of Bhāmaha.[2]

Udbhaṭa: Alaṅkārasaṁgraha

Rudraṭa wrote his *Kāvyālaṅkāra* in the first quarter of the ninth century A.D. The work which is in sixteen chapters, deals mainly with figures of poetry. In his treatment of figures Rudraṭa seems to have been the follower of a tradition different from that of Bhāmaha and Udbhaṭa. Of the three commentators of Rudraṭa, Namisādhu appears to be the most important.

Rudraṭa: Kāvyālaṅkāra

(ii) Rīti school

Daṇḍin, the author of the *Kāvyādarśa*, is the precursor of the Rīti school which was developed by Vāmana. Though Daṇḍin is usually assigned to the seventh century A.D., still the relative priority of Bhā-

[1] According to modern scholars, a comparatively late work on Indian poetics is the *Agnipurāṇa* where in as many as eleven chapters, comprehensive and authoritative information about the various schools of poetics known to the author is available.

[2] Though Udbhaṭa belongs to the Alaṅkāra school, his well-known commentator Pratihārendurāja, a pupil of Mukulabhaṭṭa, is a follower of the Rasa school. Pratihārendurāja is assigned to the first half of the tenth century A.D.

Daṇḍin: Kāvyādarśa

maha and Daṇḍin is a disputed point in the history of Sanskrit poetics. Daṇḍin appears to have been greatly influenced by the Alaṅkāra school. His most outstanding contribution to poetics is the concept of Guṇa. In his definition of poetry Daṇḍin gives more importance to the word-element than to the sense-element. The most authoritative commentator of the *Kāvyādarśa* is Taruṇavācaspati.

Vāmana: Kāvyālaṅkārasūtra

Vāmana who flourished in the latter half of the eighth century A.D., wrote his *Kāvyālaṅkārasūtra* in five chapters and twelve sections in which he boldly asserted that Rīti is the soul of poetry. The ten Guṇas are important in so far as they constitute Rīti. The *Kāmadhenu*, a late work by Gopendra Tippa Bhūpāla, is a lucid commentary on the *Kāvyālaṅkāra-sūtra*.

(iii) Rasa school

Lollaṭa

The Rasa school originated from the interpretations by different commentators of Bharata's aphorism on Rasa. Lollaṭa who is known to be the earliest interpreter, flourished in the eighth century A.D. The work of Lollaṭa is unfortunately lost to us, though a review of his opinion is found in the *Abhinava-bhāratī* of Abhinavagupta and the *Kāvyaprakāśa* of Mammaṭa. The text of Daṇḍin's Kāvyadarśa on figure, *rasavat*, leads us to presume that the rhetorician was influenced by the School of Lollaṭa.

Śrī-Śaṅkuka

Another interpreter is Śrī-Śaṅkuka who has criticized the views of Lollaṭa. The work of Śrī-Śaṇkuka also is lost to us. He is believed to be a junior contemporary of Lollaṭa.

Bhaṭṭanāyaka: Hṛdayadarpaṇa

Bhaṭṭanāyaka is the most celebrated commentator of the Rasa school. He is said to have flourished between the last quarter of the ninth century A.D. and the beginning of the tenth century A.D. His work, the *Hṛdayadarpaṇa,* is unfortunately lost to us. Bhaṭṭanāyaka has rejected the views of Lollaṭa and Śrī-Śaṅkuka. It is interesting to note that Bhaṭṭanāyaka has recognized two additional powers of word, viz., the power of generalization (*bhāvakatva*) by which the meaning is made intelligible to the audience and the power of *bhojakatva* which enables the audience to relish the enjoyment of the poem.

(iv) Dhvani school

Ānanda-vardhana: Dhvanyāloka

The doctrine of Dhvani according to which 'suggestion' is held to be the essence of poetry, was formulated by Ānandavardhana in his *Dhvanyāloka* in the middle of the ninth century A.D. Ānandavardhana informs us that the doctrine of Dhvani is very old, the dim beginnings of which are lost in oblivion. According to Ānandavardhana, a word is not only endowed with the two powers of denotation (*śakti*) and implication (*lakṣaṇā*) but also with that of suggestion (*vyañjanā*). Through the power of suggestion, either a subject, or a figure or a sentiment is revealed.

Abhinavagupta: Locana & Abhinavabhāratī

The views of Ānandavardhana found a large and definite shape in the writings of his erudite commentator Abhinavagupta who flourished at the end of the tenth and the beginning of the eleventh century A.D. Abhinavagupta has to his credit two important commentaries on poetics which may be looked upon as independent treatises and these are the *Locana* on the *Dhvanyāloka* of Ānandavardhana and the *Abhinavabhāratī* on the *Nāṭyaśāstra* of Bharata. Abhinavagupta thinks that all suggestion must be of sentiment, for the suggestion of subject or that of figure may be ultimately reduced to the suggestion of sentiment.

B. WORKS ON POETICS & DRAMATURGY

Abhidhāvṛttimātṛkā: by Mukulabhaṭṭa who is generally assigned to the period between the end of the ninth and the beginning of the tenth century A.D.—a grammatico-rhetorical work.

Kāvyamīmāṁsā: by Rājaśekhara of the tenth century A.D.—written in eighteen chapters—a practical hand-book for poets.

Vakroktijīvita: by Kuntala or Kuntaka who flourished in the middle of the tenth century A.D. and belonged to a reactionary school to Dhvani—upholding Vakrokti (figurative speech) as the essence of poetry. (The Vakrokti school is an off-shoot of the older Alaṅkāra school).

Daśarūpaka: by Dhanañjaya of the tenth century A.D.—containing also a section on dramaturgy besides sections on Rasa and allied topics—commented on by Dhanika, a contemporary of Dhanañjaya in his *Avaloka*.

Aucityavicāra and *Kavikaṇṭhābharaṇa*: by Kṣemendra of the eleventh century A.D.—the first, discussing propriety as essential to sentiment and the second, discussing such topics as the possibility of becoming a poet, the issue of borrowing, etc., etc.

Sarasvatīkaṇṭhābharaṇa and *Śṛṅgāraprakāśa*: by Bhoja of the first half of the eleventh century A.D.—the first, an enclyclopaedic work containing information about different schools of poetics and the second, a supplement to the first and containing a section on dramaturgy.

Vyaktiviveka: by Mahimabhaṭṭa of the second half of the eleventh century A.D. who belonged to the reactionary school to Dhvani—containing discussions on the possibility of including Dhvani under inference.

Kāvyaprakāśa: by Mammaṭa of the eleventh century A.D.—much influenced by the writings of Ānandavardhana and Abhinavagupta—discussing Rasa as the soul of poetry—commented on by Rucaka (identified with Ruyyaka, author of the *Alaṅkārasarvasva*), Māṇikyacandra, Śrīdhara, Caṇḍīdāsa, Viśvanātha and Govinda, besides a number of minor commentators.

Bhāvaprakāśana: by Śāradātanaya who flourished in the first half of the twelfth century A.D. and was one of the later writers on Rasa—much influenced by the works of Bhoja—dealing with topics of drama.

Alaṅkārasarvasva: by Ruyyaka of the latter half of the twelfth century A.D.—written in the line of Udbhaṭa—discussing the importance of Dhvani in so far as it embellishes the expressed meaning—commented on by Jayaratha, Vidyācakravartin and others.

Kāvyānuśāsana: by Hemacandra, belonging to the twelfth century A.D. who has borrowed from the writings of Abhinavagupta, Mammaṭa, Kuntala and others.

Vāgbhaṭālaṅkāra: by Vāgbhaṭa of the twelfth century A.D.—a work in verse.

Candrāloka: by Jayadeva who was not earlier than the twelfth century A.D.—a convenient manual of figures of speech with happy illustrations.

Rasamañjarī and *Rasataraṅgiṇī*: by Bhānudatta who was not earlier than the twelfth century A.D.—the two works treating of Rasa and allied topics.

Nāṭyadarpaṇa: by Rāmacandra and Guṇacandra of the twelfth century A.D.—a work on dramaturgy differing widely from the *Nāṭyaśāstra* of Bharata.

Kāvyānuśāsana: by Vāgbhaṭa of the thirteenth century A.D., who follows Hemacandra.

Kavitārahasya or *Kāvyakalpalatā*: by Arisiṁha and his pupil Amaracandra, two Śvetāmbara Jainas, belonging to the thirteenth century A.D.

Kavikalpalatā: by Deveśvara, a Jaina writer, probably belonging to the thirteenth century A.D.

Nāṭakalakṣaṇaratnakośa: by Sāgaranandin of the thirteenth century A.D.—a work on dramaturgy—strictly following the *Nāṭyaśāstra*.

Ekāvalī: by Vidyādhara of the fourteenth century A.D.—written for King Narasiṁha of Orissa—belonging to the Dhvani school—commented on by Mallinātha in his *Taralā*.

Pratāparudrayaśobhūṣaṇa: by Vidyānātha of the fourteenth century A.D.—written for King Pratāparudra of Warangal—a voluminous treatise containing various informations about poetics and dramaturgy.

Sāhityadarpaṇa: by Viśvanātha of the fourteenth centurry A.D.—treating in the manner of Mammaṭa, Rasa as the soul of poetry, though fully acknowledging the importance of Dhvani—containing discussions on both poetics and dramaturgy—criticizing Mammaṭa and in turn criticized by Govinda and Jagannātha.

Ujjvalanīlamaṇi: by Rūpagosvāmin of the sixteenth century A.D. who regards the Erotic as only a different name for the Devotional (*Bhakti*)—commented on by Jīvagosvāmin who flourished after him in the same century, in his *Locanarocanī*.

Alaṅkāraśekhara: by Keśavamiśra of the sixteenth century A.D.—a short treatise on poetics, the Kārikās of which according to the author are the composition of Śauddhodani.

Citramīmāṁsā and *Kuvalayānanda*: by Appayyadīkṣita of the seventeenth century A.D., who is noted for his critical insight and originality of appreciation. The first has been criticized by Jagannātha and the second is based on the *Candrāloka* of Jayadeva.

Rasagaṅgādhara: by Jagannātha of the seventeenth century A.D. who is the last of the Titans in Indian poetics and evinces a superb power of criticism and presentation—an important work on the dialectics of Indian poetics in particular.

REFERENCES

De, S. K.: *Sanskrit Poetics*, Vols. I & II
Kane, P. V.: *Sāhityadarpaṇa* (Introduction)
Keith, A. B.: *A History of Sanskrit Literature*

CHAPTER XV

METRICS

A. INTRODUCTION

Metrics: a Vedāṅga

In the Brāhmaṇas we find discussions on metrical matters and it may be presumed that at that time the study of metrics was deemed essential as one of the six Vedāṅgas.

Piṅgala: his Sūtra

Piṅgala is, however, the earliest known author on prosody. In his work which is of the Sūtra-type, we find for the first time the use of algebraic symbols. The book discusses both Vedic and Classical metres. Scholars opine that Piṅgala's work is surely earlier than the chapters on metre (chs. XIV, XV) in the *Nāṭyaśāstra* and the metrical section of the *Agni-purāṇa*. The text attributed to this author on Prākrit metres (*Prākṛta-Paiṅgala*) is undoubtedly a later work.

B. WORKS ON METRICS

Śrutabodha: ascribed to Kālidāsa and often attributed to Vararuci—a manual of Classical metres.

Suvṛttatilaka: by Kṣemendra of the eleventh century A.D.—containing a variety of Classical metres.

Chando'nuśāsana: by Hemacandra of the twelfth century A.D.—a compilation and not an original work.

Vṛttaratnākara: by Kedārabhaṭṭa (earlier than the fifteenth century A.D.)—a bulky book dealing with one hundred and thirty-six metres.

Vṛttaratnākara: by Nārāyaṇa of the sixteenth century A.D.

Chandomañjarī: by Gaṅgādāsa—a late and yet popular work on prosody.

REFERENCES

Keith, A. B.: *A History of Sanskrit Literature*
Macdonell, A. A.: *A History of Sanskrit Literature*
Weber, A.: *The History of Indian Literature*

CHAPTER XVI

LEXICOGRAPHY

A. INTRODUCTION

Yāska: Nirukta

Yāska's *Nirukta* is the oldest extant lexicographic work which contains a collection of Vedic terms. The lexicons of Classical Sanskrit literature are in many respects different from the *Nirukta*. One of the salient points of difference is that the Classical dictionaries treat of nouns and indeclinables while the Nighaṇṭus contain both nominal and verbal forms. Almost all the lexicographical works of Classical Sanskrit are written in verse.

Amarasiṁha: Amarakośa

The *Nāmaliṅgānuśāsana* or the *Amarakośa* is one of the earliest lexicographical works in Classical Sanskrit. Amarasiṁha, the author, probably flourished in the seventh century A.D. He is, however, believed to have been one of the 'nine gems' in the court of the famous Vikramāditya. Of the many commentators of this work, Kṣīrasvāmin, Sarvānanda, Bhānuji and Maheśvara are well-known.

B. LESS IMPORTANT LEXICONS

Trikāṇḍaśeṣa and Hārāvalī: by Puruṣottama—both early lexicons, containing collections of many rare words.
Anekārthasamuccaya: by Śāśvata, a contemporary of Amarasiṁha.
Abhidhānaratnamālā: by Halāyudha of the tenth century A.D.
Vaijayantī: by Yādava of the eleventh century A.D.
Abhidhānacintāmaṇi and Anekārthasaṁgraha: by Hemacandra of the twelfth century A.D.—both containing a rich variety of words.
Viśvaprakāśa: by Meheśvara of the twelfth century A.D.
Anekārthaśabdakośa: by Medinīkāra of the fourteenth century A.D.
Vācaspatya: by Tārānātha Tarkavācaspati of the nineteenth century A.D.—an encyclopaedic work of outstanding merit.

Śabdakalpadruma: an encyclopaedic compilation made by a batch of Sanskrit Pundits in the nineteenth century A.D., under the patronage of Rājā Sir Rādhakānta Deva.

REFERENCES

Keith, A. B.: *A History of Sanskrit Literature*
Macdonell, A. A.: *A History of Sanskrit Literature*
Weber, A.: *The History of Indian Literature*

CHAPTER XVII

CIVIL AND RELIGIOUS LAW

A. GROWTH AND DEVELOPMENT OF LEGAL WORKS

Besides the Śrautasūtras and the Gṛhyasūtras there were in ancient times a number of Dharmasūtras which may be viewed as rudimentary texts on civil and religious law. Among these Dharmasūtras mention must be made of the *Dharmasūtras* of Gautama, Hārīta, Vaśiṣṭha, Bodhāyana, Āpastamba, Hiraṇyakeśin and others. It is not definitely known when these Sūtras were composed but it is generally believed that their age must be approximately the fifth or the fourth century B.C. Two other Dharmasūtras, the *Vaiṣṇavadharmasūtra* and the *Vaikhānasadharmasūtra* were written at a later period, the former being assigned to the third century A.D. Grave doubt exists as to the antiquity of the alleged Dharmasūtras of Paiṭhīnasi, Śaṅkhalikhita, Uśanas, Kāśyapa, Bṛhaspati and others.

Early Dharmasūtras

The most outstanding and popular work on Brāhmaṇical laws is the *Mānavadharmaśāstra* or the *Manusmṛti.* Though the author of this work is generally known to be Manu, still the present text is said to have been the work of Bhṛgu. Again, from certain references it becomes evident that the present version of the *Manusmṛti* was narrated by one of Bhṛgu's students and not even by Bhṛgu himself. Dr. Bühler suggests that the *Mānavadharmaśāstra* or the *Manu-*

Manusmṛti: authorship

smṛti is a recast and versification of an original work of the type of Sūtra works known as the *Mānavasūtra-karaṇa*, a subdivision of the Maitrāyaṇīya school which adheres to a redaction of the *Kṛṣṇa-Yajurveda*. The work itself ascribes its origin to Brahmā whence it came to men via Manu and Bhṛgu while the Nārada *Smṛti* tells of a smṛti in 100,000 verses by Manu reduced to 12,000 by Nārada, 8,000 by Mārkaṇḍeya and 4,000 by Sumati, son of Bhṛgu. This account is suggestive of a successive series of redactions of some original sūtra and the inconsistencies in the Smṛti as well as allusions to a Vṛddha-Manu and Bṛhan-Manu have been adduced in support of this view.

Age

It has been argued that the present text of the *Manusmṛti* contains various facts about the supremacy of the Brāhmaṇas over other castes. The presumption, therefore, is that the work was written at a time when the Brāhmaṇas were kings of India and had great power in their hands. History tells us that there were Brāhmaṇa kings in India after the fall of the Śuṅgas. It is known that the Kāṇvas ruled in ancient India for forty-five years in the first century B.C. It is suggested that the present text of the *Manusmṛti* was prepared during the reign of the Kāṇvas.

Contents & commentators

The Manusmṛti is written in lucid Sanskrit verse which comprises 2684 couplets arranged in twelve chapters. The work discusses at length the duties of the four castes and the four orders of Hindu society, the duties of the king in particular and civil and criminal law. The work has been commented on by numerous scholars including Medhātithi, Govindarāja, Nārāyaṇa, Kullūka, Rāghavānanda and Nandana.

B. IMPORTANT WORKS ON LAW

Nāradasmṛti: Presumably a late work which has its individual merits but cannot stand comparison with the work of Manu—usually regarded as the legal supplement to the *Manusmṛti.*

Bṛhaspatismṛti: A supplementary work to the *Manusmṛti*—belonging to the sixth or the seventh century A.D.

Yājñavalkyasmṛti: An important work in the style of the *Manusmṛti*—containing a methodical and very satisfactory treatment with a stamp of individuality—not earlier than the third century A.D.—commented on by Vijñāneśvara of the eleventh century A.D. in his *Mitākṣarā.*

Saṁskārapaddhati and Prāyaścittaprakaraṇa: by Bhavadevabhaṭṭa (eleventh century A.D.), the famous minister of King Harivarman of south Bengal.

Smṛtikalpataru: by Lakṣmīdhara. minister of Govindacandra of Kanauj (twelfth century A.D.).

Parāśarasmṛti: The author of this work is not the same person quoted as an authority by Yājñavalkya—commented on by Mādhava, of the fourteenth century A.D.. in his *Parāśaramādhava.*

Brāhmaṇasarvasva: by Halāyudha, of the twelfth century A.D.—written for King Lakṣmaṇasena of Bengal.

Daśakarmapaddhati: by Paśupati of the twelfth century A.D.

Pitṛdayitā: by Aniruddha of the twelfth century A.D.

Caturvargacintāmaṇi: by Hemādri of the thirteenth century A.D.—a voluminous work.

Dharmaratna: by Jīmūtavāhana of the fourteenth century A.D.—an important work containing the famous *Dāyabhāgā* which dominates the views of Bengal on inheritance.

Dīpakalikā: by Śūlapāṇi of the fourteenth century A.D.—a commentary on the *Yājñavalkyasmṛti.*

Madanapārijāta: by Viśveśvara of the fourteenth century A.D.—a work on religious laws.

Vivādaratnākara, Smṛtiratnākara and other *Ratnākaras*: by Caṇḍeśvara, grand-uncle of Vidyāpati, minister of Harisiṁha of the fourteenth century A.D.—very important law books.

Raghunandanasmṛtis: by Raghunandana of the sixteenth century A.D.—twenty-eight in number—all bearing the appellation of *Tattva*, e.g., *Tithitattva, Udvāhatattva*, etc.—highly authoritative, specially in Bengal.

Vivādacintāmaṇi, Vyavahāracintāmaṇi and other *Cintāmaṇis*: by Vācaspati who wrote for Bhairavasiṁha (Harinārāyaṇa) and Rāmabhadra (Rūpanārāyaṇa) of Mithilā (fifteenth century A.D.)—highly important law books.

Vīramitrodaya: by Mitramiśra of the seventeenth century A.D.—a voluminous work.

Nirṇayasindhu: by Kamalākarabhaṭṭa of the seventeenth century A.D.

REFERENCES

Bühler, G.: SBE Vol. XXV

Kane, P. V.: *History of Dharmaśāstra*

Keith, A. B.: *A History of Sanskrit Literature*

Weber, A.: *The History of Indian Literature*

CHAPTER XVIII

POLITICS

A. INTRODUCTION

Kauṭilya: Artha-śāstra

Kauṭilya's work is an outstanding work in the field of Indian politics and is claimed by some modern scholars to have been composed sometime in the third century A.D., though traditionally the author is believed to have been none other than Cāṇakya or Viṣṇugupta, the able minister of Maurya Candragupta (fourth century B.C.), who has been unanimously recognized by all scholars as the Machiavelli of India. It is, however, a controversial matter as to whether Kauṭilya himself wrote the book in the Maurya age, or it was the production in a late period of any other author or a board of authors belonging to the Kauṭilyān school of political and economic thoughts. The *Arthaśāstra* mentions Bṛhaspati, Bāhudantiputra, Viśālākṣa and Uśanas as authorities and thus exhibits every sign of a long prior development of this science. The book is a perfect manual for the conduct of kings in their political existence. It is divided into fifteen great sections, adhikaraṇas, and 180 sub-divisions, prakaraṇas. The subdivision is crossed by one into chapters, Adhyāyas, which are marked off from the prose of the treatise by the insertion of verses summing up the doctrine expounded before. Later works on this science are mainly based on the *Arthaśāstra*.

It is not true to say that the Vedic Indian occupied himself with religious practices alone and ignored practical life and temporal topics. The *Gṛhyasūtra* of Hiraṇyakeśin and the Mahābhārata recognise Dharma, Artha and Kāma as the three ends of human existence. Doctrines of Artha appear to have found their first expressions in didactic verse. The *Mahābhārata* informs us that Brahmā, the creator was the author of an Arthaśāstra in 100,000 sections, that Śiva as Viśālākṣa reduced it to 10,000, that Indra brought it down to 5,000 and that Bṛhaspati and Uśanas gradually reduced the same to 3,000 and 1,000 sections respectively. The epic itself contains certain sections dealing with polity and scholars have traced the actual use of a formal Arthaśāstra in it.

The discovery, nearly half a century ago, of the *Arthaśāstra* of Kauṭilya, the lost jewel from the treasure-house of Indian political literature, brought a revolution in the study of ancient Indian politico-economic topics. The work was first published in 1909 by the late Dr R. Shamasastry of Mysore and its value may be guessed from the comment of a scholar who described it as 'a library of ancient India'.

Kauṭilya bases his own political theories and discourses on a monarchical form of government, but not an absolute monarchy. All early teachers of political science were of opinion that the king's supreme duty was to contribute to the happiness and welfare of his own people and to maintain peacefully law and order in his own kingdom so that the life and property of his people might be well protected and secured. The king's other higher duty was to remain ever vigilant over the activities of neighbouring rulers of foreign states and ready for launching direct hostility by war, if need be. The above two duties respectively known as *tantra* and *'āvāpa'* have been elaborately treated by Kauṭilya. And one may presume that in the *Arthaśāstra* Kauṭilya probably wanted to state the principles and regulations of state-craft as also laws and ordinances which may be regarded as an ideal for an ambitious king (*vijigīṣu*) who aspires to build an empire under himself as the lord-paramount.

B. MINOR WORKS ON POLITICS

Nītisāra: by Kāmandaka—written in verse with the character of a Kāvya—not later than the eighth century A.D.

Nītivākyāmṛta: by Somadeva, the author of Yaśastilaka—the details of war and kindred topics are meagrely dealt with and the author appears to be a great moral teacher.

Laghu Arhannīti: by the great Jaina writer Hemacandra (A.D. 1088-A.D. 1172)—written in verse—an abbreviation of another bigger work of the author written in Prakrit.

Yuktikalpataru: ascribed to Bhoja.

Nītiratnākara: by Caṇḍeśvara, a jurist—grand-uncle of Vidyāpati.

Śukranīti: of unknown authorship—a work of a very late date, mentioning the use of gunpowder.

REFERENCES

Keith, A. B.: *A History of Sanskrit Literature*
Macdonell, A. A.: *A History of Sanskrit Literature*
Weber, A.: *The History of Indian Literature*

CHAPTER XIX

EROTICS

A. INTRODUCTION

EROTICS or the science of love was specially studied in ancient India. The most outstanding work on the subject is the *Kāmasūtra* of Vātsyāyana who is placed somewhere in the third century A.D. The work is divided into seven parts and is written in prose interspersed with stray verses. The work does not claim to have been the first to be written on that subject. The work is a mine of information on matters relating to the social order and customs of the day.

Vātsyāyana: Kāmasūtra

Yaśodhara of the thirteenth century A.D., wrote a commentary, the *Jayamaṅgalā*, on the *Kāmasūtra* of Vātsyāyana. Credit is due to this commentator who has explained many technical terms used by Vātsyāyana.

Yaśodhara: Jayamaṅgalā

B. MINOR WORKS ON EROTICS

Pañcasāyaka: by Jyotirīśvara, later than Kṣemendra.
Ratirahasya: by Kokkoka—prior to A.D. 1200.
Ratimañjarī: by one Jayadeva of unknown date—sometimes identified with the poet of the *Gītagovinda*.
Anaṅgaraṅga: by Kalyāṇamalla of the sixteenth century A.D.
Ratiśāstra: by Nāgārjuna of unknown date—often wrongly identified with the great Buddhist thinker.

REFERENCE

Keith, A. B.: *A History of Sanskrit Literature*

CHAPTER XX

MEDICINE

A. HISTORY OF MEDICAL WORKS

Introduction

A STUDY of Vedic literature will reveal that Anatomy, Embryology and Hygiene were known to Vedic Indians. The science of Āyurveda was also looked upon as one of the auxiliary sciences to the Vedas. There are references in early literature to ancient sages who delivered instruction on the science of medicine. Ātreya is one of these sages who is usually held to be the founder of the science, and Cāṇakya is said to have written on medicine. According to Buddhist tradition, Jīvaka, a student of Ātreya, was a specialist in the diseases of children.

Caraka

The earliest extant literature on medicine is the *Carakasaṁhitā*. Caraka, according to Professor Lévi, was a contemporary of King Kaniṣka. It is, however, known that the present text of Caraka was revised by one Dṛḍhabala, a Kāshmirian, who lived as late as the eighth or the ninth century A.D.

Suśruta & his commentators

Suśruta is another great teacher of Indian medicine whose name occurs in the famous Bower Manuscript and who is mentioned as the son of Viśvāmitra in the *Mahābhārata*. As early as the ninth and the tenth centuries his reputation travelled far beyond India. Among his commentators, mention must be made of Cakrapāṇidatta (eleventh century A.D.), besides Jaiyyaṭa, Gayadāsa and Ḍallana.

Bhela

Bhela is another authority who is said to have

written a *Saṁhitā* which, in the opinion of some scholars, is earlier than the work of Caraka.

B. LATE MEDICAL WORKS

Aṣṭāṅgasaṁgraha and *Aṣṭāṅgahṛdayasaṁhitā*: by Vāgbhaṭa, the next great authority after Suśruta—often identified with the medical authority referred to by I-tsing.

Rasaratnākara: by Nāgārjuna, probably of the seventh or the eighth century A.D.—containing a section on the practical application of mercury.

Nidāna: by Mādhavakara of the eighth or the ninth century A.D.—an important treatise on Pathology.

Cikitsāsārasaṁgraha: by Cakrapāṇidatta: a work on Therapeutics.

Cikitsākalikā: by Tīsata of the fourteenth century A.D.

Bhāvaprakāśa: by Bhāvamiśra of the sixteenth century A.D.

Vaidyajīvana: by Lolimbarāja of the seventeenth century A.D.

REFERENCES

Keith, A. B.: *A History of Sanskrit Literature*

Macdonell, A. A.: *A History of Sanskrit Literature*

Weber, A.: *The History of Indian Literature*

CHAPTER XXI

ASTRONOMY, MATHEMATICS AND ASTROLOGY

A. HISTORY OF ASTRONOMY

Astronomy: an early science

It is not definitely known whether Astronomy was systematically studied as a science in Vedic times. It is as late as the sixth century A.D. in the *Pañcasiddhāntikā* of Varāhamihira that we get information about the contents of five Siddhāntas of an earlier date. It is, however, a fact that the lunar mansions were known to Vedic Indians. Dr Weber says that the names of some asterisms occur in the *Ṛgveda,* the *Śatapathabrāhmaṇa,* the *Taittirīyasaṁhitā* and the *Atharvaveda.* It is presumed that with the discovery of planets, the science of Astronomy made a significant advance. Planets are mentioned in the *Taittirīyāraṇyaka,* the two Great Epics, and the Law-books of Manu. It still remains an open question, however, whether the ancient Indians discovered the planets independently of others or whether the knowledge came to them from a foreign source. Nevertheless, it cannot be denied that Indian Astronomy thrived well under Greek influence.

B. WORKS ON ASTRONOMY

Āryabhaṭa: his works

Before the discovery of the *Pañcasiddhāntikā,* Āryabhaṭa was regarded as the only authority on Indian Astronomy. Āryabhaṭa wrote towards the close of the fifth century A.D. Three of his works now available to us are the *Āryabhaṭīya*, in ten stanzas, the *Daśagītikāsūtra* and the *Āryāṣṭaśata* in which there is a section on Mathematics.

Āryabhaṭa
Ārya-siddhānta

Āryabhaṭa is to be carefully distinguished from another author of the same name who wrote the *Āryasiddhānta* in the tenth century A.D. and was known to Alberūnī.

Brahma-gupta: his works

Brahmagupta is another great name in Indian Astronomy who in the seventh century A.D. wrote two important works, the *Brahmasphuṭasiddhānta* and the *Khaṇḍakhādyaka*.

Lalla: Śiṣyadhīvṛ-ddhitantra

Lalla who is later than Brahmagupta, has to his credit one work the *Śiṣyadhīvṛddhitantra*.

Bhoja & Śatānanda: their works

To the eleventh century belong two writers Bhoja and Śatānanda whose works are respectively, the *Rājamṛgāṅka* and the *Bhāsvatī*.

Bhāskara: his works

Bhāskarācārya of A.D. 1150 wrote his masterpiece, the *Siddhāntaśiromaṇi*, which is divided into four sections. A second work of his is the *Karaṇakutūhala*.

C. WORKS ON MATHEMATICS

Āryabhaṭa, Brahma-gupta, Mahāvīra & Bhāskara

In the field of Indian Mathematics, there are only a few names. Āryabhata was the first to include in his work a section on Mathematics. Brahmagupta has discussed the principles of ordinary Arithmetic in a brief manner. In the ninth century A.D. Mahāvīrā-cārya wrote an elementary but comprehensive work on Indian Mathematics. In the tenth century A.D. he wrote his *Triśatī* which discusses quadratic equations. It was Bhāskarācārya who in the two sections viz., *Līlāvatī* and *Bījagaṇita* of his work, the *Siddhāntaśiro-*

maṇi, made some lasting contributions to Indian Mathematics.

D. WORKS ON ASTROLOGY

Early works: In India Astrology has been studied as a science from very ancient times. The works of Varāhamihira, of course, eclipsed the fame of earlier authorities whose writings are lost to us. Fragments of one *Vṛddhagargasaṁhitā* are still available. Varāhamihira classified Astrology into the three branches of *Tantra* —the astronomical and mathematical foundations, *Horā*—that dealing with horoscope and *Saṁhitā*—that discussing natural Astrology. The most outstanding contribution of Varāhamihira is the *Bṛhatsaṁhitā* which was commented on by Bhaṭṭotpala. On the *Horā* section Varāhamihira wrote two works, the *Bṛhajjātaka* and the *Laghujātaka*. Besides the works of Varāhamihira, we find a reference to a *Yavanajātaka* of dubious authorship.

Later works Among later works on Astrology, mention may be made of the *Horāśatapañcāśikā* by Pṛthuyaśas, son of Varāhamihira, the *Horāśāstra* by Bhaṭṭotpala, the *Vidyāmādhavīya* (before A.D. 1350 the *Vṛddhavāśiṣṭhasaṁhitā* of unknown authorship, the *Jyotiṣasāroddhāra* of Harṣakīrti, the *Jyotirvidyābharaṇa* of unknown authorship (not later than the sixteenth century A.D.) and the *Tājikā* in two parts (the *Saṁjñātantra* and the *Varṣatantra*) of Nīlakaṇṭha (sixteenth century A.D.).[1]

[1] Closely associated with works on Astrology are treatises on omens and prognostications. Among such treatises are the *Adbhutasāgara* (twelfth century A.D.) and the *Samudratilaka* (twelfth century A.D.) by Durlabharāja and Jagaddeva. The *Ramalarahasya* of Bhayabhañjanaśarman is a work on geomancy and under the style of the *Pāśakakevalī*, preserved in the Bower Manuscript, are the two treatises on cubomancy.

REFERENCES

Keith, A. B.: *A History of Sanskrit Literature*
Macdonell, A. A.: *A History of Sanskrit Literature*
Weber, A.: *The History of Indian Literature*

CHAPTER XXII

MISCELLANEOUS SCIENCES

Archery

It is a pity that though the Indians specialized in almost every branch of Sanskrit literature, the literature on a considerable number of minor sciences is little known to us. Thus there are no extant works on Archery. Among the authoritative writers on Archery the names of Vikramāditya, Sadāśiva and Śārṅgadatta have reached us.

Sciences of elephants & horses

On the sciences of elephants and horses which are associated with the names of two ancient sages Pālakāpya and Śālihotra respectively, a few works are available. The *Hastyāyurveda* of uncertain date and the *Mātaṅgalīlā* of Nārāyaṇa are the two known works on the science of elephants. The *Aśvāyurveda* of Gaṇa, the *Aśvavaidyaka* of Jayadatta and of Dīpaṅkara, the *Yogamañjarī* of Vardhamāna and the *Aśvacikitsā* of Nakula are extant works on the science of horses.

Architecture

The literature on Architecture is represented by the *Vāstuvidyā*, the *Manuṣyālayacandrikā* in seven chapters, the *Mayamata* in thirty-four chapters, the *Yuktikalpataru* in twenty-three chapters, the *Samarāṅgaṇasūtradhāra* of Bhoja, the *Viśvakarmaprakāśa* and some sections of the *Bṛhatsaṁhitā*, the *Matsyapurāṇa*, the *Agnipurāṇa*, the *Garuḍapurāṇa*, the *Viṣṇudharmottara*, the *Kāśyapasaṁhitā*, the *Śilparatna* of Śrīkumāra and such other works.

Science of Jewels

The science of jewels has been discussed in such works as the *Agastimata*, the *Ratnaparīkṣā* of Buddhabhaṭṭa and the *Navaratnaparīkṣā* of Nārāyaṇapaṇḍita.

Mention may be made of the *Ṣaṇmukhakalpa,* a treatise on the science of stealing. Science of Stealing

Mention should also be made of the *Nalapāka* which treats of the art of cooking. Science of Cooking

On music there have been many important works besides the *Nāṭyaśāstra.* Among the more important works on this subject, mention may be made of the *Saṅgītamakaranda,* the *Saṅgītasudarśana* of Sudarśana, the *Saṅgītaratnākara* of Śārṅgadeva, the *Saṅgītadarpaṇa* of Dāmodara and the *Rāgavibodha* of Somanātha. Science of Music

On dancing the literature is not very extensive. Besides the *Nāṭyaśāstra,* we have the *Abhinayadarpaṇa* of Nandikeśvara, the *Śrīhastamuktāvalī,* the *Nartananirṇaya* and a few other works. Science of Dancing

On painting the *Viṣṇudharmottara,* of uncertain date, contains a chapter. Science of Painting

REFERENCES

Keith, A. B.: *A History of Sanskrit Literature*
Weber, A.: *The History of Indian Literature*

CHAPTER XXIII

PHILOSOPHY

A. ORTHODOX SYSTEMS

I
Nyāya

Introduction

THE Nyāya system which represents the analytic type of philosophy like the Vaiśeṣika system, has a long history that extends over the vast period of twenty centuries. Indian tradition has assigned a unique status to this system and it has been universally held in high esteem and reverence.

Works on Nyāya: (a) Old school

There are two well-known schools of the Nyāya systems, the old and the new. The earliest known literature of the old school is the *Nyāyasūtras* of Gautama which are divided into five books. It is believed that the *Nyāyasūtras* are as old as the third century B.C.[1] Vātsyāyana's *Nyāyabhāṣya* is the most important commentary on the *Nyāyasūtras* of Gautama and it is presumed that the work was written before A.D. 400. Vātsyāyana's views were vehemently criticized by Diṅnāga, the famous Buddhist logician,

[1] Dr S. C. Vidyābhūṣaṇa believes that Gautama wrote only the first chapter of the work, and was a contemporary of Buddha. He further thinks that this Gautama is the same as the author of the *Dharmasūtras* who lived in Mithilā in the sixth century B.C. He suggests that Gautama's original views are contained in the *Carakasaṁhitā* (*Vimānasthāna*). But the *Carakasaṁhitā* itself has suffered considerable refashioning and its date is uncertain. Professor Jacobi believes that the *Nyāyasūtras* and the *Nyāyabhāṣya* belong to about the same time perhaps separated by a generation. He places them between the second century A.D. when the doctrine of Śūnya developed, and the fifth century A.D. when the doctrine of Vijñāna was systematized. Professor Suali also supports Professor Jacobi and refers the work to A.D. 300. According to Professor Garbe the date is A.D. 100. MM. Haraprasāda Śāstrin believes that the work has undergone several redactions. Professor Radhakrishnan places it (though not in the present form) in the fourth century B.C.

whose probable date is not later than the fifth century A.D. Uddyotakara wrote his *Nyāyavārttika* in the sixth century A.D. with the sole object of defending Vātsyāyana against the criticisms of Diṅnāga. It was Dharmakīrti, another noted Buddhist logician, who took up the cause of Diṅnāga and wrote his *Nyāyabindu* in the latter part of the sixth century A.D. Probably Uddyotakara and Dharmakīrti were contemporaries who mutually referred to each other. A commentary on the *Nyāyabindu* was written in the ninth century by the Buddhist logician Dharmottara. It was in the first half of the ninth century A.D. that Vācaspati, a versatile genius and most prolific writer, came to write his *Nyāyavārttikatātparyaṭīkā*, a super-commentary on the *Nyāyavārttika* of Uddyotakara and gave a sufficient stimulus to the orthodox line of thought by writing his *Nyāyasūcīnibandha* (A.D. 841) and *Nyāyasūtroddhāra*. Udayana who is noted for his trenchant logic and convincing presentation of facts, wrote a commentary on Vācaspati's *Nyāyavārttikatātparyaṭīkā*, known as the *Nyāyavārttikatātparyapariśuddhi* in the last part of the tenth century (A.D. 984). The *Nyāyakusumāñjali*, the *Ātmatattvaviveka*, the *Kiraṇāvalī* and the *Nyāyapariśiṣṭa* are four other well-known works of Udayana. Jayanta is another great name of this school and he wrote the *Nyāyamañjarī* in the tenth century A.D. He is admitted to have been a Bengali by origin. Bhāsarvajña's *Nyāyasāra* is a survey of Indian logic. The author was a Kāshmir Saivite of the tenth century A.D.

Works of Nyāya: (b) New school

Gaṅgeśa is the father of the new school of the Nyāya system (Navyanyāya) which flourished mainly in Bengal. His *Tattvacintāmaṇi* is a *magnum opus* which was written in the last quarter of the twelfth century A.D. The work discusses primarily the four means of knowledge admitted in the Nyāya system. His son Vardhamāna (A.D. 1225) continued the tradition by writing commentaries on the treatises of Udayana and Vallabha. Jayadeva (sometimes identified with Pakṣadhara Miśra) of Mithilā wrote his *Āloka* on the *Tattavacintāmaṇi* in the latter part of the thirteenth century A.D. Vāsudeva Sārvabhauma, a Bengali Brāhmaṇa, wrote his *Tattvacintāmaṇivyākhyā*—the first great work of the Navadvīpa (Nadia) school. He had at least three distinguished pupils: Śrī-Caitanya Mahāprabhu, the famous Vaiṣṇava saint and founder of the Gauḍīya Vaiṣṇava school, Raghunātha Śiromaṇi, the great logician and Kṛṣṇānanda Āgamavāgīśa, the author of the *Tantrasāra*. Raghunātha wrote two outstanding works, viz., the *Dīdhīti* and the *Padārthakhaṇḍana* in the fifteenth century A.D. Jagadīśa (end of the sixteenth century A.D.) and Gadādhara (seventeenth century A.D.) are reputed thinkers of the modern school, who wrote beside many commentaries, the *Śabdaśaktiprakāśikā* and the *Vyāptipañcaka* respectively. Viśvanātha's *Nyāyasūtravṛtti* (A.D. 1634) is another important work.

Fundamental concepts of Nyāya

The logicians of the old school recognize sixteen categories while those of the modern school who have been greatly influenced by the Vaiśeṣika system, reduce them to seven only. The logicians of both schools accept four means of proof, viz., perception (*pratyakṣa*), inference (*anumāna*), analogy (*upamāna*) and verbal testimony (*śabda*). They do not admit the self-manifestation of a cognition. Like the Vaiśeṣika, the Nyāya regards the world as a composite of external, unchangeable and causeless atoms. The soul in the Nyāya system is a 'real substantive being' which has certain qualities. The God (Īśvara) is the Supreme Spirit or the Universal Soul who acts as the Creator of the universe in the capacity of an efficient cause (*nimittakāraṇa*), while the atoms are the material cause (*upādānakāraṇa*). A true knowledge (*tattvajñāna*) of the categories leads to the liberation (*mukti*) of the soul in bondage, and the liberated soul is essentially conscious.

II Vaiśeṣika

Introduction

The Vaiśeṣika system which is also called the Aulukya philosophy, is closely akin to the Nyāya system. It is, however, presumed that the earliest extant literature of this system is older than what is available in the Nyāya system. Thus while the *Vaiśeṣikasūtras* of Kaṇāda (Kaṇabhakṣa, Kaṇabhuk or Kāśyapa) and the *Padārthadharmasaṁgraha* of Praśastapāda, evince no influence of the Nyāya system, the *Nyāyasūtras* of Gautama and the *Bhāṣya* of Vātsyāyana betray the fact that they have been greatly influenced by the views of the Vaiśeṣika system.

Works on Vaiśeṣika

The *Vaiśeṣikasūtras* of Kaṇāda which are of unknown date but are generally considered to be later than 300 B.C., received additions from time to time. They are divided into *ten* books. The work of Praśastapāda which is generally regarded as a commentary on the *Vaiśeṣikasūtras* may be viewed as an original contribution to the Vaiśeṣika system. Praśastapāda is usually assigned to the end of the fourth century A.D., though Dr Keith makes him later than Diṅnāga, but earlier than Uddyotakara. There are four noted commentaries on the work of Praśastapāda and they are (1) the *Vyomavatī* by Vyomaśivācārya alias

Vyomaśekhara or Śivāditya (of unknown date, probably of the ninth century A.D.), (2) the *Nyāyakandalī* by Śrīdhara (last part of the tenth century A.D.), (3) the *Kiraṇāvalī* and the *Lakṣaṇāvalī* by Udayana (last part of the tenth century A.D.) and (4) the *Nyāyalīlāvatī* by Śrīvatsa or Vallabha (probably towards the end of the tenth or the beginning of the eleventh century A.D.). Śaṅkara's *Upaskāra* (latter half of the fifteenth century A.D.) is one important commentary on the *Vaiśeṣikasūtras* of Kaṇāda. Laugākṣi Bhāskara's *Tarkakaumudī* is another work based on Praśastapāda's treatise.

Manuals of Nyāya & Vaiśeṣika

Among manuals belonging to both Nyāya and Vaiśeṣika systems of Indian philosophy, may be mentioned Śivāditya's *Saptapadārthī* (eleventh century A.D.), Varadarāja's *Tārkikarakṣā*, Keśavamiśra's *Tarkabhāṣā* (thirteenth or fourteenth century A.D.), Annambhaṭṭa's *Tarkasaṁgraha* and *Dīpikā* (sixteenth or seventeenth century A.D.), Jagadīśa's *Tarkāmṛta* (A.D. 1635) and Viśvanātha's *Bhāṣāpariccheda* or *Kārikāvalī* (seventeenth century A.D.) and its famous commentary *Siddhāntamuktāvalī* by himself. Jayanārāyaṇa's (seventeenth century A.D.) *Vivṛti* is another important compendium of the Vaiśeṣika school.

Fundamental concepts of Vaiśeṣika

The Vaiśeṣika system which in broader details agrees with the Nyāya, accepts six categories to which a seventh was added later on. It recognizes only two means of knowledge, viz.. perception and inference. It does not accept verbal testimony as an independent means of proof, but as one included in inference. Both the Vaiśeṣika and the Naiyāyika are advocates of what is known in philosophical terms as Asatkāryavāda (the doctrine of the creation of the non-existent effect) and Ārambhavāda (the doctrine of initiation which makes the universe an effect newly produced from the eternal atoms). In the state of liberation, the soul in Vaiśeṣika conception retains no consciousness (*jñāna*), while in the Nyāya view the released soul is conscious.

III
Sāṅkhya

Introduction

The Sāṅkhya system is universally believed to be the oldest of the existing systems of Indian philosophy. The Sāṅkhya views are found in the Upaniṣads, in the *Mahābhārata*, in the law-books of Manu and in the medical works of Caraka and others. Indian tradition ascribes the authorship of the system to the sage Kapila, an incarnation of Lord Viṣṇu. The successors of Kapila were Āsuri, Pañcaśikha, Gārgya and Ulūka. Professor Garbe makes Pañcaśikha a contemporary of the great Mīmāṁsist Śabarasvāmin (sometime between A.D. 100 and A.D. 300). Chinese tradition ascribes the authorship of the *Ṣaṣṭhītantra* to Pañcaśikha, while Vārṣagaṇya gets the same credit in others' opinion.

Works on Sāṅkhya

The *Sāṅkhyakārikā* is the earliest known work of the Sāṅkhya system. It is believed that Īśvarakṛṣṇa wrote this work in the third century A.D.[1] An important commentary on the *Kārikā* is that of Gauḍapāda.[2] The *Māṭharavṛtti* is another commentary which is regarded by some as the source of Gauḍa-

[1] A Chinese tradition ascribes to Vindhyavāsin the writing of a work of Vārṣagaṇya. Professor Takakusu identifies Vindhyavāsin with Īśvarakṛṣṇa. In that case the *Kārikā* of Īśvarakṛṣṇa has an earlier basis. Guṇaratna, however, regards Vindhyavāsin and Īśvarakṛṣṇa as different. Īśvarakṛṣṇa was earlier than Vasubandhu who is now assigned to the fourth century A.D. The *Kārikā* was translated into Chinese by Paramārtha (sixth century A.D.).

[2] Whether he is the same as the author of the *Māṇḍūkyakārikā* cannot be decided, and some seek to place him in the eighth century A.D.

pāda's commentary while others assign a later date to it. Yet another commentary on the *Sāṅkhya-kārikā* is the *Yuktidīpikā* which is wrongly ascribed to Vācaspati. The *Sāṅkhyatattvakaumudī* of Vācaspati (middle of the ninth century A.D.) is a most popular work of this system. Another popular work is the *Sāṅkhyapravacanasūtra* which contains six chapters. The authorship of this work is attributed to one Kapila. But this Kapila cannot be identical with the founder sage of this system, for the work cannot but be assigned to such a late date as the fourteenth century A.D., since it is not referred to even in the *Sarvadarśanasaṁgraha* of Mādhava (fourteenth century A.D.). Aniruddha's *Sāṅkhyasūtra-vṛtti*, which was composed in the fifteenth century A.D., is an important work commenting on the *Sāṅkhya-pravacanasūtra*. But the *Sāṅkhyapravacanabhāṣya* of Vijñānabhikṣu, (sixteenth century A.D.) a commentary on the *Sāṅkhyapravacanasūtra*, is the most important work of the system. Vijñāṇabhikṣu wrote another work on Sāṅkhya known as the *Sāṅkhyasāra*.

Fundamental concepts of Sāṅkhya

The Sāṅkhya system is essentially dualistic, inasmuch as it speaks of Puruṣa (Spirit) and Prakṛti (Matter) as the two Ultimate Realities. The fundamental position of this system is that 'cause' is the entity in which 'effect' lies in a subtle form. Thus this system advocates the doctrine of Satkāryavāda. The world is said to be the evolution of Prakṛti which is its material cause. Prakṛti has been described to be of the nature of equilibrium of the triple Guṇas, *sattva* (purity-stuff), *rajas* (passion-stuff) and *tamas* (inertia-stuff). Puruṣa is defined as Pure Spirit which is different from Prakṛti and Puruṣas are many in number. A Supreme Spirit (Īśvara) or God is not admitted to exist in so many words. The Sāṅkhya system acknowledges the authority of three means of knowledge, viz., perception, inference and verbal testimony.

IV Yoga

Introduction

The Yoga and the Sāṅkhya systems are used as complementary aspects of one whole system. While the Sāṅkhya system signifies 'theory', the Yoga signifies 'practice'. In the Upaniṣads, the *Mahābhārata*, the Jaina and the Buddhist literatures, Yoga practices have been mentioned.

Works on Yoga

The *Yogasūtras* of Patañjali[1] form the earliest extant literature on the Yoga system. The *Yogasūtras* are divided into four chapters known as *samādhi* (concentration), *sādhana* (practice), *vibhūti* (miraculous powers) and *kaivalya* (emancipation). It is Vyāṣa who, according to modern scholars, is said to have written a masterly commentary on the *Yogasūtras* about the fourth century A.D., though traditionally he is believed to be the same as the author of the *Mahābhārata*. Vācaspati wrote an interesting and learned gloss on the *Vyāsabhāṣya* known as the *Tattvavaiśāradī*. Nāgeśabhaṭṭa of the eighteenth century A.D., wrote another gloss on the *Vyāsabhāṣya* known as the *Chāyā*. Other important works on the Yoga system are the *Rājamārtaṇḍa* of Bhoja (eleventh century A.D.) and the *Yogavārttika* and the *Yogasārasaṁgraha* of Vijñānabhikṣu (sixteenth century A.D.). Vijñānabhikṣu criticizes Vācaspati and brings the Yoga system nearer to the philosophy of the Upaniṣads.

[1] It is traditionally believed that Patañjali, the author of the *Yogasūtras* is the same person as the great grammarian of that name who wrote the *Mahābhāṣya* in the middle of the second century B.C. But there is no positive evidence to prove the identity and some modern

Rājayoga & Haṭhayoga

The Yoga system discusses how through methodical effort of concentration of mind we can attain perfection. It teaches us how to control the different elements of human nature both physical and psychical. The Yoga system explains fully the principles according to which 'the physical body, the active will and the understanding mind are to be harmonically brought under control'. This is technically known by the name Royal Yoga (Rājayoga). There is yet a physical side of Yoga (Haṭhayoga) which describes how to control the body in various ways. Too much indulgence in this Haṭhayoga serves as an obstacle to the attainment of real Perfection.

Yoga & Sāṅkhya: comparison

The Yoga system materially differs from the Sāṅkhya at least in one essential point, viz., that while the latter system does not explicitly say anything of God, the former regards God as a third category besides Prakṛti and Puruṣa and holds that devotion to the Lord is also one of the means of Release (*Kaivalya*).

V Purvamīmāṁsā

The Pūrvamīmāṁsā, Karmamīmāṁsā or Mīmāṁsā system mainly interprets and explains Vedic injunctions and their applications, and thus has a unique importance of its own.

Works on Purvamīmāṁsā

The earliest literature on the Pūrvamīmāṁsā is the *Pūrvamīmāṁsāsūtras* of Jaimini who, according to modern scholars, wrote in all probability in the fourth century B.C. The orthodox tradition, however, makes Jaimini a disciple of Vyāsa, the author of the *Mahābhārata*. It is held by some that the *Mīmāṁsāsūtras* are later than both the *Nyāyasūtras* and the *Yoga-*

scholars are positively against this view. Bhoja in the introductory verses of the *Rājamārtaṇḍa* makes a suggestion to the effect that Patañjali (author of the *Mahābhāṣya*), Patañjali (author of the *Yogasūtras*), and Caraka (author of the *Carakasaṁhitā*) are identical.

sūtras. Śabara wrote his commentary on the *Mīmāṁsā-sūtras* probably in the first century B.C. Professor Jacobi thinks that the *Vṛtti* quoted by Śabara, belongs to a period between A.D. 200 and A.D. 500, while Dr Keith holds A.D. 400 to be the earlier date for it. Śabara's predecessors were Upavarṣa, Bodhāyana, Bhartṛmitra, Bhavadāsa and Hari. MM Ganganath Jha identifies Bhavadāsa with the Vṛttikāra referred to in the *Śābarabhāṣya*. Both the *Mīmāṁsāsūtras* and the *Bhāṣya* were interpreted differently by three different schools of thought associated with the names of Prabhākara, Kumārila and Murāri. The school of Murāri is known by name alone.

Prābhākara school

Prabhākara who was called 'Gauḍamīmāṁsaka' and 'Guru' wrote the *Bṛhatī* a commentary on the *Bhāṣya* of Śabara, probably about A.D. 600. According to some, Prabhākara preceded Kumārila, but tradition runs that he was a pupil of Kumārila. Śālikanātha's *Ṛjuvimalā* which is a commentary on the *Bṛhatī*, was written about the ninth century A.D. Another important work of the same author is the *Prakaraṇapañcikā*, a good and useful manual of the Prābhākara system. Śālikanātha has referred to Dharmakīrti. Bhavanātha's *Nayaviveka* (*c*. A.D. 1050-A.D. 1150) is another important work of this school. Vācaspati in his *Nyāyakaṇikā* differentiates between two sub-schools of the Prābhākaras, viz., old and new.

Bhāṭṭa school

Kumārila is a great name in Indian philosophy, noted for his spirited zeal for Brāhmaṇical orthodoxy. It was he who fought courageously against the onslaughts of Buddhism, and but for the stand he took up, much of Brāhmaṇical heritage of which we feel proud today, would have been lost. Kumārila's *Ślokavārttika, Tantravārttika* and *Ṭupṭīkā* are the three great works. The first, which is in verse, is a commentary on the first part of the first chapter of the *Mīmāṁsāsūtras*. The second, which is in prose occasionally interspersed with verses, takes us to the end of the third chapter, and the third covers the rest. Kumārila is earlier than Śaṅkara and is usually assigned to A.D. 750, though some new data point to the fact that he lived in the seventh century A.D. The *Ślokavārttika* was commented upon by Umbeka or Bhavabhūti (eighth century A.D.), by Sucaritamiśra (not later than the middle of the thirteenth century A.D.) in his *Kāśikā* and by Pārthasārathimiśra (according to the orthodox tradition, tenth century A.D. ; according to Professor Radhakrishnan, A.D. 1300) in his *Nyāyaratnākara*. The *Tantravārttika* was commented upon by Bhavadevabhaṭṭa (eleventh century A.D.) in his *Tautātitamatatilaka* and by Someśvarabhaṭṭa (*c.* A.D. 1200) in his *Nyāyasudhā*. Veṅkaṭadīkṣita wrote his commentary on the *Ṭupṭīkā* known as the *Vārttikābharaṇa*. Maṇḍana (eighth century A.D.) is the next great name after Kumārila who is reported to be Maṇḍana's teacher and father-in-law. Maṇḍana who is earlier than Vācaspati and is traditionally identified with Sureśvara and Viśvarūpa, wrote his *Vidhiviveka, Bhāvanāviveka, Vibhramaviveka* and *Mīmāṁsānukramaṇī*.[1] The first was commented upon by Vācaspati in his *Nyāyakaṇikā*.

Independent works on Mīmāṁsā

Among independent works on the Mīmāṁsā system, may be mentioned the *Śāstradīpikā* of Pārthasārathimiśra, the *Jaiminīyanyāyamālā* of Mādhava

[1] The *Sphoṭasiddhi* of Maṇḍana which explains the grammarian's doctrine of Sphoṭa is an important work.

(fourteenth century A.D.), the *Upakramaparākrama* and the *Vidhirasāyana* of Appayyadīkṣita, the *Mīmāṁsā-nyāyaprakāśa* of Āpodeva (seventeenth century A.D.), the *Arthasaṁgraha* of Laugākṣibhāskara (seventeenth century A.D.), the *Bhāṭṭadīpikā*, the *Mīmāṁsākaustubha* and the *Bhāṭṭarahasya* of Khaṇḍadeva (seventeenth century A.D.), the *Bhāṭṭacintāmaṇi* of Gāgābhaṭṭa (seventeenth century A.D.), the *Mānameyodaya* of Nārāyaṇabhaṭṭa (seventeenth century A.D.) and the *Mīmāṁsa-paribhāṣā* of Kṛṇṣayajvan (eighteenth century A.D.). Rāmakṛṣṇabhaṭṭa, author of the *Yuktiṣnehaprapūraṇī*, Somanātha, author of the *Mayūkhamālikā*, Dinakarabhaṭṭa and Kamalākarabhaṭṭa belong to the Bhāṭṭa school.

Important concepts of Mīmāṁsā

The Pūrvamīmāṁsā system recognizes the self-validity of knowledge. Jaimini accepts only three means of knowledge—perception, inference and verbal testimony. To these three Prabhākara adds two more, viz., comparison (*upamāna*) and implication (*arthāpatti*). Kumārila also recognizes non-apprehension (*anupalabdhi*) as a means of knowledge. It is generally believed that the Pūrvamīmāṁsā has not accorded any significant status to God, though, in the *Vedāntasūtras*, Jaimini has been represented as theistic in views.[1]

VI Vedānta

Introduction

The Uttaramīmāṁsā, Brahmamīmāṁsā or the Vedānta is the most popular of all orthodox systems of Indian philosophy. The earliest teachers of the school were Āśmarathya, Bādari, Kārṣṇājini, Kāśakṛtsna, Auḍulomi and Ātreya. These teachers along with Jaimini are mentioned in the *Vedāntasūtras*.

[1] *Introduction to the Pūrvamīmāṁsā*, Dr Pashupatinath Shastri, pp. 132-8.

Scholars differ with regard to the age when the *Vedāntasūtras* or the *Brahmasūtras* of Bādarāyaṇa were composed. Modern Indian scholars are inclined to assign as early a date as the sixth century B.C. while others would prefer to fix the date between 400 B.C. and A.D. 200[1].

The Vedāntasūtras

The *Vedāntasūtras* contain four chapters. The first discusses the Brahman as the Ultimate Reality. The second deals with objections raised by rival schools of philosophy. The third proposes to study the means of attaining Brahmavidyā, while the fourth discusses the results of Brahmavidyā. The *Vedāntasūtras* are in intimate agreement with the teachings of the Upaniṣads. Thus Bādarāyaṇa has evinced his great and abiding reverence for the Vedas. Unlike the Sāṅkhya, the Vedānta of Bādarāyaṇa champions the cause of monism when he holds that it is the One Brahman which is the Transcendent Reality. Bādarāyaṇa openly refutes the Sāṅkhya doctrine which conceives Puruṣa and Prakṛti as two independent entities. The conception of māyā as the illusory principle which shuts out the vision of the Brahman and reflects It as many, is a great contribution to the philosophical thought of the world. The world exists so long as the vision of the Brahman does not dawn upon us. While the Sāṅkhya maintains that the world is an evolution (*pariṇāma*) of Prakṛti, the Vedānta holds

[1] The orthodox Indian tradition makes the author identical with Vyāsa, the author of the *Mahābhārata*. Śaṅkarācārya, however, does not clearly state anywhere that Vyāsa (or, Kṛṣṇadvaipāyana born as an incarnation of the Vedic sage Apāntaratamas by the direction of Lord Viṣṇu) was the author of the *Brahmasūtras*. He invariably calls this author Bādarāyaṇa and never Vyāsa and does not explicitly say that the two are identical. But Vācaspati, Ānandagiri, Rāmānuja, Mādhava, Vallabha and Baladeva identify Bādarāyaṇa with Vyāsa.

that the world is an appearance (*vivarta*) of the Brahman.

Among the early teachers of Vedānta mention must be made of Gauḍapāda who in his famous *Kārikās* has attempted a systematic treatment of the monistic Vedānta. Another important author is Bhartṛhari (probably belonging to the first part of the seventh century A.D.) who is said to have written a commentary on the *Brahmasūtras*. Yet another author hinted at by Śaṅkara is Bhartṛprapañca, according to whom the Brahman is at once one and dual. Besides him Śaṅkara speaks of one Vrttikāra, who remains even now unidentified.[1]

Early teachers of Vedānta

The greatest of all thinkers on monistic Vedānta is Śaṅkara who, according to Professor Max Müller and other modern scholars, wrote his immortal *Śārīrakabhāṣya* between A.D. 788-A.D. 820. The orthodox tradition, however, assigns him to the latter half of the seventh century (A.D. 686-A.D. 720). Besides the philosophical insight which marks his writings his style and diction have always lent a unique distinction to them. Śaṅkara has written commentaries on the ten major Upaniṣads and his commentary on the *Bṛhadāraṇyakopaniṣad* has, in particular, attracted the attention of many an able thinker. Śaṅkara's expositions have earned for him such distinction that by the expression Vedānta we seem invariably to understand his views on it.

Śaṅkara: age & works

The *Śārīrakabhāṣya* was commented upon by *two* schools of thought known as the Vivaraṇa school

Vivaraṇa school

[1] Whether he is the same as Upavarṣa, a brother of Varṣa, the teacher of Pāṇini, or Bodhāyana, or whether the two sages are identical, or whether there was a third author who passed as Vṛttikāra, cannot be definitely ascertained.

and the Bhāmatī school. The original source of the former school is found in the *Pañcapādikā* of Padmapāda who is said to have composed the commentary on the first five quarters (pādas) of the *Brahmasūtraśārīrakabhāṣya* of which only the commentary on the first four Sūtras are now available. The age of Padmapāda is about the end of the seventh and the beginning of the eighth century A.D., as he is represented as the senior-most disciple of Śaṅkara. The *Vivaraṇa* which is a gloss on the *Pañcapādikā*, was composed by Prakāśātman (probably ninth century A.D. ; 1200 A.D. according to Professor Radhakrishnan). According to him the Brahman is both the content (*viṣaya*) and the locus (*āśraya*) of Māyā. Vidyāraṇya who is generally identified with Mādhava (fourteenth century A.D.), wrote a summary on the Vivaraṇa known as the *Vivaraṇaprameyasaṁgraha*.

Bhāmatī school

The Bhāmatī school has been well represented in the *Bhāmatī* of Vācaspati, the *Kalpataru* and the *Śāstradarpaṇa* of Amalānanda (thirteenth century A.D.) and the Parimala of Appayyadīkṣita (sixteenth—seventeenth century A.D.).

Works on Monistic Vedānta

The literature on monistic Vedānta, as interpreted by Śaṅkara, is extremely rich. Sureśvara (who is traditionally identified with Maṇḍana who later became a disciple of Śaṅkara), wrote his *Taittirīyopaniṣadbhāṣyavārttika*, *Bṛhadāraṇyakabhāṣyavārttika* and *Naiṣkarmyasiddhi* about the end of the seventh or the beginning of the eighth century A.D.[1] Maṇḍana's *Brahmasiddhi* is an outstanding work in which he puts forward many original ideas. The *Saṁkṣepaśārīraka*

[1] Some would rather place him in the first half of the ninth century A.D.

was written in verse by Sarvajñātmamuni in the ninth century A.D. The *Iṣṭasiddhi* of Avimuktātman (or Vimuktātman) is another notable work of the school. In A.D. 1190 Śrī-Harṣa who is noted for his trenchant logic and Advaita polemics, composed his *Khaṇḍana-khaṇḍakhādya*—a masterly contribution. In the thirteenth century A.D. Citsukha wrote on the same lines his *Pratyaktattvapradīpikā* or *Citsukhī*. In the fourteenth century A.D. Vidyāraṇya wrote his *Pañcadaśī*, a highly popular work in verse, and the *Jīvanmukti-viveka*, a work of considerable importance. Vidyāraṇya and his teacher Bhāratītīrtha jointly wrote the *Vaiyāsikanyāyamālā*. The *Vedāntasāra* of Sadānanda, is a good manual of monistic Vedānta. It was composed in the fifteenth century A.D. Another epistemological manual on monistic Vedānta is the *Vedāntaparibhāṣā* which was composed by Dharmarājādhvarīndra in the sixteenth century A.D. His son Rāmakṛṣṇa (sixteenth-seventeenth century A.D.) wrote the commentary *Śikhāmaṇi* on it. Ānandagiri's *Nyāyanirṇaya* (fourteenth century A.D.) and Govindānanda's *Ratnaprabhā* (fifteenth century A.D.) are two other commentaries on Śaṅkara's *Brahmasūtrabhāṣya*. Prakāśānanda's *Siddhāntamuktāvalī* (fifteenth century A.D.) and Appayyadīkṣita's *Nyāyarakṣāmaṇi* and *Siddhāntaleśasaṁgraha* are other valuable manuals of the monistic school. Madhusūdana Sarasvatī, a Bengali of the sixteenth century A.D., wrote his monumental work the *Advaitasiddhi* which contains an intricate and abstruse criticism of the rival school of Madhva as represented in the *Nyāyāmṛta* of Vyāsatīrtha or Vyāsarāja (last part of the fifteenth century A.D.). The *Gauḍabrahmānandī* or *Laghucandrikā* of

Brahmānanda, is a defence of the *Advaitasiddhi* against the criticism of Rāmācārya (alias Rāmatīrtha or Vyāsarāma) in his *Taraṅgiṇī* (latter part of the sixteenth century A.D.).

The *Brahmasūtras* of Bādarāyaṇa have been differently interpreted by a number of great thinkers of different schools, all of whom wrote after Śaṅkara. One such thinker was Bhāskara who wrote his *Bhāṣya* sometime about the end of the eighth or the first part of the ninth century A.D. Bhāskara was a champion of the doctrine of simultaneous identity and difference (Bhedābhedavāda).

School of Vedānta: (i) Bhāskara

Rāmānuja is another great commentator on the *Brahmasūtras* who is assigned to the eleventh century A.D. His philosophy is based on the doctrine of qualified monism (Viśiṣṭādvaitavāda) according to which God is the one Reality, but is a composite of the conscious individual selves and the non-conscious material world. Rāmānuja's chief sources of inspiration were the Tāmil Gāthās of the Āḷvāras or Vaiṣṇava saints of South India, the chief of them being Nāthamani and Yāmunācārya (tenth century A.D.). The name of his commentary is the *Śrībhāṣya*. The *Śrutaprakāśikā* of Sudarśana (thirteenth century A.D.) is a well-known gloss on the *Śrībhāṣya*. Veṅkaṭanātha Vedāntadeśika (thirteenth century A.D.) was perhaps the greatest successor of Rāmānuja. He was the author of the *Śatadūṣaṇī*, the *Tattvaṭīkā* (a commentary on the *Śrībhāṣya*) and the *Seśvaramīmāṁsā*.

(ii) Rāmānuja

Nimbārka is another commentator on the *Brahmasūtras*. His commentary is called the *Vedāntapārijātasaurabha*. He advocates the doctrine of dualistic non-dualism (Dvaitādvaitavāda) which is somewhat

(iii) Nimbārka

akin to the view of Bhāskara with but minor technical differences. Nimbārka lived about the eleventh century A.D. His disciple Śrīnivāsācārya wrote a commentary known as the *Vedāntakaustubha*. Keśavakāśmīrin, a follower of this school (fifteenth century A.D.), wrote a commentary on the *Gītā* known as the *Tattvaprakāśikā*.

(iv) Madhva

Another commentator on the *Brahmasūtras* is Madhva who was born in A.D. 1199. Besides the commentary he wrote, he justified his interpretation in another work called the *Aṇuvyākhyāna*. He advocates the theory of pure dualism (Dvaitavāda).

Yet another commentator is Vallabha who lived in the last part of the fifteenth century and the first part of the sixteenth century A.D. His commentary is called the *Aṇubhāṣya*. The theory he advocates is pure non-dualism (Śuddhādvaitavāda). He looks upon the world as a reality which is in its subtlest form the Brahman.

(v) Gauḍīya

Last, though not the least, is the school of the Gauḍīya Vaiṣṇavas who advocate the doctrine of inscrutable identity and difference (Acintyabhedābhedavāda). Though they call themselves a branch of the Mādhva school yet in views they are more akin to the school of Nimbārka and sometimes follow Śaṅkara also. The school traces its origin to the teachings of Śrī-Kṛṣṇa-Caitanya who flourished in Bengal in the sixteenth century A.D. In the Gauḍīya Vaiṣṇava school, Rūpagosvāmin, a contemporary and disciple of Śrī-Caitanya, was a versatile scholar who wrote many works on drama, rhetoric and philosophy. His *Vaiṣṇavatoṣiṇī*, a commentary on the tenth chapter of the *Bhāgavata*, is an important contribution to the literature of the Gauḍīya Vaiṣṇavas. His nephew and disciple Jīvagosvāmin was also a great scholar and prolific writer. His six *Sandarbhas* (*Kramasandarbha, Tattvasandarbha, Bhaktisandarbha,* etc.,) and the *Sarvasaṁvādinī* are outstanding works on Gauḍīya Vaiṣṇava philosophy. Baladeva Vidyābhūṣaṇa (eighteenth century A.D.) wrote the *Govindabhāṣya,* the commentary on the *Brahmasūtras,* according to the Gauḍīya Vaiṣṇava point of view. His *Prameyaratnāvalī* is also a popular work.

B. HETERODOX SYSTEMS

I
Buddhism

Introduction

The Buddhists are the followers of Gotama Buddha who preached his doctrines in the language of the people sometime in the sixth and fifth centuries B.C. The Buddhist Canonical literature or the *Tipiṭaka* which was written in Pāli, has three divisions: (1) the *Vinayapiṭaka,* (2) the *Suttapiṭaka* and (3) the *Abhidhammapiṭaka.* Besides the Canonical works, the Buddhist literature is rich in non-Canonical works which were also written in Pāli. It must be mentioned here that Buddhist literature has a still wider scope and includes a fairly long list of Sanskrit works, an account of which has already been set forth in a previous chapter.[1]

Four schools of Buddhism

The Buddhist philosophers are broadly divided into four schools—the Sautrāntikas, the Vaibhāṣikas, the Mādhyamikas and the Yogācāras. Like Jainism, Buddhism also does not accept the authority of the Vedas. The Buddhists acknowledge only two means of knowledge—perception and inference. Though

[1] Chap. V, pp. 51-75.

there are sharp lines of difference among the four schools referred to above, they are unanimous in their attitude against Brāhmaṇic culture. I-tsing, the Chinese traveller, says—Those who worship the Bodhisattvas and read the Mahāyānasūtras are the Mahāyānists and those who do not perform such acts, are the Hīnayānists. The Mahāyānists are divided into two branches—(1) Mādhyamika and (2) Yogācāra. The Hīnayānists also have two divisions—(1) Vaibhāṣika and (2) Sautrāntika. Both are called Sarvāstivādins.

(i) Vaibhāṣika

The Vaibhāṣikas reject the authority of the Sūtras and attach themselves to the *Vibhāṣā*, the commentary on the *Abhidhamma*. Kātyāyanīputra's *Jñānaprasthāna* (composed about three hundred years after Buddha's Nirvāṇa) is their chief work. The commentary *Mahāvibhāṣā* was compiled by five hundred Arhats led by Vasumitra, probably after the great council under Kaniṣka. Fragments of *Udānavagga*, *Dhammapada*, *Ekottarāgama*, Aśvaghoṣa's *Buddhacarita* and Āryaśūra's *Jātakamālā* seem to belong to this school. Bhadanta (third century A.D.) Dharmatrāta and Ghoṣaka are other prominent exponents of this school.

(ii) Sautrāntika

According to Hiuen Tsang (Yuan Chwang) Kumāralāta (or Kumāralabdha), a contemporary of Nāgārjuna, was the founder of the Sautrāntika school. The Sautrāntikas derive their name from the fact that they take their stand on the Sūtras. To be precise, unlike the Vaibhāṣikas, they adhere to the *Suttapiṭaka*, (the section consisting of the discourses of Lord Buddha) to the rejection of the two other Piṭakas. It is unfortunate that none of the works of this school are extant. Dharmottara, the logician, and Yaśomitra, the author of the commentary on Vasubandhu's *Abhidharmakośa*, are said to be the followers of this school.

(iii) Mādhyamika

The founder of the Mādhyamika school was Nāgārjuna who is said to have written the *Śatasāhasrikā-prajñāpāramitā*, the latest of the Mahāyāna-sūtras. It may be mentioned in this connexion that the *Prajñāpāramitās* declare that the highest wisdom consists of the knowledge of Void (*Śūnyatā*). The most representative work of the Mādhyamika school is the *Mādhyamikakārikā* or the *Mādhyamikasūtra* of Nāgārjuna which consists of four hundred verses in twenty-seven chapters. Nāgārjuna wrote a commentary on his own work, which is named the *Akutobhaya*. Unfortunately the work has not come down to us in Sanskrit. Among other works written by Nāgārjuna are the *Yuktiṣaṣṭikā*, the *Śūnyatāsaptati*, the *Pratītyasamutpādahṛdaya*, the *Mahāyānaviṁśaka* and the *Vigrahavyāvartanī*. Nāgārjuna is usually placed between the first century B.C. (according to the tradition preserved in the archives of the Dalai-Lama) and the fourth century A.D. (according to Dr S. C. Vidyābhūṣaṇa). In any case he cannot be later than A.D. 401, when Kumārajīva translated his life into Chinese. Śāntideva (seventh century A.D.), the author of the *Bodhicaryāvatāra* and the *Śikṣāsamuccaya*, is sometimes called a Mādhyamika and sometimes an advocate of the Yogācāra doctrine. The commentary named the *Prasannapadā*, written by Candrakīrti in the sixth or the seventh century A.D., is an important contribution to the Mādhyamika literature. Āryadeva who is a disciple of Nāgārjuna, wrote the *Catuśśataka* which is another important work of the Mādhyamika school. It was commented on by Candrakīrti. Other works by Āryadeva are the *Cittaviśuddhiprakaraṇa*, the *Hastavālaprakaraṇa* and two other small treatises constituting a kind of commentary on some sections of the *Laṅkāvatāra*.

(iv) Yogācāra

The founder of the Yogācāra school was Maitreyanātha, the teacher of Asaṅga who is generally believed to have clearly expressed the implications of his system. Asaṅga is at least as late as the third century A.D., though some would place him in the fourth or the fifth century A.D. According to the Yogācāra school nothing exists beyond consciousness (*vijñāna*). The *Abhisamayālaṅkārakārikās* and probably the text of the *Mahāyānasūtrālaṅkāra* attributed by Professor Lévi to Asaṅga and the *Yogācārabhūmiśāstra*, a prose work after the manner of the *Abhidharma* text, are the work of Maitreyanātha.[1] Aśvaghoṣa was a follower of the Yogācāra school who wrote among other works the *Mahāyānaśraddhotpādasūtra* as detailed in a previous chapter.[2] Vasubandhu Asaṅga is a great name in Buddhist literature who is assigned to the fourth century A.D., though some place him in the fifth century A.D. His work the *Abhidharmakośa* in six hundred verses, which has not reached us in the Sanskrit original, is a lasting contribution to Buddhist philosophy. In this work the author has refuted chiefly the views of the Vaiśeṣikas. The Sāṅkhya theory has been criticized in his *Paramārtha-*

[1] The name of Asaṅga has become more famous than that of his teacher Maitreyanātha. This explains why the works of the latter are attributed to the former. According to the Tibetans and Hiuen Tsang the *Yogācārabhūmiśāstra* has been ascribed to Asaṅga.

[2] Ch. VI., p. 68.

saptati. Yaśomitra wrote a commentary on the *Abhidharmakośa* known as the *Abhidharmakośavyākhyā*, the earliest translation of which into Chinese was done in the sixth century A.D. The work is extremely important as it enables us to know the views of the Vaibhāṣikas and the Sautrāntikas. Vasubandhu wrote a monumental treatise, the *Vijñaptimātratāsiddhi* consisting of two works the *Viṁśatikā* and the *Triṁśikā* which explain the doctrine of the reality of consciousness. A few other works, viz., *Pañcaskandhaprakaraṇa*, the *Vyākhyāyukti*, the *Karmasiddhiprakaraṇa* and two commentaries on the *Mahāyānasūtrālaṅkāra* and the *Pratītyasamutpādasūtra*, the *Madhyāntavibhāga* and the *Aparimitāyussūtropadeśa* are said to have been written by Vasubandhu. Among the adherents to the school of Vasubandhu mention must be made of Sthiramati, Diṅnāga, Dharmapāla and Śīlabhadra. Sthiramati wrote a commentary on Vasubandhu's *Triṁśikā-Vijñapti*, and Dharmapāla made a commentary on the *Viṁśatikā-Vijñapti*. Diṅnāga was the disciple of Vasubandhu, brother of Ārya Asaṅga. Diṅnāga's date also is not accurately fixed. Thus while some assign him to the fifth century A.D., others place him between A.D. 520 and A.D. 600, and make him a contemporary of Guṇaprabha, the teacher of King Śrī-Harṣa of Kanauj. Mallinātha, the famous commentator of the fifteenth century A.D., seems to find a reference to this Diṅnāga in Kālidāsa's *Meghadūta*. Diṅnāga's *Pramāṇasamuccaya*, *Pramāṇaśāstrapraveśa* and other works are preserved in Tibetan translations, and are very popular in Japan. The only Sanskrit work of Diṅnāga which has come down to recent times is the *Nyāyapraveśa*. Dharmakīrti (sixth or seventh century A.D.) wrote a valuable work—the *Nyāyabindu*—which was commented on by Dharmottara (ninth century A.D.) in his *Nyāyabindu-ṭīkā*. Śīlabhadra (seventh century A.D.) was the head of the Buddhist Vihāra at Nālandā and Yuan Chwang (Hiuen Tsang) acquired from him his knowledge of Buddhist philosophy. Śāntarakṣita in the eighth century A.D. wrote a voluminous work, the *Tattvasaṁgraha*, in which he has criticized the views of many rival schools of philosophers. His work was commented on by Kamalaśīla in his *Pañjikā*.[1]

II Jainism

The Jainas are the followers of Jina which is a title applied to Vardhamāna, the last prophet. Vardhamāna said that he was the expounder of tenets that had been successively held by twenty-three earlier sages. The Jainas are divided into two schools: (1) Śvetāmbara (white-robed) and (2) the Digambara (sky-robed or nude). We are told that this division took place as early as the first century A.D. The Śvetāmbara Jainas possess both Canonical and philosophical works, while the Digambara Jainas have no Canonical literature. The Canonical literature of the Śvetāmbara sect comprises eighty-four books among which forty-one are Sūtras. Both the schools disregard the authority of the Veda and are, therefore, called heterodox schools of philosophy by the orthodox Hindu philosophers.

Two schools

(i) Digambara

The earliest Digambara author who is also held in high esteem by the Śvetāmbara sect, is Kundakunda whose works are all written in Prākrit. The first known Digambara writer in Sanskrit, is Umāsvāmin,

[1] A late treatise on the Buddhist philosophy is the work of Advayavajra who is assigned to the close of the eleventh or the beginning of the twelfth century A.D.

also called Umāsvāti (third century A.D.) whose *Tattvārthādhigamasūtra* (in ten chapters) is regarded as an authoritative text by both sects. Siddhasena Divākara is also a well-known Digambara philosopher who wrote probably in the fifth century A.D. His commentary on the *Tattvārthādhigamasūtra* and his two other works the *Nyāyāvatāra* and the *Sammatitarkasūtra* are all important contributions. In the first half of the eighth century A.D., Samantabhadra, a Digambara, wrote a commentary on the *Tattvārthādhigamasūtra* which contains an introduction called the *Āptamīmāṁsā* which was known both to Kumārila and Vācaspati. Samantabhadra's other works are *Yuktyanuśāsana* and *Ratnakāraṇḍaśrāvakācāra*. To the same century, in all probability, lived Akalaṅka among whose works the *Tattvārtharājavārttika* and the *Aṣṭaśatī*, commentaries on the *Tattvārthādhigamasūtra* and the *Āptamīmāṁsā* respectively, may be mentioned. His views were strongly opposed by Kumārila. It was Vidyānanda who defended Akalaṅka against the criticisms of Kumārila by writing the *Aṣṭasāhasrī*, the *Tattvārthaślokavārttika*, the *Āptaparīkṣā*, the *Patraparīkṣā*, the *pramāṇaparīkṣā* and the *Pramāṇanirṇaya*. Māṇikyanandin wrote his *Parīkṣāmukhasūtra* which is based on the *Nyāyaviniścaya* of Akalaṅka. Prabhācandra who is said to be a pupil of Kundakunda, wrote two independent works on logic, the *Prameyakamalamārtaṇḍa* and the *Nyāyakumudacandrodaya*. It is usually believed that Prabhācandra was a pupil of Akalaṅka, but it is stated in the epilogue of the *Prameyakamalamārtaṇḍa* that the work was composed during the reign of Bhoja of Dhārā. Śubhacandra is another

Digambara Jaina who wrote his *Jñānārṇava*, a philosophical work in verse, at the close of the eighth or the beginning of the ninth century A.D.

(ii) Svetāmbara

Haribhadra is the earliest Śvetāmbara Jaina philosopher who wrote two important works, the *Ṣaḍdarśanasamuccaya* and the *Lokatattvanirṇaya*, besides a commentary on the *Nyāyapraveśa* of Diṅnāga, the *Yogadṛṣṭisamuccaya*, the *Yogabindu* and the *Dharmabindu*. His date is believed to be the ninth century A.D. Towards the close of the ninth century A.D. Amṛtacandra wrote the *Tattvārthasāra* and the *Puruṣārthasiddhyupāya* besides a few commentaries. Hemacandra is a great Jaina philosopher whose *Pramāṇamīmāṁsā* is an important work on Jaina philosophy. Malliṣeṇa in the thirteenth century A.D. wrote his *Syādvādamañjarī*, a commentary on Hemacandra's *Anyayogavyavacchedikā*. To the same century belongs Āśādhara among whose works mention should be made of the *Dharmāmṛta*. Devendrasūri, another writer of the same century, wrote the *Siddhapañcāśikā*, the *Vandāruvṛtti* and the *Upamitibhavaprapañca-kathā-sāroddhāra*. In the fifteenth century Sakalakīrti wrote a voluminous work the *Tattvārthasāradīpaka* in twelve chapters. To the same century belonged Śrutasāgara who wrote the *Jinendrayajñavidhi* and the *Tattvārthadīpikā*. In the seventeenth century flourished Yaśovijaya who wrote the *Jñānabinduprakaraṇa* and the *Jñānasāra*.

III Materialism (Cārvāka)

The substance of the doctrine of the Indian materialists is aptly and very briefly summed up in the allegorical drama, the *Prabodhacandrodaya*—'Lokāyata is the only Śāstra. In this system perceptual evidence is the only authority. The elements are

Introduction

four in number—earth, water, fire and wind. Wealth and enjoyment are the objects of human existence. Matter can think; there is no other world. Death is the end of all.'[1] 'Lokāyata' (directed to the world of enjoyment through senses) is the Sanskrit expression for materialism. It is the name of the Śāstra. The materialists are called Lokāyatikas or Cārvākas called as such after the name of the founder of the school.

References to Cārvāka philosophy

Cārvāka's story is found in the *Mahābhārata* while the doctrine is referred to in the *Mahābhārata* (*Śalyaparvan* and *Śāntiparvan*), the *Viṣṇupurāṇa* and the *Manusmṛti*, as that of the Nihilists and the Heretics. Sometimes Cārvāka is identified with Bṛhaspati, who incarnated himself as an atheist in order to bring ruin unto the demons. The classic authority on the materialist theory is said to be the *Sūtras* of Bṛhaspati, which have perished. The *Sarvadarśanasaṁgraha* of Mādhava gives a summary of the teaching of the school in its first chapter. Fragmentary quotations of Sūtras and passages from works of the school now lost to us, can be traced in the polemical works of other philosophical schools.

Early teachers

Among the earlier heretical teachers, mention may be made of Sañjaya the sceptic, Ajita Keśakambalin the materialist, Purāṇa Kāśyapa the indifferentist, Maskarin Gosāla the fatalist and Kakuḍa Kātyāyana the elementalist.

Schools of Materialism

The materialists, again, were subdivided into several schools—those who identified the body with the self, those who confused the self with the external senses, those who regarded the internal organ (*antaḥkaraṇa*)

[1] Act II.

as their self and so on. The oft-quoted verses quoted by Mādhava, give a popular view of the materialists —'While the life regains, let a man live happily; let him feed on ghee, even if he runs in debt; when once the body becomes ashes, how can it ever return again?' 'The three authors of the Vedas were the hypocrites, knaves and nightprowlers', etc., etc.

C. MISCELLANEOUS WORKS ON PHILOSOPHY

Śrīkaṇṭhabhāṣya: a commentary on the *Brahmasūtras* by Śrīkaṇṭha *alias* Nīlakaṇṭha (thirteenth or fourteenth century A.D.).—written from the Viśiṣṭaśivādvaita point of view—much in the same line as that adopted by Rāmānuja.—commented on by Appayya-dīkṣita in his *Śivārkamaṇidīpikā*. (It is said that Appayya was at first a Śaivaite and later was converted into an Advaita-Vedāntin.)

Śrīkarabhāṣya: a commentary on the *Brahmasūtras* by Śrīpati Paṇḍita representing the Dvaitādvaita point of view.

Commentaries on the Gītā (named Subodhinī), the Bhāgavata, and the Viṣṇupurāṇa: by Śrīdharaśvāmin (twelfth or thirteenth century A.D.)—who is claimed to be an exponent of the Śuddhādvaita school, inasmuch as he refers to Viṣṇusvāmin, the founder of the Śuddhādvaita school in his commentary on the *Bhāgavata*. [Vallabhācārya (fifteenth-sixteenth century A.D.) was a later exponent of this school. But as he has also referred to Citsukha, it may also be possible that he was a thinker of the Advaita school, who had his leanings towards the doctrine of devotion (*bhakti*). This sort of compromise between the doctrines of devotion (*bhakti*) and knowledge (*jñāna*), is also found in the *Bhaktirasāyana* of Madhusūdana Sarasvatī who was a sturdy champion of the Advaita philosophy].

Sarvadarśanasaṁgraha: by Mādhavācārya who along with his brother Sāyaṇa, the celebrated commentator of Vedic literature, was in the court of Kings Harihara and Vīra Bukka of Vijayanagara (fourteenth century A.D.) and subsequently turned a Sannyāsin and passed his days in the Śṛṅgerī Maṭha,—a valuable encyclopaedia of Indian philosophy, which contains the summary of the views of at least seventeen different orthodox and heterodox schools of Indian philosophy.

Sarvasiddāntasārasaṁgraha: ascribed to Śaṅkarācārya but seems to be the work of a more modern hand who was possibly one of the later chiefs of a Śaṅkara Maṭha—a work in the line of the *Sarvadarśanasaṁgraha* though written in easy verses.

Vijñānāmṛtabhāṣya: by Vijñānabhikṣu (sixteenth century A.D.) who by writing this commentary on the *Brahmasūtras* sought to establish a compromise between the Sāṅkhya and Yoga views on one hand and the Vedāntic (Upaniṣadic) views on the other.

Śaktibhāṣya: by Pañcānana Tarkaratna of the twentieth century A.D.—an ingenious work in the form of a commentary on the *Brahmasūtras*. It does not, however, strictly conform to the orthodox Śāktāgama standpoint.

REFERENCES

Das Gupta, S. N.: *History of Indian Philosophy*, Vols. I, II & III
Keith, A. B.: *A History of Sanskrit Literature*
Radhakrishnan, S.: *Indian Philosophy*, Vols. I & II
Winternitz, M.: *A History of Indian Literature*, Vol. II

INDEX

Abhayanandin, 146.
Abhidhammapiṭaka, 192.
Abhidhānaratnamālā, 157.
Abhidhānacintāmaṇi, 157.
Abhidharma, 193, 195.
Abhidharmakośa, 72, 195, 196, 199.
Abhidharmakośavyākhyā, 196.
Abhidhāvṛttimātṛkā, 154.
Abhijñānaśakuntala, 93, 10 .
Abhinanda, son of Jayanta, 98.
Abhinanda, son of Śatānanda, 83.
Abhinavabhāratī, 152, 153.
Abhinavagupta, 49, 75n., 116, 153-4.
Abhinayadarpaṇa, 173.
Abhisamayālaṅkārakārikā, 71, 195.
Abhiṣeka, 96n, 99.
Abhyankar, 98n.
Acintyabhedābhedavāda, 191.
Adbhutadarpaṇa, 117.
Adbhutasāgara, 170n.
Ādipurāṇa, 83.
Advayavajra, 197n.
Ādyā Śakti, 45.
Āgama, 47, 49.
Agastimata, 172.
Agnipurāṇa, 44, 151n, 156, 172.
Ahirbudhnya Saṁhitā, 49.
Aihole inscription, 80.
Aiyer, G., 59.
Ajita Keśakambalin, 200.
Akalaṅka, 198.
Ākhyāyikā, 131.
Akṣobhyavyūha, 70.
Akutobhaya, 71, 194.
Alaṅkāra, minister of Jayasiṁha, 84.
Alaṅkāra (lit.), 145, 151-2, 154.
Alaṅkārakāṇḍa of *Bhaṭṭikāvya*, 80.
Alaṅkārasaṁgraha, 151.
Alaṅkārasarvasva, 154.
Alaṅkāraśekhara, 155.
Albērūnī, 33, 40, 169.
Alexander, 86.
Allahabad Stone Pillar Inscription, 55.
Āloka, 176.
Āḷvāras, 190.
Amalānanda, 188.
Amaracandra, 84, 155.
Amarakośa, 2, 157.
Amaramaṅgala, 117.
Amarasiṁha, 42, 43, 131, 157.
Amaru, 122, 123.
Amaruśataka, 122, 123.
Amitābha, 70.
Amitagati, 124.
Amoghavṛtti, 146.
Amṛtabhāratī, 147.
Amṛtacandra, 199.
Amṛtamanthana, 85.
Amṛtānanda, 65.
Ānandabhairava, 49.
Ānandagiri, 186n, 189.
Ānandalaharī, 124.
Ānandavardhana, 9, 81, 112, 123-4, 150, 153-4.
Ānandavṛndāvanacampū, 140.
Anaṅgaharṣa Mātrarāja, 116.
Anaṅgaraṅga, 165.
Ananta, 140.
Anargharāghava, 112-3.
Anekārthaśabdakośa, 157.
Anekārthasaṁgraha, 157.
Anekārthasamuccaya, 157.
Aniruddha, *Pitṛdayitā*, 161.
Aniruddha, com. on *Sāṅkhyasūtra*, 180.
Annaṁbhaṭṭa, 178.
Aṇubhāṣya, 191.
Anubhūtisvarūpācārya, 147.
Aṇuvyākhyāna, 191.
Anyayogavyavacchedikā, 199.
Anyoktimuktālatā-śataka, 125.
Apāntaratamas, 186n.
Aparimitāyussūtropadeśa, 196.
Āpastamba, 41, 149, 159.
Āpiśali, 141.
Āpodeva, 185.
Appayyadīkṣita, 155, 185, 188-9, 198, 201.
Āptamīmāṁsā, 198.
Āptaparīkṣā, 198.
Ārambhavāda, 179.
Arisiṁha, 128, 155.
Arjunarāvaṇīya, 83.
Arjunavarman, 123.
Arthasaṁgraha, 185.
Arthaśāstra, 94, 95, 137, 150, 162, 164.

Āryabhaṭa, 168-9.
Āryabhaṭa, *Āryasiddhānta*, 169.
Āryabhaṭīya, 169.
Āryacandra, 69.
Āryadeva, 71, 194.
Āryāsaptaśatī, 125.
Āryasiddhānta, 169.
Āryāṣṭaśata, 169.
Āryaśūra, 69, 140, 193.
Āśādhara, 199.
Asaṅga, 71, 195-6.
Asatkāryavāda, 178.
Āścarya-upapurāṇa, 46.
Āśmarathya, 185.
Aśoka, 8, 12, 59, 73.
Aśokāvadāna, 73.
Aṣṭādhyāyī, 2, 5, 21, 141-2, 144, 148.
Aṣṭamahāśrīcaitya-stotra, 124.
Aṣṭāṅgahṛdayasaṁhitā, 167.
Aṣṭāṅgasaṁgraha, 167.
Aṣṭasāhasrī, 198.
Aṣṭaśatī, 198.
Āsurī, 179.
Aśvacikitsā, 172.
Aśvaghoṣa, 27, 57, 62-9, 71, 76, 77n, 95n, 193, 195.
Āśvalāyana, 36.
Aśvavaidyaka, 172.
Aśvāyurveda, 172.
Atharvaveda, 36, 40, 85, 130, 168.
Ātmatattvaviveka, 175.
Ātreya, ritual authority, 166.
Ātreya, authority on medicine, 185.
Aucityavicāra, 154.
Auḍulomi, 185.
Aufrecht, T., 3.
Aulūkya Philosophy, 77.
Avadāna, 67, 72-3.
Avadānakalpalatā, 73.
Avadānaśataka, 72-3, 83.
Avaloka, 154.
Avalokiteśvara, 70.
Avantīsundarīkathā, 97n.
Avantivarman, 83.
Avimāraka, 102.
Avimuktātman, 189.

Bādarāyaṇa, 186, 190.
Bādari, 185.
Bāhudantiputra, 162.
Bālabhārata, Amaracandra, 84.
Bālabhārata, Bhāsa, 113.
Bālacarita, 101, 103.
Baladeva, 186n, 192.
Bālamanoramā, 144.
Bālarāmāyaṇa, 133.
Bālasubrahmanyam, I.R., 77n.
Balibandha, 95.
Ballālasena, 138.
Bāṇabhaṭṭa, 36, 40, 83, 96n, 97n, 98, 107, 117, 120, 122, 124, 134-5, 139.
Banerji, R. D., 64n, 65n.
Banerji Sastri, A., 98n.
Barnett, L. D., 4, 98n.
Bauddhasaṁgatyalaṅkāra, 133.
Belvalkar, S. K., 98n.
Bhadanta, 193.
Bhadrakalpāvadāna, 73.
Bhagavadajjukīya, 116.
Bhagavadgītā, 1, 2, 33-4.
Bhāgavata, 44, 45, 84, 115, 130, 191, 201.
Bhaimarathī, 52.
Bhairavasiṁha, 161.
Bhaktāmarastotra, 124.
Bhaktirasāyana, 201.
Bhaktiśataka, 125.
Bhallaṭa, 124.
Bhallaṭaśataka, 127.
Bhāmaha, 81, 132, 143, 151-2.
Bhāmatī, 188.
Bhāminīvilāsa, 125.
Bhandarkar, R. G., 33, 64n.
Bhānudatta, 155.
Bhānuji, 157.
Bharata, 19, 75n, 85, 104, 149, 150-3, 155.
Bhāratacampū, 140.
Bhāratacandra, 123.
Bhāratamañjarī, 83.
Bhāratītīrtha, 189.
Bhāravi, 80, 82.
Bhartṛhari, 1, 80, 121-2, 125, 143, 145.
Bhartṛmeṇṭha, 83.
Bhartṛmitra, 183.
Bhartṛprapañca, 187.
Bhāsa, 93, 95-102.
Bhāṣāpariccheda, 178.
Bhāsarvajña, 175.
Bhāṣāvṛtti, 148.
Bhāskarācārya, 169.
Bhāskara, Philosopher, 190-91.
Bhāskara, *Unmattarāghava*, 117.
Bhāskara-upapurāṇa, 46.
Bhāskara, *Varivasyārahasya*, 50.
Bhāsvatī, 169.
Bhāṭṭacintāmaṇi, 185.

Bhāṭṭadīpikā, 185.
Bhaṭṭanārāyaṇa, 112.
Bhaṭṭanāyaka, 152-3.
Bhāṭṭarahasya, 185.
Bhaṭṭi, 27, 80-81, 83, 132, 143.
Bhaṭṭikāvya, 76n, 80, 132, 147.
Bhaṭṭoji, 144-5, 148.
Bhaṭṭotpala, 170.
Bhaumaka, 83.
Bhavabhūti, 27, 86, 88, 93, 104, 108-110, 112, 127, 184.
Bhavadāsa, 183.
Bhavadevabhaṭṭa, 161, 184.
Bhavadevasūri, 84.
Bhāvakatva, 153.
Bhāvamiśra, 167.
Bhavanātha, 183.
Bhāvanāviveka, 184.
Bhāvaprakāśa, 167.
Bhāvaprakāśana, 154.
Bhaviṣyapurāṇa, 44.
Bhavabhañjanaśarman, 170n.
Bhedābhedavāda, 190.
Bhela, 166.
Bhikkhuṇīpācittīya, 6.
Bhikkhupācittīya, 6.
Bhīma, 127.
Bhīmaṭa, 116.
Bhītā medallion, 77n.
Bhoja, 154, 164, 169, 172, 181-2, 198.
Bhojadeva, 123.
Bhojakatva, 153.
Bhojaprabandha, 138.
Bhojarāja, 140.
Bhṛgu, 160.
Bhūdevaśukla, 115.
Bījagaṇita, 169.
Bilhaṇa, 116, 123, 127.
Bilvamaṅgala, 124.
Bindumatī, 94.
Blan, A., 42.
Bloomfield, M., 4.
Bodhāyana, 159, 183, 187n.
Bodhāyanakavi, 116.
Bodhicaryāvatāra, 194.
Böhtlingk, O., 3.
Bopp, F., 2.
Brahmadatta, 61.
Brahmagupta, 169.
Brahmānanda, 190.
Brāhmaṇasarvasva, 161.
Brahmāṇḍapurāṇa, 42, 44.
Brahmapurāṇa, 44.
Brahmasiddhi, 188.
Brahmasphuṭasiddhānta, 169.
Brahmasūtra, 131, 186n, 187-8, 190, 201-2.
Brahmasūtrabhāṣya, 189.
Brahmavaivartapurāṇa, 42.
Bṛhacchabdenduśekhara, 145.
Bṛhadāraṇyakabhāṣyavārttika, 188.
Bṛhadāraṇyakopaniṣad, 40, 187.
Bṛhadbrahmasaṁhitā, 50.
Bṛhajjātaka, 170.
Bṛhaspati, 159, 162-3, 200.
Bṛhaspatismṛti, 161.
Bṛhaspatisūtra, 200.
Bṛhatī, 183.
Bṛhatkathā, 99, 101, 103, 136-7.
Bṛhatkathāmañjarī, 136.
Bṛhatsaṁhitā, 170, 172.
Buddha, 18, 59, 63, 66-7, 70, 192-3.
Buddhabhaṭṭa, 172.
Buddhacarita, 27, 62, 65-7, 76, 77n, 83, 193.
Buddhaghoṣa, 83.
Buddhāvataṁśaka, 70.
Buddhism, 192-7.
Buddhist Tantra, 48.
Budhasvāmin, 136.
Bühler, G., 4, 5, 8-10, 12, 14n, 5[illegible] 121n, 136, 159.
Burnell, A. C., 4, 141n.
Burnouf, E., 3.

Caitanyacandrodaya, 115.
Caitanyāmṛta, 147-8.
Cakrapāṇidatta, 166-7.
Cambridge History of India, 37n.
Campakaśreṣṭhikathānaka, 138.
Campū, 55.
Cāṇakya, 137, 162, 166.
Caṇḍakauśika, 113.
Caṇḍeśvara, 161, 164.
Caṇḍī, 45.
Caṇḍīdāsa, 154.
Caṇḍīśataka, 124.
Candra, Candraka, 116.
Candragomin, 116, 143, 145.
Candragupta, 43, 76, 133, 162.
Candrakīrti, 72n., 195.
Candrāloka, 154-5.
Cāndra school, 145.
Caraka, 130, 166, 167, 179, 182n.
Carakasaṁhitā, 166, 174n, 182n.
Cārucaryāśataka, 125.
Cārudatta, 93, 97n, 102-3.

Cārvāka, 199-200.
Catalogus Catalogorum, 3.
Caturbhāṇī, 92.
Caturvargacintāmaṇi, 161.
Caturvargasaṁgraha, 125.
Catuśśataka, 71, 194.
Catuśśatakastotra, 69.
Caurapañcāśikā, 123.
Chandasūtra, 53.
Chandomañjarī, 156.
Chando'nuśāsana, 156.
Chāyā, on *Vyāsabhāṣya*, 181.
Charpentier, J., 98n.
Chézy, A. L., 2.
Cidambara, 84.
Cikitsākalikā, 167.
Cikitsāsārasaṁgraha, 167.
Citrabhārata, 116.
Citramīmāṁsā, 155.
Citsukha, 189, 201.
Citsukhī, 189.
Cittaviśuddhiprakaraṇa, 71, 195.
Colebrooke, T., 1, 148.
Court epics, 75-84.
Cowell, E. B., 4, 77n.
Cunninghum, A., 4, 11, 59.

Dalai Lama, 194.
Ḍallana, 166.
Dāmodara, 173.
Dāmodaragupta, 124.
Dāmodaramiśra, 113.
Dānastuti, 51.
Daṇḍin, 54, 56, 97n, 103n, 131-2, 151-2.
Darpadalana, 125.
Daśabhūmaka, 70.
Daśagītikāsūtra, 169.
Daśakarmapaddhati, 161.
Daśakumāracarita, 103n, 132.
Daśarathajātaka, 29.
Daśarūpaka, 116, 154.
Dattakasarvāśraya, 81.
Davids, R., 10.
Dāyabhāga, 161.
Deussen, P., 4.
Devadhara, C. R., 98n.
Devaprabhāsūri, 84.
Devaputra, 65n.
Devendrasūri, 199.
Deveśvara, 155.
Devīmahādeva, 94.
Devīmāhātmya, 45.
Devīśataka, 124.
Devī upapurāṇa, 46.
Dhanañjaya, 154.
Dhanapāla, 140.
Dhaneśvara, 84.
Dhanika, 154.
Dharasena, 81.
Dharmābhyudaya, 116.
Dharmabindu, 199.
Dharmakīrti, 69, 72n., 75, 133, 183, 196.
Dharmāmṛta, 199.
Dharmapada, 193.
Dharmapāla, 72, 196.
Dharmaparīkṣā, 124.
Dharmarājādhvarīndra, 189.
Dharmaratna, 161.
Dharmasaṁgraha, 71.
Dharmaśarmābhyudaya, 84.
Dharmasūtra, 5, 41, 159, 174.
Dharmatrāta, 193.
Dharmavijaya, 115.
Dharmottara, 72n, 175, 194, 197.
Dhātupāṭha, 140.
Dhātupradīpa, 148.
Dhātuvṛttī, 148.
Dhavalacandra, 137.
Dhīranāga, 117.
Dhoyī, 124.
Dhruva, K. H., 98n.
Dhūrtanartaka, 117.
Dhūrtasamāgama, 117.
Dhūrtaviṭasaṃvāda, 92n.
Dhvani school, 153.
Dhvanyāloka, 150-51, 153.
Dīdhīti, 176.
Digambara, 197.
Dinakarabhaṭṭa, 185.
Diṅnāga, 72. 77n, 117, 174-5, 177, 196, 199.
Dīpakalikā, 161.
Dīpaṅkara, 172.
Dīpikā, 178.
Diringer, 11.
Divyāvadāna, 59, 73.
Dṛḍhabala, 166.
Dsanglun, 73.
Dubreuil, J., 64n, 65n.
Durgasiṁha, 146.
Durghaṭavṛtti, 148.
Durlabharāja, 170n.
Dūtaghaṭotkaca, 100.
Dūtāṅgada, 117.
Dūtavākya, 100.
Dvādaśanikāyaśāstra, 71.
Dvaitavāda, 191.

Dvaitādvaita, 190, 201.
Dvāvimśatyavadāna, 73.
Dvyāśrayakāvya. 128.

editio princeps of Ṛgveda, 3
Eggeling, J., 4.
Ekaślokaśāstra, 71.
Ekāvalī, 155.
Ekottarāgama, 193.
Elizabethan drama, 86.
Erotics, 165.

Fergusson, J., 4, 64n, 77n, 78n, 104n.
Fleet, J. F., 4, 54, 64n, 78n, 103.
Forster, G., 1.
Frank, 64n.

Gadādhara, 176.
Gāgābhaṭṭa, 185.
Gajendragadkar, 121n.
Gālava, 141.
Gaṇa, 172.
Gaṇapāṭha, 146.
Gaṇaratnamahodadhi, 148.
Gaṇasūtras, 21n.
Gaṇḍavyūha, 70.
Gaṇḍīstotragāthā, 67.
Gaṅgādāsa, 156.
Gaṅgālaharī, 125.
Gaṅgeśa, 175-6.
Garbe, R., 4, 174n, 179.
Gārgya, 141, 179.
Garuḍapurāṇa, 44, 172.
Gāthā, 58, 62, 70.
Gāthā Nārāśaṁsī, 25.
Gāthāsaptaśatī, 119.
Gauḍa style, 57, 109.
Gauḍabrahmānandī, 189.
Gauḍapāda, 179, 187.
Gauḍapādakārikā, 187.
Gauḍavaho, 109. 127.
Gauḍīya Vaiṣṇavas, 191-2.
Gautama, 41, 159, 174-5, 177.
Gayādāsa, 166.
Geldner, F., 3, 88.
Gentoo law, A Code of, 1.
Ghaṭakarpara, 121.
Ghaṭakarparakāvya, 121.
Ghaṭak, J. C., 98n, 104n.
Ghorī Shahabuddin, 128.
Ghoṣaka, 193.
Ghosh, Arabinda, 121n.
Girnar Inscription, 55.
Gītā, 33, 191.
Gītagovinda, 123, 165.
Goethe, 1, 104, 120.
Gokulanātha, 115.
Gokulikas, 60.
Goldstücker, T., 4, 5, 142.
Gopālacampū, 140.
Gopatha-Brāhmaṇa, 40.
Gopendra Tippa Bhūpāla, 152.
Gopīnātha, 117.
Govardhana, 125.
Govinda, 154-5.
Govindabhāṣya, 192.
Govindacandra, 161.
Govindānanda, 189.
Govindarāja, 160.
Grassmann, H., 3.
Gṛhyasūtra, 30, 36, 159.
Grierson, G., 4.
Guṇabhadra, 83.
Guṇacandra, 155.
Guṇāḍhya, 99, 136.
Guṇaprabhā, 196.
Guṇaratna, 179n.

Hāla, 120, 125.
Halāyudha, 83, 157, 161.
Hamilton, A., 2.
Hammīramadamardana, 117.
Haṁsadūta, 120n.
Haṁsasandeśa, 120n.
Hanumannāṭaka, 113.
Hanxleden, J. E., 1.
Haradatta, 144.
Haradattasūri, 84.
Harakelināṭaka, 116.
Hārāvalī, 157.
Haravijaya, 76n, 83.
Hari, 81, 183.
Haribhadra, 199.
Haricandra, 84, 140.
Haridīkṣita, 148.
Harihara, King of Vijayanagara, 201.
Harināmāmṛta, 147.
Hariṣeṇa, 55-6.
Harisiṁha, 161.
Hārīta, 159.
Harivaṁśa, 32, 34-5, 41, 95, 97n, 99, 101.
Harivaṁśa, court epic, 84.
Harivaṁśapurāṇa, 83.

Harivarman, King of South Bengal, 161.
Harivilāsa, 83.
Harṣa, 41, 107-8, 124-5, 128, 134, 196.
Harṣacarita, 40, 107, 120, 134.
Harṣadeva, King of Kashmir, 125, 128.
Harṣakīrti, 170.
Hastabālaprakaraṇa, 195.
Hastimalla, 117.
Hastings, W., 1.
Hastyāyurveda, 172.
Hāsyacūḍāmaṇi, 116.
Hāsyārṇava, 117.
Haṭha Yoga, 182.
Hayagrīvavadha, 83.
Helen, 30.
Hemacandra, 84, 125, 128, 146, 148, 154-7, 164, 199.
Hemādri, 46n, 161.
Hemavijayagaṇi, 138.
Herder, 1.
Heretics, 201.
Hertel, J., 88n, 137.
Hillebrandt, A., 88 n.
Hīnayāna, 54, 61-2, 73.
Hindu Law on Contracts and Succession, A Digest, 2.
Hiraṇyakeśin, 163.
History of Indian Literature, 3.
Hitopadeśa, 1, 2, 137.
Hittite, 11.
Hiuen Tsang, 22, 64 n, 193, 195 n, 197.
Hopkins, E. W., 4, 37 n.
Horā, 170.
Horāśāstra, 170.
Horāśatapañcāśikā, 170.
Hṛdayadarpaṇa, 153.
Hrozny, 11.
Hultzsch, E., 4.
Humboldt, W. von, 2.
Hunter, 11.
Huviṣka, 64.

Indra, 141.
Indradhvaja, 85, 87.
Inscriptional Kāvyas, 54.
Introduction to Pūrvamīmāṁsā, 185.
Iṣṭasiddhi, 189.
Iśvaradatta, 92 n.
Iśvarakṛṣṇa, 179.
Iśvarasaṁhitā, 49.
Iśvarasena, 104.
I-tsing, 64, 65, 143, 193.

Jackson, A. M. T., 42.
Jacobi, H., 4, 25-6, 28, 30, 37, 39, 98 174 n, 183.
Jagaddeva, 170 n.
Jagadīśa, 176, 178.
Jagadīśvara, 117.
Jagaḍucarita, 128.
Jagannātha, 125, 148, 155.
Jaimini, 182, 185, 197-9.
Jaiminīyanyāyamālā, 184.
Jaina-Mahābhārata, 84.
Jaina-Rāmāyaṇa, 84.
Jaina Tantras, 48.
Jaiyyaṭa, 166.
Jalhaṇa, 125.
Jāmbavatīvijaya, 83.
Jānakīharaṇa, 81.
Jānakīpariṇaya, 117.
Jātaka literature, 29-30, 61.
Jātakamālā, 68, 140, 193.
Jayadatta, 172.
Jayadeva, 123-5, 165, 176.
Jayadeva, Berar, 116.
Jayadeva, *Candrāloka*, 154-5.
Jayāditya, 143.
Jayamaṅgalā, 165.
Jayanārāyaṇa, 178.
Jayantabhaṭṭa, 83, 175.
Jayāpīḍa, 124.
Jayaratha, 154.
Jayasiṁha, 117.
Jayasiṁha, King of Kashmir, 84.
Jayaswal, K. P., 98 n.
Jha, Gaṅgānāth, 183.
Jīmūtavāhana, 161.
Jinadāsa, 84.
Jinakīrti, 138.
Jinasena, *Harivaṁśapurāṇa*, 83.
Jinasena, *Mahāpurāṇa*, 83.
Jinendra, 145-6.
Jinendrabuddhi, 81, 143.
Jinendrayajñavidhi, 199.
Jīvagosvāmin, 140, 147, 155, 192.
Jīvaka, 166.
Jīvānanda, 115.
Jīvandharacampū, 140.
Jīvanmuktiviveka, 189.
Jñānabinduprakaraṇa, 199.
Jñānāmṛtasārasaṃhitā, 50.
Jñānaprasthāna, 193.

Jñānārṇava, 50. 199.
Jñānasāra, 199.
Jñanendrasarasvatī, 144.
Jolly, J., 4, 28 n, 98 n.
Jones, W., 1, 77 n, 123.
Jumaranandin, 147.
Junagadh Inscription, 64n.
Jyotirīśvara, 165.
Jyotirvidābharaṇa, 170.
Jyotiṣasāroddhāra, 170.

Kādambarī, 133-4.
Kādamba Kāmadeva, 83.
Kadphises I, 64 n.
Kadphises II, 64 n.
Kaiyaṭa, 144-5.
Kakudakātyāyana, 200.
Kalāpa, 146.
Kālāśoka, 38.
Kalāvilāsa, 125.
Kale, M. R., 98 n.
Kalhaṇa, 108, 126, 128.
Kālidāsa, 1, 56-7, 76-83, 94, 96 n, 98, 104-108, 112, 120-1, 124, 156, 196.
Kālikāpurāṇa, 46.
Kālīvilāsa, 50.
Kalkipurāṇa, 46.
Kalpadrumāvadānamālā, 73.
Kalpanālaṅkṛtikā, 67 n.
Kalpanāmaṇḍitikā, 76n.
Kalpataru, 188.
Kalyāṇamalla, 165.
Kalyāṇamandirastotra, 124.
Kāmadatta, 94.
Kāmadhenu, 152.
Kamalākarabhaṭṭa, 161, 185.
Kamalaśīla, 197.
Kāmandaka, 164.
Kāmasūtra, 22, 165.
Kaṁsavadha, 52, 95.
Kaṁsavadha, Śeṣakṛṣṇa, 117.
Kanakāvatīmādhava, 94.
Kaniṣka, 63, 64n, 71, 166, 193.
Kaṇabhakṣa, 177.
Kaṇabhuk, 177.
Kaṇāda, 177.
Kane, P. V., 98 n.
Kant, 3.
Kapila, 179, 180.
Kapilapurāṇa, 46.
Kapphaṇābhyudaya, 83.
Karṇakutūhala, 169.
Kārikāvalī, 178.
Karmaśataka, 72.
Karmasiddhiprakaraṇa, 196.
Karṇabhāra, 100.
Karṇa, King of Chedī, 114.
Karṇasundarī, 116.
Karpūracarita, 93, 116.
Karpūramañjarī, 94, 113.
Kārṣṇājini, 185.
Kāśakṛtsna, 185.
Kāsikāvivaraṇapañjikā, 143.
Kāśikāvṛtti, 81, 143, 184.
Kāśipatikavirāja, 117.
Kāśyapa, 141, 159, 177.
Kāśyapasaṁhitā, 172.
Kātantrasūtra, 146.
Kathā, 131.
Kāṭhasaṁhitā, 36.
Kathākautuka, 138.
Kathākośa, 138.
Kaṭhāratnākara, 138.
Kathārṇava, 138.
Kathāsaritsāgara, 103, 136, 151n.
Kātyāyana, 21, 96 n, 142.
Kātyāyanīputra, 193.
Kaumāra, 146.
Kaumudīmitrānanda, 116.
Kauṭilya, 94, 95 n, 137, 162-4.
Kautukaratnākara, 117.
Kautukasarvasva, 117.
Kavi, R., 97 n.
Kavikalpalatā, 155.
Kavikaṇṭhābharaṇa, 154.
Kavikarṇapūra, 115, 140.
Kavīndravacanasamuccaya, 125.
Kaviputra, 103.
Kavirahasya, 83.
Kavirāja, 83.
Kaviśekhara, 117.
Kavitārahasya, 155.
Kavitārkika, 117
Kāvyādarśa, 103, 131-2, 136, 139n, 151
Kāvyālaṅkāra, Bhāmaha, 151.
Kāvyamīmāṁsā, 154.
Kāvyānuśāsana, Hemacandra, 154.
Kāvyānuśāsana, Vāgbhaṭa, 155.
Kāvyaprakāśa, 152, 154.
Kedārabhaṭṭa, 156.
Keith, A. B., 4, 81, 95, 97 n, 98 n, 116, 136-7, 177, 183.
Keliraivataka, 94.
Kennedy, 64 n.
Kern, H., 62-3, 70.

Keśavakāśmirin, 191.
Keśavamiśra, rhetorician, 155.
Keśavamiśra, naiyāyika, 178.
Khaṇḍadeva, 185.
Khaṇḍakhādyaka, 169.
Khaṇḍanakhaṇḍakhādya, 189.
Khāravela, Hāthigumphā Inscription, 19.
Kharoṣṭha, 9.
Kharoṣṭhi, 8, 9, 14.
Kielhorn, F., 4, 54, 121 n.
Kiraṇāvalī, 175.
Kirātārjunīya, court epic, 2, 80.
Kirātārjunīya, drama, 116.
Kīrtikaumudī, 128.
Kīrtilatā, 129.
Kīrtivarman, 114.
Kokkoka, 165.
Koṇḍabhaṭṭa, 148.
Konow, S., 4, 64 n, 98 n, 103, 107 n.
Korur theory, 78 n.
Kramadīśvara, 147.
Kramasandarbha, 192.
Krīḍārasātala, 94.
Kṛṣṇakarṇāmṛta, 124.
Kṛṣṇamiśra, 114-6.
Kṛṣṇānanda Āgamavāgīśa, 176.
Kṛṣṇānanda, *Padāṅkadūta*, 120n.
Kṛṣṇānanda, *Sahṛdayānanda*, 84.
Kṛṣṇānanda, *Tantrasāra*, 50.
Kṛṣṇa-yajurveda, 130, 160.
Kṛṣṇayajvan, 185.
Kṣemarāja, 4.
Kṣemendra, 73, 83, 113, 116, 125, 136, 154, 156, 165.
Kṣemendra, grammarian, 147.
Kṣemiśvara, 113.
Kṣīrasvāmin, 157.
Kulacūḍāmaṇi, 50.
Kulārṇava, 50.
Kullūka, 160.
Kumāradāsa, 81.
Kumāragupta, 76, 78 n.
Kumārajīva, 194.
Kumāralabdha, 193.
Kumāralāta, 193.
Kumārapālacarita, 128.
Kumārasambhava, 78-9.
Kumārilabhaṭṭa, 36, 40, 183-5, 198.
Kundakunda, 197-8.
Kundamālā, 116.
Kuntaka, Kuntala, 154.
Kunteśvaradautya, 83.
Kūrmapurāṇa, 44.
Kuṭṭanīmata, 124.
Kuvalayānanda, 155.

Laghu Arhannīti, 164.
Laghucandrikā, 189.
Laghu-Jātaka, 170.
Laghuśabdenduśekhara, 145.
Laghusiddhāntakaumudī, 145.
Lakṣaṇā, 153.
Lakṣaṇāvalī, 178.
Lakṣmaṇabhaṭṭa, 140.
Lakṣmaṇasena, 123-4, 161.
Lakṣmīdhara, 161.
Lalitāditya Muktāpīḍa, 127.
Lalitamādhava, 117.
Lalitavistara, 41, 59, 61-3, 66, 83.
Lalla, 169.
Laṅkāvatāra, 71, 195.
Lanman, C. R., 4.
Lassen, C., 2, 30, 123.
Laṭakamelaka, 115.
Laugākṣibhāskara, 178, 185.
Lesny, V., 98 n.
Levy, S., 4, 9, 68, 98n, 107n, 123, 166, 195.
Līlāśuka, 127.
Līlāvatī, 169.
Lindanau, M., 98 n.
Liṅgānuśāsana, 146.
Liṅgapurāṇa, 44.
Lipikāra, 5.
Locana, 153.
Locanarocanī, 155.
Lacote, F., 98 n.
Lokānanda, 116.
Lokatattvanirṇaya, 232.
Lokāyata, 200.
Lokeśvaraśataka, 122 n.
Lokottaravādin, 59, 60.
Lolimbarāja, 83, 167.
Lollaṭa, 152-3.
Lomaharṣaṇa, 34, 42.
Lorinser, F., 33.
Lüders, H., 4, 68.
Ludwig, A., 3.

Macdonell, A. A., 4, 104 n, 120, 121 n, 123.
Machiavelli, 162.
Madālasā-campū, 140.
Madanapārijāta, 161.
Mādhava, 148, 161, 180, 184, 200-1.

Mādhavakara, 167.
Mādhavaṣādhana, 117.
Madhusūdana Sarasvatī, 189, 201.
Mādhva, 186 n, 191.
Madhyamavyāyoga, 23, 99-100.
Mādhyamika, 71-2, 192, 194-5.
Mādhyamikakārikā, 71, 194.
Mādhyamikasūtra, 194.
Madhyāntavibhāga, 196.
Madhyasiddhāntakaumudī, 145.
Māgha, 81-3, 144.
Mahābhārata, 1, 2, 28, 32-9, 41, 48, 51, 75 n, 80, 82-4, 95, 99, 102, 112, 130, 137, 163, 166, 179, 186.
Mahābhāṣya, 52, 95, 130, 141-2, 144, 149, 181 n.
Mahādeva, 117.
Mahānāṭaka, 113-4.
Mahānirvāṇatantra, 50.
Mahāpurāṇa, 83.
Mahārāja-Kanikalekha, 69.
Mahāsāṅghika, 59, 60.
Mahāvagga, 7.
Mahāvaṁśa, 59, 60.
Mahāvastu, 41, 59, 60-1, 66.
Mahāvibhāṣā, 193.
Mahāvīra, 18.
Mahāvīrācārya, 169.
Mahāvīracarita, 84, 109.
Mahāvīrastotra, 125.
Mahāyāna, 41, 58, 61-2, 68-9, 72.
Mahāyānaśraddhotpādasūtra, 68, 195.
Mahāyānasūtra, 69, 70, 193.
Mahāyānasūtrālaṅkāra, 195-6.
Mahāyānaviṁśaka, 71, 194.
Mahendale, 104 n.
Mahendrapāla, 113.
Mahendravikrama Varman, 94, 108.
Maheśvara-upapurāṇa, 46.
Maheśvara, lexicographer, 157.
Mahimabhaṭṭa, 154.
Mahimnastotra, 124.
Mahīpāla, 113.
Maithilīkalyāṇa, 117.
Maitrāyaṇīya, 160.
Maitreyanātha, 71, 195.
Maitreyarakṣita, 148.
Maitreyasamiti, 69.
Maitreya-vyākaraṇa, 69.
Mālinīvijaya, 49.
Mālinīvijayottaravārttika, 49.
Mālatīmādhava, 93, 109, 110.
Mālavikā, 94.
Mālavikāgnimitra, 77 n, 105, 109.
Mallikāmāruta, 117.
Mallinātha, 78, 129, 144, 155, 196.
Malliṣeṇa, 199.
Mammaṭa, 152, 154-5.
Mānameyodaya, 185.
Mānatuṅga, 124.
Mānavadharmaśāstra, 159.
Mānavasūtrakaraṇa, 160.
Maṇḍana, 184, 188.
Mandasor Inscription, 56.
Māṇḍūkyakārikā, 179 n.
Māṇikyacandra, 83, 154.
Māṇikyanandin, 198.
Māṇikyasūri, 86.
Maṅkha, 84.
Mānsehrā Inscription, 8.
Manu, 43, 159, 160, 168.
Manusmṛti, 1, 2, 131, 160-1, 200.
Manuṣyālayacandrikā, 172.
Maskari Gosāla, 200.
Maria Stuart, 121.
Marīci-upapurāṇa, 46.
Mārkaṇḍeya-purāṇa, 44-5.
Markāṇḍeya, smṛtiśāstrakāra, 160.
Marshall, J. H., 4, 64 n, 65 n, 77 n.
Mataṅga, 49.
Mataṅgalīlā, 172.
Mātṛcetā, 69.
Mātṛgupta, 83.
Matsyapurāṇa, 43-4, 172.
Māṭharavṛtti, 179.
Mattavilāsa, 94, 108.
Maudgalyāyana, 68.
Maurya era, 19.
Max Müller, F., 3, 54, 59, 77 n, 142, 187.
Māyākapālikā, 94.
Mayamata, 172.
May-Pole (dance), 87.
Mayūkhamālikā, 185.
Mayūra, 122.
Māyurāja, 116.
Mazumdar, R. C., 64 n.
Medhātithi, 131, 160.
Medinīkāra, 157.
Megasthenes, 38.
Meghadūta, 77 n, 78, 83, 120-1, 124, 196.
Meghaprabhācārya, 116.
Menakāhita, 94.
Merutuṅga, 129.
Mīmāṁsā, philosophy, 184-5.
Mīmāṁsākaustubha, 185.
Mīmāṁsānukramaṇī, 184.

Mīmāṁsānyāyaprakāśa, 185.
Mīmāṁsāparibhāṣā, 185.
Mīmaṁsasūtra, 130.
Mitākṣarā, 161.
Mitramiśra, 161.
Mohamudgara, 124.
Mohaparājaya, 115.
Morgenstierne, G., 98n.
Mṛcchakaṭika, 90, 93, 97 n, 102-4.
Mṛgāvatīcaritra, 84.
Mṛgendra, 49.
Mudrārākṣasa, 102. 111.
Mudritakumudacandra, 116.
Muir, J., 4.
Mugdhabodha, 147.
Mukulabhaṭṭa, 151n, 154.
Mukundānanda, 117.
Murāri, poet, 112-3.
Murāri, philosopher, 183.
Murwarth, A. M., 98n.

Nāgānanda, 108.
Nāgārjuna, 63, 71, 165, 167, 193-4.
Nāgeśabhaṭṭa, 145, 148, 181.
Naiṣadhacarita, *Naiṣadhīyacarita*, 76n, 82.
Naiṣkarmyasiddhi, 188.
Naiśvāsa, 49.
Nakula, 172.
Nalābhyudaya, 84.
Nalacampū, 140.
Nalapāka, 173.
Nāmaliṅgānuśāsana, 157.
Namisādhu, 151.
Nandana, 160.
Nandikeśvara, 173.
Nandikeśvara-upapurāṇa, 46.
Nañjarāja, 117.
Napoleon Bonaparte, 2.
Nāradasmṛti, 160-1.
Nārada-upapurāṇa, 46.
Nāradīyapurāṇa, 44.
Narasiṁha, King of Orissa, 155.
Narasiṁhapurāṇa, 46.
Nārāśaṁsī, 51.
Nārāyaṇa, commentator on *Manusmṛti*, 160.
Nārāyaṇa, *Mataṅgalīlā*, 172.
Nārāyaṇa, *Svāhāsudhākara-campū*, 140.
Nārāyaṇa, *Vṛttaratnākara*, 156.
Nārāyaṇabhaṭṭa, *Mānameyodaya*, 185.
Nārāyaṇapaṇḍita, *Navaratnaparīkṣā*, 172.
Nārāyaṇapaṇḍita, *Hitopadeśa*, 137.
Nariman, G. K., 63.
Nartananirṇaya, 173.
Nasik Cave Inscription, 8, 55.
Nāṭakalakṣaṇaratnakośa, 155.
Nāthamuni, 190.
Nāṭyadarpaṇa, 155.
Nāṭyaśāstra, 19, 75n, 85, 96n, 104, 149, 150, 153, 155-6, 173.
Navaratnaparīkṣā, 172.
Navasāhasāṅkacarita, 127.
Nayaviveka, 183.
Neminirvāṇa, 84.
Netrāgama, 49.
New Testament, 33.
Nicula, 77n.
Nidāna, 167.
Nigama, 47n.
Nighaṇṭu, 149.
Nihilist, 200.
Nīlakaṇṭha, philosopher, 201.
Nīlakaṇṭha, Tājikā, 170.
Nīlamatapurāṇa, 128.
Nimbārka, 190-1.
Nirbhayabhīmavyāyoga, 116.
Nirṇayasindhu, 161.
Nirukta, 149, 157.
Nītiratnākara, 164.
Nītisāra, 164.
Nītiśataka, 121.
Nītivākyāmṛta, 164.
Nṛtyagopāla Kaviratna, 117.
Nyāsa, 81, 143.
Nyāya, 174-7.
Nyāyabhāṣya, 174-5.
Nyāyabindu, 175, 197.
Nyāyabinduṭīkā, 197.
Nyāyakandalī, 178.
Nyāyakaṇikā, 184.
Nyāyakumudacandrodaya, 198.
Nyāyakusumāñjali, 175.
Nyāyalīlāvatī, 178.
Nyāyamañjarī, 175.
Nyāyāmṛta, 189.
Nyāyanirṇaya, 189.
Nyāyapariśiṣṭa, 175.
Nyāyapraveśa, 72, 196, 199.
Nyāyarakṣāmaṇi, 189.
Nyāyaratnākara, 184.
Nyāyasāra, 175.
Nyāyasūcīnibandha, 175.
Nyāyasudhā, 184.

Nyāyasūtra, 130, 174, 177, 182.
Nyāyasūtravṛtti, 176.
Nyāyasūtroddhāra, 175.
Nyāyavārttika, 175.
Nyāyavārttikatātparyaṭīkā, 175.
Nyāyavārttikatātparyapariśuddhi, 175.
Nyāyāvatāra, 198.
Nyāyaviniścaya, 198.

Oldenberg, H., 39n, 64n, 88, 140.
On the Language and Wisdom of the Indians, 2.

Padamañjarī, 144.
Padāṅkadūta, 120n.
Padārthadharmasaṁgraha, 177.
Padārthakhaṇḍana, 176.
Pādatāḍitaka, 92n.
Padmagupta, 127.
Padmanābha, 147.
Padmapāda, 188.
Padmaprābhṛtaka, 92n.
Padmapurāṇa, 44, 83, 97n, 107.
Padyacūḍāmaṇi, 83.
Padyāvalī, 125.
Paiṭhīnasī, 159.
Pakṣadharamiśra, 176.
Pālagopālakathānaka, 138.
Pālakāpya, 172.
Pāli Jātakas, 136.
Pañcadaśī, 189.
Pañcānana Tarkaratna, 117, 202.
Pañcapādikā, 188.
Pañcarātra, 100.
Pañcasāyaka, 165.
Pañcasiddhāntikā, 168.
Pañcaśikha, 179.
Pañcaskandhaprakaraṇa, 196.
Pañcatantra, 22, 137.
Pāṇḍavacarita, 84.
Pāṇḍavapurāṇa, 84.
Pāṇini, 5, 14, 21, 36, 52, 83, 94, 96n, 141-7, 149, 187n.
Pañjikā, 197.
Pannavāṇasūtra, 13.
Paranjape, S. M., 98n.
Parākramabāhu, King of Ceylon, 125.
Paramalaghumañjūṣā, 145.
Paramārtha, 179n.
Paramārthasaptati, 172, 195-6.
Paramārthasāra, 49.
Paramasaṁhitā, 49.
Parāśaramādhava, 161.
Parāśarasmṛti, 161.
Parāśara-upapurāṇa, 46.
Paribhāṣāsūtra, 146.
Paribhāṣāvṛtti, 148.
Paribhāṣenduśekhara, 145.
Pārijātaharaṇacampū, 140.
Parīkṣāmukhasūtra, 198.
Parimala, 188.
Parimala, 127.
Pariśiṣṭaparvan, 128.
Pārśvābhyudaya, 83.
Pārśvanāthacarita, 84.
Pārthaparākrama, 116.
Pārthasārathimiśra, 184.
Pārvatīpariṇaya, 97n, 117.
Pāśakakevalī, 170n.
Paśupati, 161.
Paspaśāhnika, 21n.
Pātālavijaya, 83.
Patañjali, 19, 21, 36, 52-3, 83, 96n, 130, 141-4, 149, 150.
Patañjali, *Yogasūtra*, 181-2.
Patraparīkṣā, 198.
Pauskarasaṁhitā, 49.
Pavanadūta, 124.
Peppe, C. C., 7.
Pargiter, F. E., 42, 45.
Petersburg Dictionary, 3.
Peterson, P., 77n.
Phuyan—King, 63.
Piṅgala, 53, 156.
Piprawa Vase Inscription, 7, 12.
Pischel, R., 3, 58, 86n, 87-8, 103n, 104n, 107, 123.
Pisharoti, K. P., 97.
Pitṛdayitā, 161.
Po-t'iao, 65n.
Poussin, V., 4, 62.
Prabandhacintāmaṇi, 129.
Prabandhakośa, 129.
Prabhācandra, 128, 198.
Prabhākara, 183, 185.
Prabhāvakacarita, 128.
Prabodhacandrodaya, 114, 199.
Prabuddharauhiṇeya, 116.
Pradīpa, 144-5.
Pradyumnasūri, 132
Prahlādanadeva, 116.
Prajñādaṇḍa, 71.
Prajñāpāramitās, 70, 194.
Prakaraṇapañcikā, 183.
Prakāśānanda, 189.
Prakāśātman, 188.
Prakīrṇaka, 143.

Prākṛta-Piṅgala, 156.
Prakriyākaumudī, 144.
Pramāṇamīmāṁsā, 199.
Pramāṇanirṇaya, 198.
Pramāṇaparīkṣā, 198.
Pramāṇapraveśaśāstra, 196.
Pramāṇasamuccaya, 72, 196.
Prameyakamalamārtaṇḍa, 198.
Prameyaratnāvalī, 192.
Prāṇatoṣiṇī, 50.
Prapañcasāra, 50.
Prasāda, 144.
Prasannapadā, 194.
Prasannarāghava, 116.
Praśastapāda, 177-8.
Prasenajit, 7.
Pratāparudrayaśobhūṣaṇa, 155.
Pratāparudra of Warangal, 155.
Pratihārendurāja, 151n.
Pratijñāyaugandharāyaṇa, 96n, 102, 111.
Pratimā, 96n, 99.
Pratītyasamutpādahṛdaya, 71, 194.
Pratītyasamutpādasūtra, 196.
Pratyabhijñā (lit.), 49.
Pratyabhijñāhṛdaya, 49.
Pratyabhijñāvimarśinī, 49.
Pratyaktattvapradīpikā, 189.
Prauḍhamanoramā, 144, 148.
Prauḍhamanoramākucamardinī, 148.
Pravarasena, 132.
Prāyaścittaprakaraṇa, 161.
Princep, 104n.
Printz, W., 98n.
Priyadarśikā, 108.
Priyaṁvadā, 125.
Pṛthuyaśas, 170.
Pṛthvīdhara, 146.
Pṛthvīrājavijaya, 128.
Puṇyarāja, 147.
Pulakeśin II, 80.
Purāṇa, 25, 40-6, 61.
Purāṇakāśyapa, 200.
Purāṇasaṁhitā, 42.
Purañjaya, 30.
Puruṣaparīkṣā, 138.
Puruṣārthasiddhyupāya, 199.
Puruṣottama, 157.
Puruṣottamadeva, 148.
Pūrvamīmāṁsā, 182-5.
Pūrvamīmāṁsāsūtra. 182.
Pusalker, A. D., 98n.
Puṣpadanta, 124.
Pusyamitra, Puṣpamitra, 73, 77n, 141.
Rabindranath, 120.
Rādhākrishnan, S., 174n, 184, 188.
Rādhākāntadeva, 158.
Rāgavivodha, 173.
Rāghavanaīṣadhīya, 84.
Rāghavānanda, 160.
Rāghavapāṇḍavīya, 83.
Rāghavapāṇḍavīyanaiṣadhīya, 84.
Raghunandana, 46n, 161.
Raghunātha Śiromaṇi, 176.
Raghuvaṁśa, 77n, 79-80, 97n.
Raivatamadanikā, 94.
Raja, Dr., 97.
Rājamārtaṇḍa, 181, 182n.
Rājamṛgāṅka, 169.
Rājaśekhara, 81, 88, 94, 98, 113, 116.
Rājaśekhara, 14th century, 129, 154.
Rājayoga, 182.
Rājataraṅgiṇī, 103, 108, 126, 128, 132.
Rājendrakarṇapūra, 128.
Rāmabhadra, 161.
Rāmabhadra Dīkṣita, 117.
Rāmabhadra Muni, 116.
Rāmacandra, *Kaumudīmitrānanda*, 116, 155.
Rāmacandra, Jaina dramatist, 116.
Rāmacandra of Bengal, 125.
Rāmacandra, *Rasikāñjana*, 84.
Rāmacandra, grammarian, 144.
Rāmacarita, 83.
Rāmācārya, 190.
Rāmakṛṣṇa, 189.
Rāmakṛṣṇabhaṭṭa, 185.
Ramalarahasya, 170n.
Rāmānuja, 40, 186n, 190, 201.
Rāmapālacarita, 127.
Rāma Tarkavāgīśa, 147.
Rāmatīrtha, 190.
Rāmāyaṇa, 2, 24-32, 37-9, 51-2, 79, 81, 83, 95, 97n, 99, 109, 114, 116, 137.
Rāmāyaṇa-campū, 140.
Rāmāyaṇamañjarī, 83.
Rāmopākhyāna, 28.
Rapson, E. J., 64n.
Rasa, 75.
Rasagaṅgādhara, 155.
Rasamañjarī, 155.
Rasaratnākara, 167.
Rasa school, 152-3.
Rasataraṅgiṇī, 155.
Rasavatī, 147.
Rasikāñjana, 84.
Rāṣṭrapāla, 70.
Ratimañjarī, 165.

Ratirahasya, 165.
Ratiśāstra, 165.
Ratnākara, 83.
Ratnakāraṇḍaśrāvakācāra, 198.
Ratnakūṭa, 70.
Ratnaparīkṣā, 172.
Ratnaprabhā, 189.
Ratnāvadānamālā, 74.
Ratnāvalī, 94, 107-8, 116, 124.
Rāvaṇārjunīya, 83.
Rāvaṇavadha, 80-1.
Raviṣeṇa, 83.
Renaissance theory, 55, 78n.
Ṛgveda, 3, 25, 30, 85, 88, 105, 149, 168.
Ridgeway, 87.
Rīti school, 151-2.
Ṛjuvimalā,183.
Roer, E., 4.
Roger, A., 1.
Rosen, F., 3.
Roth, R., 3.
Roy, S., 77n.
Roychowdhuri, H. C., 65n.
Ṛṣabha, 83.
Ṛtusaṁhāra, 1, 121.
Rucaka, 154.
Rückert, F., 3.
Rudrabhaṭṭa, 137.
Rudradāman, 9, 55, 64n.
Rudraṭa, 151.
Rudrayāmala, 49.
Rukmiṇīharaṇa, 94, 115.
Rūpagosvāmin, 117, 120n, 125, 147, 155, 191.
Ruyyaka, 84, 154.

Śābarabhāṣya, 183.
Śabarasvāmin, 130, 179, 183.
Śabdakalpadruma, 46n, 158.
Śabdakaustubha, 144.
Śabdānuśāsana, Hemacandra, 146.
Śabdānuśāsana, Śākaṭāyana, 146.
Śabdānuśāsanabṛhadvṛtti, 146.
Śabdaratna, 148.
Śabdārṇavacandrikā, 146.
Śabdaśaktiprakāśikā, 176.
Sadānanda, 189.
Sadāśiva, 172.
Ṣaḍdarśanasamuccaya, 199.
Saddharmapuṇḍarīka, 41, 69-70
Saduktikarṇāmṛta, 125.
Sāgaranandin, 155.
Sāhityadarpaṇa, 93, 94 n, 117, 155.
Sahṛdayānanda, 84.
Śaiva Tantra, 47-8.
Sakalakīrti, 84, 199.
Śākaṭāyana, 141, 146, 202.
Sākta Tantra, 47-8.
Śaktibhāṣya, 202.
Śakuntalā, 1, 77 n.
Śākyamuni, 70.
Śālihotra, 172.
Śālikanātha, 183.
Samādhirāja, 71.
Sāmarājadīkṣita, 115, 117.
Samarāṅgaṇasūtradhāra, 172.
Samavāyāṅgasūtra, 13.
Sāmaveda, 85.
Samayamātṛkā, 125.
Śāmba-upapurāṇa, 46.
Śambhū, 125, 128.
Saṁhitā literature, 49-50.
Saṁjñātantra, 170.
Saṁkṣepaśārīraka, 188.
Saṁkṣiptasāra, 147.
Sammatitarkasūtra, 198.
Saṁskārapaddhati, 161.
Samudragupta, 55.
Samudramanthana, 93, 116.
Samudratilaka, 170n.
Samantabhadra, 198.
Saṁvāda hymn, 51, 88, 105.
Samyaktakaumudī, 138.
Sanatkumāra-upapurāṇa, 46.
Sandhyākaranandin, 127.
Saṅgītadarpaṇa, 173.
Saṅgītamakaranda, 173.
Saṅgītaratnākara, 173.
Saṅgītasudarśana, 173.
Sañjaya, 200.
Saṅkalpasūryodaya, 115.
Śaṅkara, 40, 50, 125, 131, 140, 184, 186 n, 187-90, 201.
Śaṅkaracetovilāsacampū, 140.
Śaṅkaramiśra, 178.
Śaṅkhadhara Kavirāja, 116.
Śaṅkhalikhita, 159.
Sāṅkhya philosophy, 43, 72, 179-181.
Sāṅkhyakārikā, 179-80.
Sāṅkhyapravacanasūtra, 180.
Sāṅkhyasāra, 180.
Sāṅkhyasūtravṛtti, 180.
Sāṅkhyatattvakaumudī, 180.
Śāṅkhyāyanaśrautasūtra, 36.
Śaṅkuka, 152-3.

Ṣaṇmukhakalpa, 173.
Śāntarakṣita, 197.
Śāntideva, 72 n, 194.
Śāntiśataka, 125.
Saptapadārthī, 178.
Saptaśatī, 45.
Śāradātanaya, 154.
Śāradātilaka, 50.
Śaraṇadeva, 148.
Sārasvataprakriyā, 147.
Sarasvatīkaṇṭhābharaṇa, 154.
Śāriputra, 68-9.
Śāriputraprakaraṇa, 68, 95.
Śārīrakabhāṣya, 187-8.
Sarma, R., 98 n.
Śarmiṣṭhāyayāti, 94.
Śārṅgadatta, 172.
Śārṅgadeva, 173.
Śārṅgadhara, 125.
Śārṅgadharapaddhati, 125.
Sarup, 98 n.
Sarvadarśanasaṁgraha, 4, 180, 200 201.
Sarvajñamitra, 124.
Sarvajñātmamuni, 189.
Sarvānanda, 128, 192.
Sarvasaṁvādinī, 192.
Sarvasiddhāntasārasaṁgraha, 201.
Sarvāstivādin, 58, 61, 62, 71, 193.
Sarvavarman, 146.
Ṣaṣṭhītantra, 179.
Śāstradarpaṇa, 188.
Śāstradīpikā, 184.
Śāstrin, MM Haraprasad, 65, 67, 77n, 87, 97n, 174n.
Śāstrin, H., 98 n.
Śāstrin, MM. K., 96 n.
Śāstrin, Pasupatinath, 185 n.
Śāstrin, T. Ganapati, 95 n, 97-8.
Śāśvata. 157.
Śatadūṣaṇī, 190.
Śatānanda, 169.
Śatapathabrāhmaṇa, 3, 40, 149, 168.
Śatasāhasrikaprajñāpāramitā, 194.
Sātavāhana, 119-20.
Satīdāha, 38.
Śatruñjayamāhātmya, 84.
Sattasai, 119.
Sāttvatasaṁhitā, 50.
Śauddhodani, 155.
Saugandhikāharaṇa, 117.
Saumilla, 103.
Śaunaka, 34.
Saundarananda, 67, 76.
Saundaryalaharī, 124.
Sautrāntika, 192-3.
Sauvīra, 64 n.
Sāyaṇa, 3, 148. 201.
Schelling, 3.
Schiller, 3, 121.
Schlegel, F., 2, 28 n.
Schlegel, A. W. von, 2.
Schopenhauer, 3.
Schröeder, L. von, 88, 121 n, 123.
Senaka, 141.
Senart, 4, 58.
Śeṣakṛṣṇa, 117, 140.
Śeśvaramīmāṁsā, 190.
Setubandha, 132.
Sevyasevakopadeśa, 125.
Shāhbāzgarhī, Inscription, 8.
Shama Sastri, S., 163.
Siddha, Siddharsi, 138.
Siddhāntakaumudī, 144-5.
Siddhāntaleśasaṁgraha, 189.
Siddhāntamuktāvalī, 178.
Siddhāntamuktāvalī, Vedānta, 189.
Siddhāntaśiromaṇi, 169-70.
Siddhapañcāśikā, 199.
Siddhasena Divākara, 124, 198.
Śikhāmaṇi, 189.
Śikṣāsamuccaya, 194.
Śīlabhadra 196-7.
Śīlābhaṭṭārikā, 125.
Śilhaṇa, 125.
Śilparatna, 172.
Siṁhāsanadvātriṁśikā, 138.
Sīradeva, 148.
Siri Pulumayi, 55.
Śiśupālavadha, 81-2.
Śiṣyadhīvṛddhitantra, 169.
Sitābeṅgā Cave, 86.
Śivadāsa, 138.
Śivadatta, 163.
Śivadharma-upapurāṇa, 46.
Śivāditya, 178.
Śivadṛṣṭi, 49.
Śivārkamaṇidīpikā, 201.
Śivapurāṇa, 44.
Śivasvāmin, 83.
Skandagupta, 77.
Skandapurāṇa, 40, 44, 103.
Ślokasaṁgraha, 126.
Ślokavārttika, 184.
Smith, V. A., 4, 7-8, 43, 59, 63, 64 n.
Smṛtikalpataru, 161.
Smṛtiratnākara, 161.
Soḍḍhala, 140.

Sohgaura copper-plate, 7.
Somadeva, 136, 146, 164.
Somadeva, Jaina, 140.
Somānanda, 49.
Somanātha, 173.
Somaprabha, 125.
Someśvarabhaṭṭa, 184.
Someśvaradatta, 128.
Sphoṭasiddhi, 184 n.
Sphoṭāyana, 141.
Sragdharāstotra, 124.
Śrautasūtras, 159.
Śrībhāṣya, 190.
Śri Caitanya, 176, 191.
Śrīdāmacarita, 115.
Śrīdhara, 125, 154, 178.
Śrīdharasena, 81.
Śrīdharasvāmin, 201.
Śrīharṣa, 82, 189.
Śrīhastamuktāvalī, 173.
Śrīkaṇṭhabhāṣya, 201.
Śrīkaṇṭhacarita, 86.
Śrīkarabhāṣya, 201.
Śrīkumāra, 172.
Śrīnivāsācārya, 191.
Śrīpatipaṇḍita, 201.
Śrīvara, 125, 138.
Śrīvatsa, 178.
Śṛṅgāraprakāśa, 154.
Śṛṅgāraśataka, 121.
Śṛṅgāratilaka, 94, 124.
Śṛṅgāravairāgyataraṅgiṇī, 125.
Śrutabodha, 156.
Śrutaprakāśikā, 190.
Śrutasāgara, 199.
Stael-Holstein, A. von, 67.
Stein, O., 98 n.
Stein, M. A., 4.
Sthiramati, 72, 196.
Strauss, O., 4.
Suali, 174 n.
Subarṇākṣī, 65.
Subandhu, 36, 133-4, 139.
Śubhacandra, 84, 198.
Subhāṣitamuktāvalī, 125.
Subhāṣitaratnasandoha, 124.
Subhāṣitāvalī, 125.
Subhaṭa, 117.
Subodhinī, 201.
Sucaritamiśra, 184.
Sudarśana, 173, 190.
Suddhādvaitavāda, 191.
Śūdraka, 92 n, 97 n, 103-4.
Sue Vihara Inscription, 64 n.
Suhṛllekha, 71.
Śukasaptati, 138.
Sukhāvatīvyūha, 70.
Śukranīti, 164.
Sukṛtasaṅkīrtana, 128.
Sukthankar, 98 n.
Śūlapāṇi, 161.
Sumanottarā, 52.
Sumati, 160.
Śūnyatāsaptati, 71, 194.
Śūnya-upapurāṇa, 46.
Supadma, 147.
Supadmapañjikā, 147.
Suparṇādhyāya, 88 n.
Suprabhātastotra, 124.
Surathotsava, 128.
Sureśvara, 184, 188.
Sūryaśataka, 122.
Suśruta, 130, 166-7.
Sūtrālaṅkāra, 67.
Suttapiṭaka, 192-3.
Suvarṇaprabhāsa, 71.
Suvṛttatilaka, 156.
Svacchanda, 49.
Svāhāsudhākaracampū, 140.
Svapnadaśānana, 116.
Svapnavāsavadatta, 96, 101-2.
Svāyambhuva, 49.
Svétāmbara, 197.
Syādvādamañjarī, 199.

Taittirīyāraṇyaka, 168.
Taittirīya Saṃhitā, 141 n, 168.
Taittirīyopaniṣadbhāṣya-vārttika, 188.
Tājikā, 170.
Takakusu, 72, 179 n.
Tamil Gāthās, 190.
Tantras, 47-50.
Tantrākhyāyikā, 137.
Tantrāloka, 49.
Tantrarāja, 50.
Tantrasāra, 49-50, 176.
Tantravārttika, 184.
Tāpasavatsarājacarita, 116.
Taralā, 155.
Tārānātha, 69.
Tārānāth Tarkavācaspati, 157.
Taraṅgiṇī, 190.
Tarkabhāṣā, 178.
Tarkakaumudī, 178.
Tarkāmṛta, 178.
Tarkasaṃgraha, 178.
Tārkikarakṣā, 178.

Taruṇavācaspati, 152.
Tattvabodhinī, 144.
Tattvacintāmaṇi, 175-6.
Tattvacintāmaṇivyākhyā, 176.
Tattvaprakāśikā, 191.
Tattvārthādhigamasūtra, 198.
Tattvārthadīpikā, 199.
Tattvārtharājavārttika, 198.
Tattvārthasāra, 199.
Tattvārthasāradīpaka, 199.
Tattvārthaślokavārttika, 198.
Tattvasaṁgraha, 197.
Tattvasaṁgrahapañjikā, 197.
Tattvasandarbha, 192.
Tattvaṭīkā, 190.
Tattvavaiśāradī, 181.
Tautātitamatatilaka, 184
Taylor, I., 9.
Telang, 33.
Thera, 60.
Thibaut, G. 4.
Thomas, F. W., 4, 64 n, 69, 97 n.
Tilakamañjarī, 140.
Tipiṭaka, 6, 29, 36, 69, 192.
Tīṣata, 167.
Tithitattva, 161.
Trikāṇḍaśeṣa, 157.
Triṃśikāvijñapti, 196.
Triṁśikā, 196.
Tripuradāha, 85, 94, 116.
Triṣaṣṭiśalākāpuruṣacarita, 84.
Triśatī, 169.
Trivikramabhaṭṭa, 140.
Trozan War, 30.
Tscherbatsky, T., 4.
Tucci, G., 4.
Tupṭīkā, 184.

Ubhayāsārikā, 92 n.
Ucchuṣmabhairava, 49.
Udānavagga, 193.
Udāttarāghava, 116.
Udayana, 175-6.
Udayasundarīkathā, 140.
Udbhaṭa, 151, 154.
Uddaṇḍin, 117.
Uddyota, 145.
Uddyotakara, 133, 175, 177.
Udvāhatattva, 161.
Ugraśravas, 34.
Ujjvalanīlamaṇi, 155.
Ulūka, 179.
Umāsvāmin, 197.
Umāsvātī, 197.
Umbeka, 184.
Uṇādisūtras, 146.
Unmattarāghava, 117.
Upakramaparākrama, 185.
Upamitibhavaprapañcakathā, 138.
Upamitibhavaprapañcakathāsāroddhāra, 138.
Upaniṣad, 2, 131.
Upaskāra, 178.
Upavarṣa, 183, 187 n.
Ūrubhaṅga, 100.
Uśanas, 159, 162-3.
Uśanas-upapurāṇa, 46.
Utpala, 49.
Uttararāmacarita, 86, 88, 110.

Vācaspati, 161, 175, 180-1, 184, 186 n. 188, 198.
Vācaspatya, 157.
Vādirāja, 83.
Vāgbhaṭa, epic poet, 84.
Vāgbhaṭa, rhetorician, 154.
Vāgbhaṭa, medical authority, 167.
Vāgbhaṭālaṅkāra, 154.
Vaibhāṣika, 192-3.
Vaidarbha style, 55-6.
Vaidyajīvana, 167
Vaijayantī, 157.
Vaikhānasadharmasūtra, 159.
Vaipulyasūtra, 61-2.
Vairāgyaśataka, 121.
Vaiśampāyana, 34.
Vaiśeṣika philosophy, 177-9.
Vaiśeṣikasūtras, 177.
Vaiṣṇavadharmasūtra, 159.
Vaiṣṇava-tantra, 47-8.
Vaiṣṇavatoṣiṇī, 191.
Vaiyākaraṇabhūṣaṇa, 148.
Vaiyākaraṇabhūṣaṇasāra, 148.
Vaiyākaraṇasiddhāntamañjūṣā, 145.
Vaiyāsikanyāyamālā, 189.
Vajradatta, 122 n.
Vajrasūcī, 68.
Vākpati, 109, 127.
Vakroktijīvita, 154.
Vākyapadīya, 122n, 143, 145.
Vālivadha, 52, 94.
Vallabha, logician, 176, 178.
Vallabha, Vedāntin, 191, 201.
Vālmīki, 24-5, 30, 38, 52, 79, 96 n.
Vāmana, rhetorician, 81, 103 n, 112, 122, 151-2.

Vāmana, grammarian, 143.
Vāmanabhaṭṭa Bāṇa, 84, 117.
Vāmanapurāṇa, 44.
Vandāruvṛtti, 199.
Varadācārya, 116.
Varadarāja, grammarian, 145.
Varadarāja, logician, 178.
Varāhamihira, 168, 170.
Varāhapurāṇa, 44.
Vārarucakāvya, 52, 83.
Vararuci, 92 n, 156.
Vardhamāna, Kātantra school, 146.
Vardhamāna, *Gaṇaratnamahodadhi*, 148.
Vardhamāna, logician, 176.
Vardhamāna, *Yogamañjarī*, 172.
Vardhamāna, Jina, 197.
Varivasyārahasya, 50.
Varṣa, 187.
Vārṣagaṇya, 179.
Varṣatantra, 170.
Vārttikābharaṇa, 184.
Vārttikakāra, 146.
Varuṇa-upapurāṇa, 46.
Vāsavadattā, 52, 133.
Vāsiska, 64 n.
Vaśiṣṭha, 5, 159.
Vāstuvidyā, 172.
Vasubandhu, 71, 179 n, 194, 196.
Vāsudeva I, 65 n.
Vāsudeva, *Bālamanoramā*, 144.
Vāsudeva Sārvabhauma, 176.
Vasumitra, 63, 193.
Vatsabhaṭṭi, 56-7, 116.
Vatsarāja, 93-4, 116.
Vātsyāyana, *Kāmasūtra*, 22, 165.
Vātsyāyana, logician, 130, 174-5, 177.
Vāyupurāṇa, 40-3.
Vāyu-upapurāṇa, 40-3.
Vedānta, 185-92.
Vedāntadeśika, 120 n.
Vedāntadīkṣita, 184.
Vedāntakaustubha, 191.
Vedāntaparibhāṣā, 189.
Vedāntapārijātasaurabha, 190.
Vedāntasāra, 189.
Vedāntasūtra, 185-6.
Vedas, 16-8, 35, 48.
Vedic Concordance, 4.
Vedic Grammar, 4.
Vedic Index, 4.
Vedic Mythology, 4.
Vedic Studies, 3.
Vemabhūpāla, 122.
Venis, A., 4.
Veṇīsaṁhāra, 112.
Veṅkaṭadīkṣita, 184.
Veṅkaṭanātha, 115.
Vetālapañcaviṁśati, 138.
Vibhramaviveka, 184.
Vicitrakarṇikāvadāna, 73.
Vidagdhamādhava, 117.
Viddhaśālabhañjikā, 113.
Vidhirasāyana, 185.
Vidhiviveka, 184.
Vidyābhusana, S. C., 174 n, 194.
Vidyācakravartin, 154.
Vidyādhara, 155.
Vidyāmādhavīya, 170.
Vidyānanda, 198.
Vidyānātha, 155.
Vidyāpariṇaya, 115.
Vidyāpati, 129, 138, 161, 164.
Vidyāraṇya, 189.
Vidyāsundara, 123.
Vigrahavyāvartanī, 71, 194.
Vijjakā, 125.
Vijñānabhairava, 49.
Vijñānabhikṣu, 180-1, 201.
Vijñānāmṛtabhāṣya, 201.
Vijñāneśvara, 161.
Vijñaptimātratāsiddhi, 72, 196.
Vikaṭanitambā, 125.
Vikramāditya of Ujjayinī, 77n, 121.
Vikramāditya, Chandragupta II, 133.
Vikramāditya, authority on archery, 172.
Vikramāṅkadevacarita, 127.
Vikramorvaśīya, 94, 105-6.
Vikrama Sambat, 64n.
Vikrāntakaurava, 117.
Vilāsavatī, 94.
Viṁśatikā, 196.
Vimuktātman, 189.
Vinayapiṭaka, 7, 192.
Vindhyasvāmin, 179n.
Vīra Bukka, 201.
Vīramitrodaya, 161.
Virulaka, 7.
Viśākhadatta, 111-2.
Viśāladeva, Vigraharāja, 116.
Viśālakṣa, 162-3.
Viśiṣṭādvaitavāda, 190.
Viṣṇudharmottara, 172-3.
Viṣṇugupta, 162.
Viṣṇupurāṇa, 42-4, 97n, 130, 149, 200-1.
Viṣṇuśarman, 137.

Viṣṇusvāmin, 201.
Viśvakarmaprakāśa, 172.
Viśvanātha, rhetorician, 117, 154-5.
Viśvanātha, philosopher, 176, 178.
Viśvaprakāśa, 157.
Viśvarūpa, 184.
Viśveśvara, 161.
Vītarāgastotra, 125.
Viṭṭhalācārya, 144.
Vivādacintāmaṇi, 161.
Vivādaratnākara, 161.
Vivādārṇavasetu, 1.
Vivaraṇa, 187-8.
Vivaraṇaprameyasaṁgraha, 188.
Vivṛti, 178.
Vopadeva, 147.
Vratāvadānamālā, 73.
Vṛddhagargasaṁhitā, 170.
Vṛddhavaśiṣṭhasaṁhitā, 170.
Vṛddhamanu, 160.
Vṛndāvanastuti, 124.
Vṛttaratnākara, Kedāra, 156.
Vṛttaratnākara, Nārāyaṇa, 156.
Vṛtti, *Kāśikā*, 143.
Vṛtti, Durgasiṁha, 146.
Vṛtti, quoted by Śabara, 183.
Vṛttikāra, 183, 187.
Vyākhyāyukti, 196.
Vyaktiviveka, 154.
Vyāptipañcaka, 176.
Vyāsa, 34, 40, 42, 96n, 181-2, 186n.
Vyāsabhāṣya, 181-2.
Vyāsarāja, 189.
Vyāsarāma, 190.
Vyāsatīrtha, 189.
Vyavahāracintāmaṇi, 161.
Vyomaśekhara, 178.
Vyomaśivācārya, 177.
Vyomavatī, 177-8.

Weber, A. A., 3, 9, 10, 29, 30, 86n, 107n, 142, 168.
Weller, H., 98n.
Whitney, W. D., 4.
Wilford, 104n.
Wilkins, C., 1.
Williams, M., 4, 28n, 140n.
Windisch, E., 86.
Winternitz, M., 4, 28-9, 32-3, 35, 38 39n, 41, 45, 67n, 68n, 98, 107n.
Wogihara, 72.
Woolner, A. C., 98n.

Yādava, 157.
Yādavodaya, 94.
Yājñavalkya, 149, 161.
Yajurveda, 36, 85.
Yāmunācārya, 190.
Yaśaścandra, 116
Yaśastilaka, 140, 164.
Yāska, 21, 149, 157.
Yaśodhara, 165.
Yaśodharacarita, 83.
Yaśomitra, 72n, 194, 196.
Yaśovarman, 109, 127.
Yaśovijaya, 199.
Yatirājavijaya, 116.
Yavanajātaka, 170.
Yavanānī, 14.
Yoga, 181-2.
Yogabindu, 199.
Yogācāra, 71, 192, 195-7.
Yogācārabhūmiśāstra, 71, 195.
Yogadṛṣṭisamuccaya, 199.
Yogamañjarī, 172.
Yogasāra, 124.
Yogasārasaṁgraha, 181.
Yogaśāstra, 125.
Yogasūtra, 181, 183.
Yogavārttika, 181.
Yuan Chwang, 193, 197.
Yuktidīpikā, 180.
Yuktikalpataru, 164, 172.
Yuktiṣaṣṭikā, 71, 194.
Yuktisnehaprapūraṇī, 185.
Yuktyanuśāsana, 198.